A Cultural History of
British Alternative Cabaret
(1979–1991)

Liverpool Studies in the Politics of Popular Culture   2

Liverpool Studies in the Politics of Popular Culture

Sociologists and other scholars are reporting a resurgence of interest in popular culture. To engage with popular culture is to engage in any number of debates about power, ideology, hegemony, (dis)order, resistance and reproduction. The purpose of this series is to engage with these concepts, not as abstract ideas circulating in the grand corridors of government and academe, but rather, as Raymond Williams (1958) once put it, as ideas which are manifest in the everyday lives of 'ordinary' people.

This series looks at popular culture in its broadest sense, including topics such as celebrity and reality TV, popular culture and youth, race and diversity, Internet culture, television, music, cinema, social media, games, comedy, popular literature, comics and graphic novels, radio, subcultures, countercultures and celebrity cultures, advertising and consumerism, sports, and more. Proposals are welcome from across the disciplines and subject fields of sociology, cultural sociology, cultural studies, sociology of identity and community, popular music studies, youth studies, fashion studies, gender studies, and sport and leisure studies.

Series editors:
Brett Lashua, University College London
Stephen Wagg, De Montfort University

A Cultural History of British Alternative Cabaret (1979–1991)

Ray Campbell

LIVERPOOL UNIVERSITY PRESS

First published 2023 by
Liverpool University Press
4 Cambridge Street
Liverpool
L69 7ZU

Copyright © 2023 Ray Campbell

Ray Campbell has asserted the right to be identified as the author of this book in accordance with the Copyright, Designs and Patents Act 1988.

All rights reserved. No part of this book may be reproduced, stored in a retrieval system, or transmitted, in any form or by any means, electronic, mechanical, photocopying, recording, or otherwise, without the prior written permission of the publisher.

British Library Cataloguing-in-Publication data
A British Library CIP record is available

ISBN 978-1-83764-510-7

Typeset by Carnegie Book Production, Lancaster

Contents

Acknowledgements vii

1. An Introduction 1
2. A Journey through Time 11
3. The Outsider 71
4. An Ethnography of Alternative Cabaret 127
5. CAST, New Variety, and the Hackney Empire 171
6. Conclusion 215

Bibliography 227
Index 241

Acknowledgements

I would like to thank the following for their support and guidance in the writing of this book. Without them, none of this would have been possible. Roland and Claire Muldoon of CAST/New Variety Lives, Andrew Foster, British Music Hall Society archivist, Mark Hurst, and my PhD supervisors, Jane Stokes, Stephen Maddison, and Angie Voela. Finally, I would like to thank Stephen Wagg, who was instrumental in getting this book published.

Chapter 1

An Introduction

"I was looking for myself and asking everyone except myself questions which I, and only I, could answer. It took me a long time and much painful boomeranging of my expectations to achieve a realization everyone else appears to have been born with: That I am nobody but myself."

Ralph Ellison, *Invisible Man*

"Armalite rifle and the Holy Trinity
Used against you like Irish jokes on the BBC"

Gang of Four, 'Armalite Rifle', 1979a

This is not a book about stand-up comedy, although it features prominently. No. This is a book about an artistic movement that was not conscious of itself as a movement. The fact that many performers deny that they were involved in an artistic movement is neither here nor there. Alternative cabaret (which shares its name with Tony Allen and Alexei Sayle's loose network of venues) was a 1980s performance movement that incorporated a variety of performance styles, including stand-up comedy, circus, poetry, music, and so on. Although it appears at first glance to be an inheritor of Britain's music-hall and variety traditions, its performers and promoters made a conscious break with the past.

There have long been disagreements over terminology. Despite this, it is worth noting that the term 'alternative cabaret' was used by Roger Wilmut in a panel discussion and book launch at the ICA in 1989, while the word 'cabaret' was used from 1981 as a means of classifying this new entertainment form by London's listing magazines, *Time Out* (*TO*) and *City Limits*. When I started performing comedy in 1986, we didn't call ourselves comedians, we were called 'cabaret artists'. We didn't want to be associated with something so stale, so predictable, so bigoted and reactionary as the comics from the working men's club (WMC) circuit and its televisual companion, Granada Television's *The Comedians*. We marked our difference by referring to ourselves as the alternative. Thus, to avoid a possible confusion over names and the movement itself, the performance collective appears as 'Alternative Cabaret', while the movement is written in lower-case letters.

This book examines what I call the alternative performance space (shortened to 'alt-space'), an entertainment space that emerged during the 1980s, which challenged the staleness of Britain's official entertainment world by constructing a second world in opposition to what its agents perceived as the mainstream. Alternative promoters and performers, many of whom had been participants in the countercultures of the 1960s and 1970s, wrote these spaces in response to the conservatism, nostalgia, and hierarchies in the official entertainment world. Their talent in creating these spaces was informed by a DIY ethic that is shared with the post-punk counterculture and the historical avant-garde (McKay, 1996; Andrews, 2010). Hebdige (1993) argues that punk was both a form of rock music and an avant-garde movement, and this appears to reinforce the notion that the cultural forms that followed it were touched by its unstated philosophies of shock and agency. As a momentarily dominant rock genre, punk's alleged demise in 1977 had opened up a space for new cultural practices and practitioners, many of whom had taken advantage of greater access to higher education or attended arts schools (Itzin, 1986; Lidington, 1987). Amateur performers flourished in the 1980s and their use of bricolage to create new performance styles from an assortment of cultural genres marks them out as self-taught practitioners of whichever entertainment discipline they belonged to. One of these genres was alternative comedy (altcom), a new form of stand-up comedy that was performed by amateurs, many of whom were in their early twenties. Taken together, these performers, their disciplines, practices, and the venues in which they played, constitute an alt-space, which also accommodated oppositional political discourses that were denied a voice in the official world. This book discusses how this space was constructed, and thus complements and extends the work of previous researchers of the altcom genre (Double, 1991; Ritchie, 1997; Craig, 2000; Giappone, 2012, 2018) by discussing the space in which this new form of comedy was incubated and nourished.

My doctoral thesis, upon which this book is based, utilized a qualitative methodology that included ethnography, autoethnography, and textual and archive study. If there has been scant academic interest in altcom or stand-up comedy generally, then altcab is in a far worse position. This is not helped by the confusion over the terms 'altcab' and 'altcom' and what they mean. There is little mention of altcab as a live scene in its own right except as footnotes in secondary sources like the later edition of Lisa Appignanesi's (1976) *The Cabaret* and Lidington's 'New Terms for Old Turns' in the *New Theatre Quarterly* (1987). Similarly, there is little written about New Variety (NV) save for Double's thesis (1991), a few pages in his book, *Alternative Comedy: 1979 and the Reinvention of British Stand-Up* (2020), C. Craig's (2000) thesis, and in Wilmut's (1989) *Didn't You Kill My Mother-in-Law?* Bill McDonnell (2010), who worked with Cartoon Archetypal Slogan Theatre (or CAST) in the 1970s, produced a paper about them for the British Library Theatre Archives, but aside from these few works, there is a paucity of material relating directly to altcab. Therefore, my reading around the subject of cabaret has been equally, if not more, eclectic than my reading for altcom and I have found it useful to take a 'long view' with regards to cabaret and variety. I have made good use of a disappointingly small number of peer-reviewed articles (Segel, 1977; Houchin, 1984) on the cabaret-artistique of 1880s Paris, and the relationship between the two cabarets appears to have existed in name only. Their differences aside, the two cabarets emerged in similar conditions of social and political turmoil, and both can be regarded as countercultural responses to prevailing socio-cultural circumstances. If anything, a closer connection can be made between music hall and variety, and New Variety (NV). Double (1991) has argued that the comic songs of Victorian music hall formed the substrate of contemporary stand-up comedy. Yet we also find in music hall a range of performance styles that included juggling, fire-eating, sentimental ballads, and play recitals.

This study is primarily ethnographic. An ethnography is the systematic study of a particular social or cultural group or phenomenon and is usually associated with anthropology or sociology. The cultural group and phenomenon in this case is the altcab movement of the 1980s. However, if ethnography is the study of a cultural group, then autoethnography is a reflexive study of the self (Chang, n.d.; Ellis et al., 2011). I was part of the altcab movement, and I am also part of its story; therefore the use of autoethnography is an essential component. Autoethnography makes use of autobiographical materials as primary source data, which are critically analyzed rather than accepting self-generated data as *fait accompli* (Chang, n.d.; Ellis et al., 2011). I have adopted the position of commentator in relation to my autoethnography and converse with the data that I have collected elsewhere in this book. In terms of its utility as a method, autoethnography dispenses with selective memorization of past events and seeks to analyze life's experiences (Ellis et al., 2011). The intention behind the autoethnography, therefore, is to produce a thick description of personal experience that can be related to theory or serve as a means to construct theory (Geertz, 1973; Ellis et al., 2011). Tracy (2012) argues that autoethnography can be conceptually divided into the 'evocative' and 'analytical'. The latter was developed by Anderson (2006) as a means to negotiate the emotionality of the evocative autoethnography, which produces an emotional narrative. I found Ben Carrington's (2008) autoethnographic account of sport, race, and performativity useful for the fact that as a Black academic, he was forced to confront his own views about Blackness and how, experientially, they were challenged by geographical differences within Britain's African-Caribbean diaspora. For me, the difference lay in my mixed-heritage as well as having grown up as part of a military family, in which, for the most part, we were the only such family in the places in which we lived. I attended schools for the dependents of American service personnel, so my early inculturation differed markedly from the experiences of many Black British people. Where our experiences intersect is on the planes of racism and social class. My autoethnography forms a large part of this book and is in Chapter 3.

Although a great deal has been written about stand-up comedy in recent years, it has not been explored through the experiential lens of a single performer nor has there been any engagement with the issues of race, class, and difference. Such issues have taken a backseat to the poetics of comedy or appreciation of jokes and their delivery. Furthermore, the social and cultural aspects of the altcab movement have been less scrutinized and defined. This book, therefore, makes use of ethnography and autoethnography as methodological tools to excavate the ground beneath today's comedy industry. So, why autoethnography? Carrington (2008), in his autoethnography of Black sporting cultures, argues that there has been a limited engagement with ethnography as a research method.

> Reflecting the 'cultural turn' within much social science analysis, we now have numerous textual analyses that skillfully deconstruct the ways in which dominant ideologies of race become embedded within particular media texts such as films and advertisements, how such privileged ways of seeing are then reproduced through (political) discourse, and the effectivity of this in the attempts to hail individuals into particular racialized subjectivities.
>
> Carrington, 2008: 4

Yet no such analyses currently exist of stand-up comedy or the entertainment industry more widely, and although there has been greater academic interest in altcom and stand-up comedy in recent years, the work that exists is overwhelmingly written from a white perspective or from the position of a consumer or academic researcher. Only one academic, apart from myself, performed regularly on the cabaret and comedy circuits. Oliver Double performed on the comedy circuit until the mid-nineties but left to pursue an academic career. My comedy career, on the other hand, lasted a little longer and I've only recently been admitted into the academy. As a Black man of mixed-heritage, I am in a unique position to discuss both the changes that took place within the industry and how difference was regarded on the circuit. However, it should also be noted that while there is little or no mention of Black British comedians in academic texts, there is similarly no mention of whiteness. It is simply taken for granted that when stand-up comedians are discussed, they are white.

Stand-up comedy, as Mintz (1985) argues, is a form of social and cultural meditation. It stands to reason, therefore, that stand-up comedy and altcab as art forms and as a cultural movement demand the same level of attention from the social scientist as they would give to a specific youth culture. Furthermore, it also insists that it be analyzed from within, and by someone who is neither white nor a 'big name' comedian. It is still the case that when the comedy industry comes under discussion, one automatically thinks of names like Mark Thomas, Stewart Lee, Jo Brand, and Tim Vine, rather than Felix Dexter,[1] Rudi Lickwood, Curtis Walker,

---

[1] I should point out that I'd intended to interview Felix for my thesis but he sadly passed away in 2013.

or Gina Yashere. These are invisible people. My autoethnography seeks to address this gap in our knowledge. However, I should point out that when Black British comedians are discussed, my name is noticeably absent. I shall also deal with this issue in my autoethnography.

There must also be an effort to resist the straitjacket of racial homogenization. Black is often seen by politicians and the white-dominated media not only as a problem but as a means by which to elide differences of views and positions within a vast social group whose only common denominator is skin colour. Yet, as I know from personal experience, there are regionalized differences across the African diaspora and, like any other social group, it contains a wide range of attitudes, views, and tastes, and these must be considered. Carrington (2008: 8) again:

> Black identity, as with all identities, should be understood in terms of the social processes and cultural practices of narrating, representing, and performing the racial self. Its contingent character, forged from political struggle over the signification of 'Blackness' itself, is therefore not a closed secret to which only its racially coded members have access and hence why grounded empirical research is so vital to avoid further reifying racial and ethnic categories.

My autoethnography intends to draw out these complexities and examine them in greater detail. Indeed, no one would suggest that whiteness is a universal, because there are many different narratives, cultures, ethnicities, and skin tones within the Caucasian nomenclature. For the comedian of colour working in a 'white' world, however, there is an expectation on the part of white audiences that they behave according to the line-drawing of an ethnic stereotype, which is informed by a judgement that itself is taken from a Galtonian quasi-zoological taxonomy of racial stereotypes. Should the performer of colour step outside the boundaries of ethnic determinism, as set by the industry's white gatekeepers, problems can often arise. Such is the case with those of us who are from mixed backgrounds, who defy expectations simply because of the way we look, and we can often be read as one of many racial phenotypes rather than the identity that we've chosen for ourselves.

As Gilroy (1987) observes, the construction of racialized identities is bound up with nationalist discourses on citizenship and identity. Even the British Left has ventured into the territory of race, identity, and patriotism, seeking to colonize ground occupied by the British Right, as represented by the Conservative Party and fringe far-right parties like the British National Party (BNP) and the National Front (NF). The Labour Party, often seen as representing minorities, has over the course of the last 75 years swung from embracing minority settlers to adopting similar language to that of the far right. This is evident from the way ministers in the New Labour government attacked what it claimed were "bogus asylum seekers" and from Gordon Brown's exhortation, "British jobs for British workers". Brown also wanted to see a "British form of patriotism", but this was poorly articulated and relied on the usual tropes from the 'left' (Gilroy, 2002). When altcab first appeared in 1979, Thatcher had appropriated the anti-immigrant language of the National Front, and although the 1980s is seen, retrospectively, as a period of 'political correctness' when racist and sexist discourses were seemingly vanquished, I would argue that they were pushed underground and acquired a state of dormancy, only to be revived towards the end of the twentieth century.

I experienced some degree of anxiety over how to approach my autoethnography and like Wall (2008), I wasn't entirely sure how to represent myself. Should I use the first person singular and if so, how much should it be used? I was clearly a participant in the altcab movement, and yet I only entered the field towards the end of its countercultural phase and the beginning of its commercial phase. For those participants who had been involved in altcab from the beginning, I felt like an outsider and my knowledge of the scene was full of gaps. I realized that my idealism would also be challenged by those who had operated in the field from its early days, for I often saw altcab as a left-wing scene that was dominated by its opposition to Thatcherism. One aspect that I found difficult to deal with was writing about my early years as a performer. So much of this period was spent learning to perform as a stand-up comedian rather than playing an actor who was trying to be funny onstage. In those days, I was more showman than shaman. Like many of those who participated in this study, I was a bricoleur and constructed my comedy routine out of my cultural capital – a mixture of my performance training, voice talent, knowledge of American stand-ups like George Carlin and science-fiction horror films of the 1950s. I had no experience or training to become a comedian, because courses for comedians did not exist in Newcastle in 1986. Another aspect that I found difficult was dealing with the painful memories of rejection because of my skin colour and the reactions from club promoters who sought to pigeonhole me or offer me useless advice. Writing about this stirred up long-buried feelings of anger, sadness, and frustration. I had to put these feelings to one side and detach myself from my emotions and experiences and treat myself dispassionately as a subject.

What Follows

This book will proceed with a history of altcab in Chapter 2. This chapter is underpinned by a Bourdieusian conceptual paradigm, drawn principally from *Distinction* (2003) and *The Field of Cultural Production* (1993), and discusses the alt-space in terms of fields and capital, and provides a sociocultural background to the space. I have found Bourdieu's (1986, 1993, 2003) concepts of habitus, capital, and field most useful because they provide a more nuanced approach to analyzing class power than the determinism of its Marxian counterpart. Moreover, they have provided me with the tools to interrogate the dynamics of cultural transformation and the perennial struggles between social formations on the terrain of cultural production. For me, the utility of Bourdieu's concepts rests on his insistence that his theories were works in progress; this gives them their flexibility as analytical instruments. Thus, with this in mind, I have adapted Bourdieu's concept of cultural capital, in particular, to explain the countercultural practices that existed within the space. Hence, I propose to use the term 'counter*cultural* capital' to describe a particular kind of cultural capital that is produced and possessed by those who work in underground political and cultural fields. Bourdieu (1986) says:

> Cultural capital can exist in three forms: in the embodied state, i.e., in the form of long-lasting dispositions of the mind and body; in the objectified state, in the form of cultural goods (pictures, books, dictionaries, instruments, machines, etc.), which are the trace or realization of theories or critiques of these theories, problematics, etc.; and in the institutionalized state, a form of objectification which must be set apart because, as will be seen in the case of educational qualifications, it confers entirely original properties on the cultural capital which it is presumed to guarantee.

My concept of counter*cultural* capital is broadly in agreement with Bourdieu's formulation with the exception of its institutionalized state. Within countercultural formations there are no certificates or formal educational institutions, and the markers of prestige are conferred by peers upon other peers. In the alt-space's case, honours were awarded by audience plaudits and the press's praise. 'Counter*cultural* capital' is used in my doctoral thesis to refer specifically to the kind of culturalized capital that is produced by and through broadly libertarian socialist/anarchist movements and the performance spaces within the alt-space, and because this study deals with CAST, who would describe themselves as libertarian socialists (McDonnell, 2010; Muldoon, 2010 and 2011 interviews), its use is therefore germane. Likewise, the concept of the habitus has also been extended to accommodate my concept of the countercultural habitus, which informs what I refer to as the 'political-aesthetic' disposition that produces rebellious tendencies and new art forms. Therefore, I have borrowed the concept of political-aestheticism from the historic avant-garde and its oppositional cultural-political practices, which match the practices of the alt-space. Indeed, I use the term 'space' to refer to a location on the more general field of restricted production (Bourdieu, 1993), which governs small-scale production and what Bourdieu (2003) calls "art for art's sake".

To get a sense of the kinds of entertainment that were being opposed by altcab and NV, I watched hours of television footage from light-entertainment programmes like *The Comedians*, *The Wheeltappers and Shunters Social Club*, and *Seaside Special*. Altcom is generally associated with the anarchic comedy of *The Young Ones* (BBC1, 1982) and *The Comic Strip Presents…* (Channel Four, 1982) and so this was also relevant viewing. The British Library Sound Archive was useful for audio and video recordings of cabaret shows and for programmes like *The Cabaret Upstairs* (BBC Radio Four), *The Cabaret at the Jongleurs* (BBC2), and *The Late Show* (BBC2, April 1990), in which I appear briefly in a segment about Black Comedy. I have also spent some considerable time trawling the Hackney Empire Archives at the University of East London in an effort to fill in the gaps in CAST's and NV's history.

Chapter 3 is titled 'The Outsider' and is a more extensive autoethnography than that in my doctoral thesis and includes a detailed discussion of race, difference, and identity. My general findings follow in Chapter 4, in which I analyze the structure of the alt-space with a specific focus on altcab. In Chapter 4, I discuss how the alt-space was constructed. In this chapter, I make use of performers' first-hand testimonies to uncover the kind of cultural and counter*cultural* capital that were utilized in its construction. In the post-punk music field, record labels were small and owned by small-scale producers, and agreements were based on handshakes, meaning the middlemen were eliminated. Similarly, the alt-space was created for and by amateurs, and promoters opened clubs because they fetishized and loved unusual forms of entertainment and not because they identified the alt-space as a site of surplus value.

In Chapter 5, I discuss CAST's work from their origins in the anti-war movement of the 1960s, through their work in anti-racism and feminism, to the acquisition of the Hackney Empire and the end of the NV genre in the early nineties. As a political theatre company, CAST were responsible for catalyzing the alternative theatre space. Most importantly, CAST presents NV formed a bridge between the first wave of altcab/altcom and the clubs that followed. They introduced variety to the alt-space by giving space to punk poetry, music, street performers, and alt comedians. More importantly, NV provided a degree of continuity between alternative theatre and the alt-space and laid down a marker for others to follow.

I conclude this book in Chapter 6 by reflecting on my findings and discussing the implications of my work. NV and altcab were separate genres that were defined by their respective use of space. NV introduced variety to the nascent altcab circuit, while retaining a separate identity and space outside of altcab. This study has raised a number of questions that have yet to be answered and provided me with directions for future studies. Topics include areas that have thus far not been discussed, and these are: what were the contributions of punk poets and street performers to the alt-space? Black comedians were few in number but they faced a constant battle against tokenism and casual racism, and were Othered and ghettoized. How did they cope with this and why was a separate Black circuit created when the altcab circuit was supposedly an egalitarian space? The altcab scene outside of London has never been properly discussed, but was it any different to the London circuit and if so, how?

The comedy landscape has changed dramatically over the course of three decades and, for a while, popular entertainment had also changed. However, while we have new forms of stand-up comedy, the variety field was left to wither on the vine. It is this that has been lost to us. We are long overdue a variety revival.

Chapter 2

A Journey through Time

Background

Cultural change is brought about through the positioning of new agents on the field, who bring their dispositions and symbolic capital from other fields and adopt the positions that are available (Bourdieu, 1993). This is what Bourdieu (1996: 234–235) refers to as the "space of possibles". Robbins (2000) reminds us that position-taking is relational rather than intentional, and the positioning of the cabaret artists was taken in opposition to the traditional positions on the field, which were in turn influenced by the kind and amount of cultural, counter*cultural*, and social capital they possessed. The altcab space in its totality comprised a range of stylistically different venues and performance genres that were usually related to the clubs themselves. In this chapter I make use of the performers' stories, personal recollections, and industry texts like the *British Alternative Theatre Directory* to assist in filling in the gaps. To map the changes on the circuit, I made use of *TO* because it provides a near-unbroken record of the events that shaped the space and its transition from cabaret to the comedy industry that we know today. *TO* was generally seen among performers as an unofficial industry magazine in the same way *Melody Maker* was read by musicians for its 'musicians wanted' section at the back of the paper.

Altcab's appearance occurred against the twin backdrops of the political and social turmoil of the late 1970s and the ever-present Cold War. The usual starting point with a history of the altcom genre is the opening of the Comedy Store in May 1979, but as others (Double, 1991, 2020; Craig, 2000; Cook, 2001; Peters, 2013; Soan, 2013 interview) have noted, there was a small, loosely arranged alternative scene that took place in pubs and at far-flung theatre spaces like the Woolwich Tramshed, which was home to Joe Griffith's popular song and sketch show, the Foundation. There was also a regular alternative night at Manchester's Band on the Wall, which played host to Rik Mayall and Adrian Edmonson's fledgling 20th Century Coyote double act. Martin Soan and Malcolm Hardee's Greatest Show on Legs, which began on the streets as a portable Punch and Judy show, but had moved indoors by the late seventies, is another example of this pre-alternative scene. Soan (2013 interview) describes the early period as "nuts" with "stuff going on left, right and centre" in the pubs. There were other comics working in the pre-alternative period who could be described as 'proto-alternative' and this would include John Dowie, who was the product of Birmingham Arts Lab. However, Dowie rejected any direct association with altcab, although his act is often cited as an early example of a shift towards a non-racist, non-sexist form of comedy. Victoria Wood, Billy Connolly, Jasper Carrott, and Mike Harding are often cited as examples of this emerging comedy tendency, with the latter three coming from the folk clubs. However, as non-racist and non-sexist (defined in this instance by the *absence* of racist and sexist material, rather than an active positioning against such things) as they were, these performers were not, in any sense, countercultural, nor were they alternative.

Many writers and impresarios (Wilmut, 1989; Kershaw, 1992; Cook, 2001; Muldoon, 2011 interview) have noted how Lenny Bruce was adopted by the early alt comedians as the model for their comedy practices. The reason why Bruce was fetishized is because he broke with the conventions of joke-telling in favour of a free-form improvisational style that was linguistically and rhythmically related to jazz, as opposed to the straight gag-telling of Bob Hope, George Burns, and others. In this sense alone, Bruce was very much a countercultural comedian. He opposed the performative and stylistic *doxas* of the field by, on the one hand, attacking the rigid social conformity of fifties America and, on the other, his use of hip-speak. An alternative hypothesis was proposed by the ranting poet-turned-comedian Mark Hurst, who offers Trevor Griffiths' *Comedians* (1975) as a possible influence on the new comedians. Griffiths' play was originally produced in 1975 at the Nottingham Playhouse, directed by Richard Eyre, before appearing on BBC1's *Play for Today* (a 25-minute extract was broadcast on BBC1's *2nd*

House arts strand in March 1975). Mark believes *Comedians* "foresaw and predicted the alternative comedy circuit" (Hurst, 2012 questionnaire). There is some truth to this; many of my interviewees referred specifically to the "old-fashioned" nature of traditional comedy. *Comedians* also prefigures altcom in two ways: first, some of the action takes place during a stand-up comedy course at a local further education college. However, it is difficult to know for certain whether any such courses existed when Griffiths wrote his play. Traditional comedians, who wanted to perform on the club circuit, had to audition for an agent, who would then get them bookings at the clubs. Second, the kind of comedy that is being discussed in the play seems to herald, almost predict, as Hurst says, a shift away from the sexist and racist comedy of the WMCs.

Punk rock has been cited by previous writers – most notably Lidington (1987), Craig (2000), Cook (2001), and Giappone (2012; 2018) – as a catalyst of, if not a major influence on, the nascent altcab scene, and its appearance in the summer of 1976 was greeted with a mixture of horror and disgust by the national press and seemed to symbolize a nation in decline (Hebdige, 1993). However, for the legions of disaffected youths who became punks, theirs was a sonic, sartorial, and political response to the social, cultural, and political *doxas* that were generated on those fields by an old guard that was out of touch and living on past glories. A major feature of this decline was the cultural industries' penchant for nostalgia, which seeped into the thoughts of rock stars who pined for a Britain that only existed in the imagination. Some believed that the country's economic and political problems could be solved through a form of charismatic authoritarianism, while others – seduced by Enoch Powell's rhetoric – proposed to remove immigrants from the country, erroneously believing their presence had been responsible for Britain's economic crisis and industrial decline.

No more vividly was this penchant for nostalgia expressed than in the words and deeds of David Bowie, whose arrival at London's Victoria Station in June 1976 caused controversy when he appeared to give a Nazi salute from a Mercedes convertible (Stewart, 1976: 2). Bowie rejected the suggestion that he was giving a Nazi salute and claimed to have been caught in mid-wave (Gilmore, 2012). In another interview, Bowie claimed that

> Adolf Hitler was one of the first rock stars. Look at some of the films and see how he moved. I think he was quite as good as Jagger.
>
> Bowie, quoted in Gilmore, 2012

For one whose very existence has been one of frequent change, Bowie's sudden attachment to Nazi iconography was a rather worrying development that could not be lightly dismissed. However, the glamsters who followed him, and the other glam rock artists, were mainly hedonistic rather than ideological. Hebdige (1986: 61) observes "Bowie's meta-message was escape – from class, from sex, from personality, from obvious commitment – into a fantasy past [...] or a science fiction future". But was his flirtation with Nazism another escapist fantasy? It certainly appeared to be a postmodern disavowal of history, with Hitler presented as no more than a sign that had been emptied of its meaning (or at least partly divested of its ideological contents). Bowie's neo-Nazi sympathies were part of the 'Thin White Duke' persona of his *Young Americans* phase. Ultra-white and European, Bowie's character initially fetishized American soul music but eventually threw it overboard for Krautrock and electronica on his return to Europe in 1976. Bowie's views were wilfully ignorant but no less rooted in his art-school education, and differed in tone from the plain speech of Eric Clapton, Roger Daltrey, and Rod Stewart, whose positions on 'race' and immigration seemed more in tune with the thuggishness of skinhead gangs. Two months after the Bowie episode, a drunken Clapton told concertgoers in Birmingham "[I think] Enoch's right… we should send them all back. Throw the wogs out! Keep Britain white!" The volatility of these comments coincided with a rise in fortunes of the far-right National Front (NF) and the openly neo-Nazi British Movement (BM), both of which had seen a sharp increase in their respective members since Enoch Powell's 'Rivers of Blood' speech in 1968. These incidents were met with fury by those on the left and music papers like the *New Musical Express* (NME), which published an open letter from Red Saunders and Roger Huddle, formerly of CAST and Kartoon Klowns, attacking Clapton's speech and urging readers to form a rank-and-file movement to respond to the upsurge in racially motivated attacks (*New Musical Express*, 11 September 1976). The response to this letter led to the formation of Rock Against Racism (RAR), which offered a cultural response to the NF by marshalling the youthful energy of the punks, dreads, and their respective sounds, and fusing them with left-wing politics (Hebdige, 1986). RAR was supported by the Anti-Nazi League (ANL), which was formed in April 1978 as RAR's political wing. Also involved in RAR and the ANL was David Widgery, an East London GP, writer, essayist, political activist, and member of the Socialist Workers Party (SWP), who acted as chief propagandist. In turn, Widgery had connections to CAST, who were also briefly members of the SWP and were performing feminist and anti-racist plays around this time (Muldoon, 2011 interview). Thus, it is reasonable to argue that the social relations on the field of cultural production, at its autonomous pole, were directly influenced by the field of left-wing fringe politics. The discourses produced by the relationship between the various groups on this new cultural-political field partly contributed to the production of new countercultural forms of expression in a way that had not been witnessed since the anti-war movement of the late 1960s. The new countercultural formations that emerged from this unity of youth subcultures and fringe left politics led to a flowering of cultural producers (musicians, poets, comedians, and so on) who were committed to forms of revolutionary action within the arts. This also meant that they were opposed to the 'capitalist Labour' government and the Conservative opposition as much as the neo-Nazis. Thus, they refused the *doxa* of conventional politics and the channels through which dominant political discourse was articulated, and created their own spaces and channels for the circulation of alternative discourses.

The extent to which RAR succeeded in challenging far-right politics is open to debate: the ANL and RAR were not the street equivalents of the NF or BM, and the SWP officially forbade its members to engage in physical confrontations with fascists.[1] Therefore, at street level, the efficacy of the RAR and the ANL is rather marginal. Politically, the NF, which had stood candidates in almost every constituency in the country, had been outflanked at the ballot box by the Conservatives. Indeed, by the 1979 general election, Thatcher had skilfully appropriated the anti-immigration rhetoric of the NF and injected it into mainstream political discourse to the extent that phrases like 'swamped with immigrants' became normalized. Consequently, the NF was marginalized as a political force. RAR, on the other hand, was wound up in 1984 after nearly eight years of activity. However, the success of RAR cannot necessarily be measured by its street effectiveness alone, but by its fusion of culture and politics, which informed and influenced the post-punk counterculture that grew up alongside it and helped to shape the discourses of the altcab scene.

Old-fashioned attitudes towards difference – be they ethnic or sexual – figured prominently in light entertainment as joke-butts. British television

---

[1] This unofficial practice was referred to as 'squaddism', and the difference over tactics for defeating the fascists between the 'squaddists' and the SWP's Central Committee led to the expulsion of the former and the subsequent formation of Red Action.

depicted Blacks and Asians as low-status figures of fun in situation comedies like *It Ain't Half Hot Mum*[2] and *Mind Your Language*. Another light-entertainment programme, *The Black and White Minstrel Show* was based on the popular 'nigger' minstrel shows of the music-hall era, and was detached from the present through the unapologetic use of blackface make-up, which illuminated, to a large extent, the BBC's parochialism and socio-cultural insularity and seemed to belong to another era. After a series of complaints that stretched back to 1967, the show was finally cancelled in 1978. Yet it would take most of the 1980s to fully expel racism and sexism from the field of light entertainment and render it obsolete.

In Autumn 1978 the opinion polls gave James Callaghan's Labour government a respectable lead over Thatcher's Conservatives, but he lost his nerve and failed to capitalize on these ratings and call an immediate election (Turner, 2010; Stewart, 2013). Meanwhile, the relationship between the unions and the government was strained to breaking point, and when both parties failed to reach an agreement over the much-diluted social contract, a wave of public-sector strikes ensued, culminating in what the Conservative-supporting press coined "The Winter of Discontent" (Evans, 1997). With the numbers of people out of work increasing, the Conservative-supporting advertising firm Saatchi and Saatchi produced billboards with an image of a long queue of people – taken to be a 'dole' queue – that carried the strapline "Britain Isn't Working". Yet ironically, the numbers of unemployed always grew under Conservative rather than Labour governments, a fact that was ignored by the Tories, but which would return to haunt them in the next couple of years. Labour was a party in crisis, and, in government, it seemed as though it was content to be carried along by the currents of history rather than navigate its own course. Its willingness to apply for an International Monetary Fund (IMF) loan[3] to solve the Sterling crisis perhaps illustrates a fatal combination of political inertia and a lack of intellectual courage. It was Callaghan's Labour government that introduced neoliberalism to Britain through its

---

[2] In this sitcom, one character, Bearer Rangi Ram, was played by Michael Bates, who was in fact a white Anglo-Indian in Blackface. While there were Asian actors performing other roles, their characters were limited to head-wobbling and the uttering of phrases in broken/pidgin English.

[3] The IMF loan was used and continues to be used by the Conservatives to highlight Labour's alleged economic incompetence. In the end, the loan was never used and was fully repaid in 1979 by the Callaghan government before it left office.

embrace of Milton Friedman's economic theory of monetarism, rather than Thatcher and the Conservatives. It could therefore be argued that Labour 'test drove' the doctrine before the Tories accepted it as a *fait accompli* and infused it with its own authoritarian-libertarian ideology (the need for social spending cuts became an ideological imperative). Labour's bitter in-fighting was mostly caused by the leadership's acceptance of monetarism, which had led those on the left of the party to conclude that Labour had moved too far to the right. These tensions would be played out throughout the early part of the following decade, as could be witnessed, first, in the formation of the Social Democratic Party (SDP) and, second, in a series of expulsions that were instigated as a reflexive action to press hounding over the presumed and malign influence of the Militant Tendency within the Labour Party.

By March 1979 Callaghan's poll ratings had slipped further and the Liberals (who had supported Labour in a confidence and supply arrangement dubbed the Lib–Lab Pact in 1976) and the nationalist parties withdrew their support for the government, prompting a vote of confidence, which they lost. Within days of his Commons defeat, Callaghan called a general election for 3 May. Two days after the vote of no confidence, the Conservative MP, Airey Neave was killed by a bomb that had been planted beneath his car by the Irish National Liberation Army (INLA) (Stewart, 2013). Neave, a hardliner, had recently been appointed shadow Northern Ireland secretary by Thatcher and was seen as an implacable opponent of Irish republicanism. Months later, the Provisional Irish Republican Army (PIRA) would kill the Queen's cousin, Lord Mountbatten, his grandson and two others as he was holidaying on his yacht off the coast of Sligo in the west of Ireland (Stewart, 2013). For many on the Right, the numbers killed by the PIRA and the INLA could only be met with violence and there were calls to require Irish people to carry forms of identification with them at all times. Some wanted to go further and expel the Irish from the British 'mainland' altogether (Hennessy, 2013). These sentiments were shared by the far-right parties, which had fraternal links with Ulster loyalist paramilitaries, many of whom had connections to the security services (Rolston, 2005).

On the streets of Southall, New Zealand-born schoolteacher Blair Peach was clubbed to death by a member of the Metropolitan Police's Special Patrol Group (SPG) and Clarence Baker, the manager of reggae band Misty in Roots, was so badly beaten that he was left comatose at an Anti-Nazi League (ANL) demonstration against a planned NF march through this predominantly Indian neighbourhood in West London in April (Widgery, 1986; Elms, 2005). The SPG was a militarized branch of the police that had been created in 1965 and had gained a degree of notoriety for its indiscriminate use of force against protesters and striking workers. Two years earlier it had been accused of brutality while breaking up pickets in the bitter Grunwick dispute, in which the issue of race had played a large part. After considerable pressure, the SPG would be disbanded in 1987 and replaced with the Territorial Support Group (TSG). This was the world into which altcab was born.

What follows is a cultural history of the cabaret circuit that has been separated into four sections, each of which discuss a particular period in the life of altcab. The first wave is the rawest, most amateur, and avant-garde wave. The second is a reconstitution of the circuit after its near collapse and the third is a period of transition from the amateur circuit to a professional circuit that is orientated towards television. In the final section, I discuss the death of altcab. It was at this point that comedy panel shows began, with programmes like *Have I Got News for You*, whose parent was BBC Radio Four's long-running current affairs comedy panel show, *The News Quiz*.

The First Wave (1979–1982)

In the weeks before the opening of the Comedy Store, *TO* (469, 1979: 12) carried a short history of RAR by David Widgery titled 'The Rising of the Neon Star'. Widgery (469, 1979: 12) wrote that "RAR clubs" had formed up and down the country and added, "These shows exist in over 30 towns, putting on small-scale gigs and run by a mixture of culture conscious lefties and punk and Rasta kids". Widgery's article also acted as a means to publicize a forthcoming RAR festival at Alexandra Palace a couple of days later featuring Gang of Four, Misty in Roots, Tom Robinson, John Cooper Clarke, Aswad, Angelic Upstarts, and the Leyton Buzzards (469, 1979: 12). There are no comedians of any description involved, although Cooper Clarke has what could be described as a 'humorous bent'. Indeed, there seems to be few indications at this stage that the sub-fields of comedy and light entertainment would come under any kind of assault from countercultural forces.

Two weeks later, the following shows are listed in the Fringe Theatre section of *TO* (471, 1979: 25): the "Aba Daba Music Hall", about which there are no details save for its location at the Pindar of Wakefield (now called the Water Rats), on Gray's Inn Road; there is fringe theatre with Broadside [Mobile Workers] Theatre's production of *Divide and Rule Britannia,* which is billed as "an anti-racist play" at City and East London College, E1; while CAST present *What Happens Next?* at the Croydon Warehouse Theatre, which is also billed as "an anti-racist play" and is "hosted by the Croydon Anti-Nazi League". The Foundation (which had undergone a recent name change) at the Tramshed in Woolwich features "contemporary songs and sketches from Joe Griffiths and friends". Gareth Hale and Norman Pace (Hale and Pace) are involved in this show. Elsewhere, the Kings Head Theatre in Islington, N1 has "Fifty Words, Bits of Lenny Bruce conceived and compiled by Danny Brainin". This final listing is interesting because it also appears to foreshadow altcom. Bruce's influence is considerable because he provides a template from which many alt comedians based their routines. What these listings reveal to us are the seeds of what will later become a circuit. Particularly important is the relationship between CAST and the ANL, which illuminates the nexus between culture and politics that altcab would adopt as its philosophical position on the field of popular entertainment.

On 4 May, Margaret Thatcher's Conservative Party won the general election but not by a landslide (Turner, 2010; Stewart, 2013). Within days of winning the election a comprehensive spending review was announced for October. The review called for the dismantling of the welfare state, the privatization of the nationalized industries, and the sale of council houses under what became known as "Right to Buy". A week later, the Comedy Store opened, but there is no mention of it in the Fringe Theatre section or elsewhere in issue 472 of *TO* (May 1979). CAST is listed in the Agit-Prop section with a "Final Performance of *Confessions of a Socialist*" at the Star and Garter pub in Putney (472, 1979: 81). This show is also billed as a "gala variety benefit for one parent families" and seems to foreground CAST's later work in NV.

In *TO* (473), a "Music Hall evening at Hoxton Hall" is listed in the Fringe Theatre section. The Foundation continues to play the Woolwich Tramshed. A fortnight after the Comedy Store opened, the following advertisement appears on page 22 in issue 474:

Discoed to death?
Bored to tears?
Brings Ho Ho!
To Soho!

The amount of information contained in the advertisement is scant, listing only the name of the venue – the Comedy Store – and the location. It bills itself as an open event for "twenty to twenty-five comedians, aspiring comedians, frustrated dentists etc." (*TO* 472: 22). There is the illuminating mention of a "conveyor belt" and auditions "will be held on Wednesday and Thursday between 6 and 8pm". When the Store opened, British stand-up comedy and light entertainment was 20 years behind its American cousin on a stylistic and cultural level. In the United States, there's been a tradition of social and political observation in mainstream stand-up comedy stretching back to the 1950s, while in Britain this was only beginning to take place in the mainstream, with performers like Dave Allen, Billy Connolly, and Victoria Wood performing comedy that broke aesthetically with the traditional stand-up styles of the WMCs. Rosengard's intention was to replicate the verve of the stand-up comedy he had seen at the Comedy Store in Los Angeles, but his attempt to find Britain's new comedians began awkwardly: the early acts at the Store were a mixture of mainstream comics, eccentrics, and left-wing fringe theatre performers, few of whom were up to standard (Wilmut and Rosengard, 1989; Cook, 2001). However, it is reasonable to argue that the only budding comedians who had any performance experience – apart from the mainstream comedians – were those who had either been involved in underground theatre or had worked as street performers at Covent Garden. Their performance skills, knowledge of youth cultures, socio-political consciousness, and their awareness of American stand-up comedians like Lenny Bruce and Richard Pryor were forms of cultural capital that were inscribed on their countercultural habituses.

In June, the Store chose Alexei Sayle as its compère and began using the gong show format that its producers, Don Ward and Peter Rosengard, regard as their unique idea (Wilmut, 1989; Cook, 2001). In reality, the format was borrowed from *The Gong Show*, a talent show on American network television in which hopefuls would perform for as long as possible before being 'gonged off'. The show's basic premise was that it was a freak show. According to the Internet Movie Database (IMDb, 2013), *The Gong Show* was aired in the years prior to the opening of the Comedy Store from 1976 to 1980 and made an appearance on British television in 1978. Furthermore, news had travelled across the Atlantic about *The Gong Show*, which meant that many British people would have been aware of its existence. It is also likely that Rosengard had seen *The Gong Show* on television during his trips to the United States.

"Alternative Kabaret" (*sic*) appears for the first time in issue 490 (September 1979: 29) at the Pindar of Wakefield pub on Gray's Inn Road. This was usually the venue of the Aba Daba Music Hall. The use of the letter 'K' to spell the word 'cabaret' informs us there is some knowledge of continental art cabarets on the part of the organizers and is a possible reference to the Berlin *Kabaretts* of Weimar Germany. Alternative Cabaret began at the Elgin pub on Ladbroke Grove and was a loose collective of performers that was founded by Tony Allen and Alexei Sayle and included, *inter alia*, Pauline Melville, Jim Barclay, Andy de la Tour, Combo Passé (a jazz band), and others, but here we see that it was created over one month earlier. This particular listing reads:

> Featuring Rat Krisis Kabaret and Comedy Store stars Tony Allen, Alexi [*sic*] Sayle, Helen Glavin, Paul Stevens and many others.

It is interesting how the acts listed are referred to as "Comedy Store stars" this early into the circuit's history and this description can be read as a form of countercultural legitimation that has been bestowed upon the new performers by the consecrating authority of *TO*. This is also the first ever listing of an altcab show and from this point on, "Alternative Cabaret" would become the widely used means of classifying this new entertainment genre. A month later, in *TO* 495 (1979: 31), "Kabaret" has been Anglicized as "cabaret", perhaps in an effort to fully situate this new form of entertainment within a British cultural milieu.

Although the Store had pitched itself to television, they provoked an attitude of indifference and mild amusement from the media. This was reflected in the initial response to it, which was to treat it like a freak show. Peter Rosengard (Wilmut, 1989: 11) explains:

> I had hoped that agents, TV producers and journalists would regularly come to discover new people. This didn't happen. The showbiz establishment regarded us as a threat. They didn't see any wider audience for a bunch of foul-mouthed amateurs. TV was out of the question.

Rosengard's description of the novice performers recalls punks' swearing, snarling, and spitting. Here we see how the dominant agents on the sub-field of television adopted a position of dismissiveness toward the newcomers. The raw energy of punk that had caught the music industry by surprise wasn't going to be replicated on television – at least, not for the moment. Television would only take an interest in altcab when it was deemed to have marketable value. Thus, we see how the official entertainment world, which includes the BBC, follow rather than lead.

In *TO* 498 there is a short feature about the Comedy Store titled 'Quip Joint'.[4] Stan Hey (498, 1979: 25), the article's author, writes, "On my second visit, I join compère Alexei Sayle 'back stage' [*sic*]. Like many of the comedians he has a background in fringe theatre". Again, we are reminded that left-wing fringe theatre practices formed the foundations upon which the new comedy was built. The rest was assembled from bricolage: rock phraseology, street argot, physicality, politics, and continental philosophy were held together in the personality of the performer and utilized as symbolic forms of counter*cultural* capital.

> It's given a lot of us who are committed to fringe theatre a chance to get together and work on new styles of comedy. We've formed a sort of loose collective called 'Alternative Cabaret' – lousy name I know – but we've started going around pubs trying to do something different from the old racist shit and such. I don't think any of us are under the illusion that we'll make the big time.
>
> Sayle, quoted by Hey in *TO* 498, 1979: 25

Here, Sayle states that they were still involved in fringe theatre, and in the last sentence, he recognized that what he and his fellow performers were participants in was an underground scene, because none of them expected to make a living by performing stand-up. On the field of entertainment, Sayle and his fellow performers consciously take a relational position against the "racist shit" of dominant cultural hierarchy. However, Muldoon (2011 interview) sees Sayles's apparent political engagement and his proletarian stance as little more than posturing. Cook (2001) also agrees, noting that Sayle is primarily a "physical performer". What Sayle is, if he is anything, is a new kind of performer who is engaged with the present rather than a romanticized variety past. We also see that fringe theatre is not just the foundation, but the engine of this new movement. He talks about "new styles of comedy" in the way a political-aesthete may talk about his/her movement challenging the primacy and the staleness of legitimated art forms.

---

[4] The title is a sly pun on the infamous Soho institution of the 'clip joint': a 'hostess' bar where the cost of drinks is vastly inflated and leaving the premises may cost the customer more money; such bars may be attached to strip clubs.

Les Dawson was also present for Hey's visit:

> "Well" he says after a long pause "Some of the material is bad obviously and there's one or two on here who'd get murdered up north. But it's useful, because it's a place to fail, and no matter what type of comedian you want to be, you need the experience of failure."
>
> *TO* 498, 1979: 25

What's noticeable in Dawson's assessment is his observation of how the generational conflict between the young and the old is now being played out on a different field from previous generational struggles (music, for example). Although Dawson is not terribly kind to the new comics, he offers them some avuncular advice by reminding them that failure (or 'death') is important to a comedian's development. The Store had no experienced comedians who matched Rosengard's specifications and such comedians inevitably had to be produced from scratch. This approach demanded experimentation, daring, and innovation and this was provided by underground theatre performers. Dawson also reinforces the belief that there are regional variations in comedy tastes, which are primarily rooted in the social, cultural, and economic tensions between the North and South. By implication, the mainly working-class Northerners are harder to please than the 'soft' suburban Southerners, whose tastes may tend towards the middle-class end of the spectrum, with its tendency to whimsy and cultural name-dropping (Bourdieu, 2003; Friedman, 2009, 2010).

The comedy of the traditional comedians seemed to exist in a space outside of time. Thus, it often recalled memories of the immediate post-war period with its rationing and austerity, the mother-in-law joke being an example of this now-fading world (Dembina, 2012 interview). For Ronnie Golden (2012 interview), the old-school comedy was beyond its use-by date:

> So, yeah, it was a new thing. I mean, America's had stand-up for years and years and we've had character comedians... I mean, comedy was the province of older men, you know, I mean... before the so-called alternative comedy, I mean it was... comedians were just old geezers, who were left over from the '30s and the '40s and doing gags and suddenly it was... this was a brand-new thing, there were no rules. It was kinda quite exciting.

The cultural divide between American and British forms of stand-up comedy is indicated here by the respective characteristics of each form. American stand-up has, since the 1950s, been more personal-political, whereas British stand-up was notionally apolitical, with comedians concealing their inner selves behind their jokes. Ronnie's use of the phrase 'old geezers' signifies the generational gulf between the old and the new and illuminates the tension with the parental culture, in this case represented by traditional light entertainment. This is reinforced by the phrase "who were left over from the '30s and the '40s", which illustrates the official world's resistance to change. However, Ronnie may be misremembering stand-up comedy in Britain, because as Double (1997) reminds us, stand-up comedians had existed in Britain, but not in the form that we currently understand them. Ronnie uses words like 'exciting' and 'new' to mark differences between his generation and the old geezers and character comedians. When Ronnie suggests that within this movement "there were no rules", he is not referring to an absence of *doxa*, but rather to the fact that the *doxa* itself was inverted in relation to the official world's unspoken sets of rules. The idea of what constituted entertainment, like art, was in the eye of the producer and audience. Therefore, traditional stand-up could never serve as an adequate model on which to base one's performance.

Traditional stand-up of the 1970s was reactionary and often avoided any philosophical engagement with the world, and light entertainment was, generally, insular and nostalgic. Cultural products from the official world represented the decline of Britain as an industrial and imperial power, and rather than look forward, its cultural industries sought refuge in nostalgia. The young upstart comedians that challenged the dominant hierarchical principle were not only regarded as unfunny, but the old guard saw them as alien invaders who hadn't paid their dues. Bernard Manning, in a *Daily Mail* obituary that was apparently written by him before his death in 2007, claimed:

> In their obsession with turning comedy into a branch of Left-wing politics, they forgot that the only point of jokes is to make people laugh. And that was what I was good at, whether I was on the cabaret circuit in Manchester or at the MGM Grand in Las Vegas.
>
> Bernard Manning, *Daily Mail*, 20 June 2007

If what Manning says is true, then WMC comedy was a branch of right-wing politics that wore its jocularized symbolic violence on its sleeve, while at the same time denying its effect or intent. The irony of this statement lay in the fact that the racist comedy of the WMC stand-ups is illustrative of the superiority theory of humour in which the butt – always a social formation – is deemed inferior to the joke-teller and his class (Lippitt, 1995b: 54–61). Manning and his fellow comics may not have found altcom funny, but it is worth remembering that the charges that were levelled against altcom were similar to those made against ground-breaking comedies like *The Goon Show*, *That Was the Week That Was* (*TW3*), and *Monty Python's Flying Circus* by the press as well as establishment entertainment figures. Outside of its rare outings in broadcast media, subversive humour tended to be confined to the visual arts and to the pages of magazines like *Punch*. Both *The Goons* and *TW3* were broadcast on mainstream media (the Home Service and BBC1 respectively), while *Monty Python* – though produced by Oxbridge graduates – was consigned to the cultural ghetto of BBC2, the Corporation's minority interest channel, because of its leftfield content.

Manning's and his fellow comedians' technical skills were often used as a rebuttal to criticism by his defenders. Steve Gribbin (2011 interview) observes:

> Some of them were brilliant technicians… then again, I always say to people, when people say "Bernard Manning was a brilliant technician" is a bit like going to see a skinhead band, who are in the BNP saying "Oh, they got a really good lead singer" – so what?

Manning and some of his fellow comedians may have possessed the technical competency required to deliver precision-tooled jokes, but their comedy wasn't only mass-produced; it was also reactionary and at times violent. In their hands, the joke was a weapon that could be deployed against any minority group; it was an iron fist inside a velvet glove. The use of the word 'technicians' is instructive because it illuminates the divide between notions of art and the technical competence of traditional joke-tellers who see their work, not as art, but as a skill that is devoid of the creative spark. The skill of delivering the perfect joke and its timing was of paramount importance to the trad. comedian rather than the meaning or attitude that lay behind it. Steve's allusion to BNP skinhead bands (like Skrewdriver) is a valid one, because these bands may have been competent, perhaps even good musicians but their art was in the service of the far right and its unpleasant discourses on national identity. It is difficult to get past this aspect of their work in the same way that it is hard to separate the Italian Futurists' misogyny from their manifesto (Marinetti, 1909 [2010]). Manning and his fellow comedians may not have been members of far-right parties and may even have found them repugnant, but they represented a type of comedy that was informed by postcolonial discourses of difference. Traditional comedians may have deflected criticism of their jokes by attributing it to a lack of a sense of humour on the complainant's part, but this overlooks the violent symbolism of racist/sexist jokes. The playfulness or aloofness with which the racist joke is delivered does not divert from the fact that such jokes reinforce dominant power relations and are produced, not in isolation from society, but subject to its discourses. Racist/sexist comedy reinforced bonds between members of particular working-class white fractions, which felt threatened by immigration, women's rights, and a growing sense of Black consciousness. In this respect, the racist and sexist comedy of Manning et al. functioned as a distorting mirror, reflecting back the thoughts, anxieties, and beliefs of their audiences as comically warped representations of minority groups. Anti-racism and anti-sexism were thus the leading edge of altcab's counter*cultural* thrust and were produced by the movement's early associations with left-wing political theatre, RAR, and feminism particularly.

In January 1980, the Fundation at Woolwich Tramshed was replaced by Rik Mayall and Adrian Edmondson's cartoon slapstick double act, 20th Century Coyote, which was imposed on the audience by the venue's management (Wilmut, 1989). The relationship between the pair and the venue wasn't a happy one. Edmondson describes the Fundation as "a very raucous, very light entertainment – Benny Hill kind of show – very funny, not quite my taste, but a good evening out" (Wilmut, 1989: 55). Mayall was less charitable about the Tramshed: "We stuck at it for a couple of months – because we thought our Equity cards would be in it" (Wilmut, 1989: 55). The catalyst for their departure was a punk production of *Macbeth* that the venue organizer wanted to stage (Wilmut, 1989). Mayall's earlier mention of "Equity cards" is worth consideration. Membership of Equity was a pre-requisite to working in television, which was then a closed shop. However, to obtain an Equity card, one had to produce two past, present, and future contracts, which was difficult if there were long gaps between bookings. The pair successfully auditioned for the Comedy Store in early 1980 and they worked at the Tramshed and the Store until May 1980, when the Fundation was reinstated (Wilmut, 1989). Regular work at the Store and the Tramshed would have provided them with the necessary qualifications several times over. Over the years, the circuit would be used as a launch pad to television work, with many venue promoters willing to provide (non-binding) contracts to novice comedians eager to leave the circuit for greater things.

The arrival of the Thatcher government brought much uncertainty and a great deal of anxiety. The public sector came under attack and the meagre social gains that had been made in the late seventies were now under threat. Nick Revell (2013 questionnaire) likened the arrival of Thatcher and her reactionary views to a form of "counter-revolution". This counter-revolution touched all social relations and would provoke spasms of civil disobedience that would sometimes take the form of rioting. Worse still, the Thatcher government signalled its intention to destroy what it referred to as 'the permissive society'. This was a not-so-coded reference to the countercultural formations of the 1960s, and the Campaign for Nuclear Disarmament (CND), in particular, would be singled out for special attention in the early 1980s.

The St Paul's riots in April 1980 heralded a pattern of similar disturbances that would become a recurrent feature of the Thatcher period (Turner, 2010; Stewart, 2013). The riots began after the police raided the Black and White Cafe in St Paul's, a predominantly Black area of Bristol. One of the primary factors behind the riots was the police's indiscriminate use of the **Sus laws** (or **Section 4 of the Vagrancy Act (1824)**), which allowed them to stop and search anyone they suspected of having committed a crime or being in the process of committing a crime. The Sus law was seen by many to be indicative of the underlying racism in the police force, which tended to criminalize and profile Black people as well as those whose ways of life were at odds with the dominant culture: this meant that anyone wearing punk clothing was also stopped by the police. The NF had also been campaigning in the St Paul's area and this caused a great deal of tension within the community. Finally, there was urban decay and neglect, a factor that would reappear in subsequent riots over the course of the decade. The riot was roundly condemned by most sections of the media but no effort was made to understand the underlying causes.

Veteran parliamentarian, Michael Foot, was elected Labour leader at the Labour Party conference in October 1980, after seeing off a challenge from right-winger Denis Healey, the former Chancellor of the Exchequer (Turner, 2010; Stewart, 2013). Despite the claims made by sections of the media and the Tory Party, Foot was seen as a compromise candidate who could unite both right and left wings of the party. However, his election did not have the desired effect and, in turn, led to more in-fighting between the right and left wings of the party. A year later, Healey would face a challenge for his position from left-winger Tony Benn. Benn and the Left wanted revenge for what they saw as Callaghan's betrayal, especially over the issue of monetarism, and to steer the party in a more leftward direction. The country was again in recession and with Foot's election as Labour leader, the party's ratings improved in the polls and it looked, for a time, as though Labour might be returned to power at the next general election – despite the internecine struggles within the party. The Trotskyite group the Militant Tendency (simply known as 'Militant' and organized around the publication of the same name) had been operating within the Labour Party as *entryists*[5] since its foundation in the early sixties. Despite pressure from the press and the Right, the party resisted calls to expel Militant.

October 1980 marked the beginning of the first Irish hunger strike at the newly renamed Maze Prison (formerly Long Kesh) in Northern Ireland, when seven prisoners refuse to take food in response to the earlier removal of the special category status,[6] which regarded Irish republican inmates as *de facto* political prisoners. The following month, a further 25 prisoners would join the strike. These hunger strikes were the final phase of a five-year campaign that began with the 'blanket protests' and the so-called 'dirty protests' of the late seventies (Stewart, 2013). Like their post-punk musical counterparts, many alt comedians were sympathetic to the Irish struggle. Andy de la Tour (quoted in Wilmut, 1989: 40) frequently commented on Northern Ireland, and was one of the first English comedians to play republican clubs.

> I did quite a lot of stuff about Northern Ireland – it was good satire and the audience used to appreciate it – but sometimes people would respond badly, simply on the grounds of its politics, no matter how funny other people in the audience found it.

---

[5] As a political group, Militant practised the tactic of political entryism, a method that is adopted by small political groups that join a larger party with the aim of transforming the party from within. This is not a tactic that is unique to the left: for example, the Monday Club was a Conservative Party entryist group that could even boast members of the NF among its number (and vice versa). The pressure on Militant would continue until 1986, when Labour was forced to expel the Militant MPs Terry Fields and Dave Nellist.

[6] Special category status granted inmates the *de facto* status of political prisoners.

This reminds us that even old-school Irish comedians like Frank Carson found it easier to play up to their English audience's expectations of their Irishness rather than challenge age-old prejudices.

The Store suffered an early blow in October when many of its leading names (20th Century Coyote, the Outer Limits, French and Saunders, Arnold Brown, and Alexei Sayle) defected to the Comic Strip (Ritchie, 1997; Cook, 2001). Around this time, the relationship between Ward and Rosengard had reached breaking point and it looked for a time as though the Store would close. According to Cook (2001: 75), Rosengard's relationship with the performers was also strained and this was part of the reason for the formation of the Comic Strip. Another reason cited for this exodus was the hostile atmosphere at the Store, which Sayle likened to "a circus" (Cook, 2001: 76). The Store's artistic director, Kim Kinnie, admitted, "They felt they were being exploited. We were using them as fodder, which is why the rest of them moved away, because they wanted to progress with their comedy, to be allowed to develop" (Cook, 2001: 76). Ward eventually bought Rosengard out of the business and the latter established his own short-lived club on Baker Street before returning to his work as a life-insurance salesman (Wilmut, 1989).

The Comic Strip took up residence at the Boulevard Theatre, which like the Store was in an upstairs room of a popular strip club, the Raymond Revue Bar. *TO* 548 described the Comic Strip show as:

> A new cabaret featuring a selection from Alexei Sayle, Pamela Stephenson, The Outer Limits, Twentieth Century Coyote, John Dowie, Furious Pig, Arnold Brown and others too.
>
> *TO* 548, October 1980: 30

This listing belies the popular notion that the Comic Strip only featured a small group of people that gathered around Peter Richardson and Pete Richens, who were clearly the Comic Strip's driving force. It is also interesting to see John Dowie, who by now was considered a comedy veteran, included on the bill. Another interesting inclusion is the a capella post-punk band, Furious Pig, which appears to suggest a cultural bond between altcom and the post-punk music scene. On the same page, there is a caption review of the show with a black-and-white photograph of Alexei Sayle in mid-skank. His porkpie hat is pulled over his eyes and he is wearing dark Sta-Prest trousers that do not match his tight-fitting two-tone jacket. Unusually, rather than wearing Dr Marten's boots, he is wearing a pair of tasselled loafers, a favourite with skins, two-tone kids, and 'soul boys'. Nichols (*TO* 548, 1980: 30) advises us to "catch his Bertolt Brecht and Two-Tone poet acts". Two issues of *TO* later and the Comic Strip is being billed as "London's newest anarchic cabaret" (550, 1980: 28). The following week, in issue 551, the Comic Strip is described as "As fine a breeding ground for thinking person's comedy as anything since the Establishment Club" (1980: 27). Here we find the press not only selling the Comic Strip as a descendant of the Establishment Club, but also seeking to connect it to a rather middle-class audience, whose habituses possess the required level of cultural capital to decode any references contained within the comedy.

The Comic Strip's stay at the Boulevard was a relatively short one, after which they transferred to the new television station, Channel Four, in October 1982 – two years after they formed. *The Comic Strip Presents...* was the channel's debut programme and ushered in a new era of minority interest broadcasting. In the same month *The Young Ones*, starring Mayall, Edmondson, Planer, and Sayle, would begin airing on BBC Two. The Comic Strip adopted a position on the alternative sub-field that made it attractive to agents of the television comedy sub-field. The Comic Strip placed more emphasis on tight scripting rather than new material or experimentation and in this sense, it was 'readymade' for television. However, the Comic Strip was the exception rather than the rule; more cabaret clubs were starting to open in and around the heart of London and many were offering an anarchic mix of stand-up, poetry, songs, and speciality acts, and efforts by television producers to capture the spirit of the clubs were unsuccessful. This was the case with BBC2's *Boom, Boom... Out Go the Lights*, which lasted for only two shows, each a year apart.

The year 1981 began tragically: on 18 January, 14 Black teenagers were killed and 30 were injured in a house fire in New Cross, London (Goodyer, 2009). The blaze was blamed on arson but two inquests held after the tragedy returned open verdicts (Lahiri, 2001; Stewart, 2013). One reason for suspecting arson had been the presence of the NF and other far-right groups in the area. (The fire at the Albany Empire[7] in Lewisham in 1978 was also blamed on the NF, but this was never proved.) Coincidentally, according to Widgery (1986) and Renton (2006) the Albany had supported RAR and this was cited as a reason for the arson

---

[7] The Albany would later become one of early altcom's main venues. It was there that I played my first Black Comedy night in 1989.

attack. However, the police later ruled this out and ultimately failed to apprehend anyone in connection with the fire. Worse still was the media's worrying lack of interest in the deaths, which appeared to hinge on the notion that the story wasn't worth the coverage because the signifier of a "Black party" had become "entrenched as a sign of disorder and criminality" that wasn't "recognizably British" (Gilroy, 1987: 102). These crude associations had been drawn in the early 1970s by sensational newspaper headlines that connected Blacks with the crime of mugging and other forms of petty criminality (Hall, 1982; Gilroy, 2002). Instead, responsibility for the blaze was pinned onto the party-goers by sections of the press and the police alike, who problematized and criminalized the Blackness of the teenagers (Gilroy, 2002). The fire and the police's failure to properly investigate the deaths contributed to a growing sense of alienation and frustration among British Blacks, which would lead, in part, to the Brixton riots later in the year (Lahiri, 2001).

A week later, the so-called Gang of Four[8] split from the Labour Party (they were followed by nine more Labour members the following day) and formed the Social Democratic Party (SDP) in March (Stewart, 2013). The rationale behind the SDP was to create a centre-left party in the mould of European social democratic parties, which are primarily drawn from the ranks of the metropolitan middle classes rather than organized labour. Unable to attract enough votes on their own, the SDP formed an electoral alliance with the Liberal Party with the aim of displacing Labour as the Official Opposition. The SDP became the butt of Alexei Sayle's humour and he savaged them on *OTT*, Central Television's (1981) short-lived adult version of the popular Saturday morning children's show *Tiswas*.

> They're great, the Social Democrats. They're the K-Tel[9] of British politics. Same shit, different package.
>
> Alexei Sayle, *OTT*, 2 January 1981

A small number of cabaret shows are beginning to appear in the Fringe section, while some of the same shows also appear in the "Agit-prop" section. CAST straddles the "Fringe Theatre" and "Agit-prop"

---

[8] Roy Jenkins, Shirley Williams, Bill Rodgers, and David Owen were leading figures on the right of the Labour Party.

[9] K-Tel is an 'as-seen-on-TV' company that specializes in compilation albums of pop chart hits, which were ridiculed by 'serious' music collectors for their apparent lack of imagination.

sections because they continue to work as a radical theatre troupe, while promoting their NV shows at the Old White Horse in Brixton (see Chapter 5). What is noticeable is the number of clubs that were opening in areas outside of central London. One such club was the long-running Earth Exchange (billed as Archway Cabaret), which opened in January and was situated in a small vegetarian café in Highgate (McGillivray, 1989: 151). The club had no PA system and was fairly typical of many of the clubs of the period: it was a basic space that attracted a politicized, if rather ideologically sensitive audience (Gribbin, 2011 interview; Revell, 2013 questionnaire). Another club that opened was the Culture Bunker in Crouch End, North London (McGillivray, 1989: 151). In 1985, Peter Grahame and Huw Thomas, a folk musician and lecturer in performing arts at Middlesex Polytechnic, would assume control of the venue and rename it Cabaret at the Kings Head. Grahame was and continues to be the booker and organizer, and Thomas was compère. The club would later be renamed Downstairs at the Kings Head after a refurbishment in 1988 and continues to the present day.

The official unemployment figures for January 1982 showed that three million people were out of work (Turner, 2010; Stewart, 2013). The primary reason for this lay in the decline of the traditional heavy industries like steel and shipbuilding, which had been nationalized after the war and were running at a loss. However, the reasons for the industries' losses were never properly discussed and were often blamed on union militancy rather than poor management and a lack of investment. Government's rationale for privatizing the nationalized industries centred on the notion that private control of this sector would lead to greater efficiency and productivity. These industries, along with coal mining, had large numbers of unionized members. However, we should also remember that much of the private sector at this time was also unionized, so while it was easy for the government to suggest that great sums of money were being lost by the nationalized sector through industrial action, the private sector was equally prone to strikes (Grunwick being a notable example) and no more efficient or productive than the state-owned industries.

March 1982 saw the beginning of the second Maze Prison hunger strike. Bobby Sands, the strike leader, was elected MP in the Fermanagh and South Tyrone by-election the following month (Hennessy, 2013). Thatcher had no intention of accommodating the demands of republicans and responded by declaring, "We are not prepared to consider special category status for certain groups of people serving sentences for crime.

Crime is crime is crime, it is not political" (University of Ulster, CAIN, 2011); but this proved to be a Pyrrhic victory for Thatcher and the deaths of the hunger strikers earned them the status of martyrs, which in turn acted as a recruiting sergeant for proscribed republican organizations and led to an escalation in attacks on the British mainland (Hennessy, 2013).

In April 1982 the first in a series of riots began in Brixton, South London. The catalyst for the riot was the police's intimidatory behaviour toward African-Caribbean residents. Of particular concern was the Met's arbitrary use of the Sus laws to stop and search people. Other contributory factors included the lack of employment opportunities and the neglected state of the area, as well as the Met's inaction over the New Cross house fire in January. The Brixton riots were followed three months later by the Toxteth riots in Liverpool, the cause of which can be attributed to many of the same factors that had contributed to the Brixton riots. The mainly Black and mixed-race population of Toxteth had also seen an increase in the use of Sus laws. Another causal factor was the damaging effect that the containerization of Liverpool docks was having on the local economy (Boyle and Charles, 2011). This had led to mass redundancies: as many of those living in Toxteth had been employed on the docks, they were now forced onto the unemployment queues to look for jobs that did not exist. The press and the local police blamed Toxteth and the previous riots on race, but there is evidence that white youths from other parts of the city had travelled in to fight side by side with Black youths (Boyle and Charles, 2011). In the same month, the Handsworth riot erupted in Birmingham and would be the first of three such riots that would occur there in the space of ten years. In this case as in the last, similar socio-economic circumstances were causal factors in the disturbances, but the right-wing press chose to frame the riots as an outbreak of criminality. On *OTT*, Alexei Sayle's response to the rioting and the continuing impoverishment of Liverpudlians was to produce this scathing attack on the government's response to the crisis, nationalism, and the way in which they continued to attack working-class communities:

> I'm gonna be Willie Whitelaw [the Home Secretary]: the human tortoise [makes physical impression of a tortoise retreating into its shell] "Riots! Oh! Back to sleep!"
>
> I've been travelling around Britain looking at what's trendy for you. You'll notice, by the way, that I don't say "Great Britain", you know… because I think it's a really imperialistic concept – Great

Britain [contorts body]. I mean, nobody says "Bloody Brilliant France", do they? Or "Not Bad Italy". Stupid, isn't it? It can't be that great... Three million unemployed and the country run by a lunatic!

By April 1982 (*TO* 606, 1982), a recognizable altcab circuit was beginning to develop. The cabaret clubs that I have teased out of the Fringe Theatre section are as follows:

The Crown and Castle, Dalston: The Flying Pickets, Silly Boy Lemon Jazz

Earth Exchange Cabaret, Highgate: Randolph the Remarkable, Peter Weir, Headless Wonder Theatre

Gate Theatre, Notting Hill Gate: The Wow Show with Lee Cornes, Steve Frost, Mark Arden, and Mark Elliot

Karno's Kabaret, Black Horse pub, Catford: Flying Pickets, John Holt, DIY Cabaret, MC Nick Edmett

CAST presents New Variety at the Old White Horse, Brixton: Roland Muldoon + Mr Clean, The Flying Pickets, Chip Shop Show, Felix and the Cats, Little Brother

Last Laugh at the Barracuda Club, Baker Street: The Three Courgettes, Brian Bailey, Helen Lederer

TO 606, 1982: 69

Helen Lederer and Peter Weir (sometimes spelled 'Wear') are the only two straight stand-up comedians on these bills and it is not clear if the "John Holt" listed here is a comic or the popular lovers rock[10] singer of the same name. Roland Muldoon, who performs stand-up comedy, tends to be thought of as a compère and actor. Lee Cornes is usually a compère, while Steve Frost and Mark Arden were collectively known as "The Oblivion Boys" and were an improvising double act. The rest of the

---

[10] Lovers rock was a popular form of reggae that had its origins in a type of reggae called 'rocksteady' that represented a break with the more politically conscious forms of reggae from artistes like Bob Marley and the Wailers, Peter Tosh, and Steel Pulse as well as the dub reggae of DJs like U Roy and Mikey Dread. As its name suggests, lovers rock was romantic in its lyrical content and sonically smooth. Popular lovers rock singers included Carroll Thompson, Janet Kay, Sugar Minott, and Freddie McGregor.

acts are comprised of a capella groups, poets, musicians, and speciality acts. What is also noticeable is the number of acts on these bills who were actors or performers with left-wing theatre companies. The Flying Pickets, for example, were formed by former members of 7:84 Theatre Company, while The Three Courgettes were a cabaret vocal group formed by Barb Jungr, Michael Parker, and Jerry Kreeger. Jungr and Parker would later form an eponymous musical partnership and play the cabaret circuit as a duo. Felix and the Cats is a swing band and acts like these were top of the bill at CAST/NV shows. Karno's Kabaret made a conscious association with the past by taking its name from music-hall comedian and theatre impresario Fred Karno (real name Fred Westcott), who invented the 'custard-pie-in-the-face' routine. What these bills also tell us is that the audiences who attended these shows did not go expecting an evening of stand-up comedy; these were variety shows – perhaps a new form of music hall, like the music halls before 1880, before they were commercialized (Kift, 1996). Other clubs would open at various points during the year and one of the most popular cabarets was the Figment at the Finborough in Earl's Court, which opened towards the end of 1982 (Wilmut, 1989: 79). This is the home of the Finborough Theatre Club, which has an upstairs room in the pub of the same name (McGillivray, 1990: 151). Like the Earth Exchange, it is a modestly sized venue, seating an audience of 60, though the facilities are rather more professional. Each of these clubs, along with CAST's NV circuit, would last well into the next waves.

Labour's poll ratings had fallen again and in April, Argentina invaded and occupied the Falkland Islands and the island of South Georgia in the South Atlantic. A task force was immediately dispatched to recover the territories, which were little known outside Foreign and Commonwealth Office circles. The conflict proved to be a godsend to the Thatcher government, which had been performing poorly in the polls, for within a couple of months, the conflict was over and the government benefitted from a huge surge in popularity.

In December 1982, the Comedy Store closed when the lease expired at the Gargoyle Club (Wilmut, 1989; Cook, 2001). This marked the end of the first wave of altcom/altcab. The first wave was a period of experimentation with the entertainment format as much as it was with the comedy itself. Everything, including stand-up comedy, was referred to as 'cabaret' and that would continue to be the case until the early 1990s. Even the Comedy Store, which self-consciously markets itself as a comedy club, is drawn into the orbit of this new kind of variety entertainment, for the Store at this stage also featured performers who were not stand-up comedians. The Store's listing in a previous issue of *TO* is revealing and tells us that it is an "Alternative cabaret with eight comedians each night" (617, 1982: 76). The policy of having all kinds of comedy on the Store's stage would also end, because when it reopened the following year, it would begin to phase out the unusual and eccentric acts.

The Second Wave (1983–1986)

TO's Cabaret section appears for the first time in January 1983 (648), a few months after its rival, *City Limits*. The front page announces "NEW CABARET LISTINGS" in a triangle in the top right-hand corner. Nevertheless, the Cabaret section is still part of the Fringe Theatre section and it is half a page in length with about a dozen shows, most of which are run by CAST, who are listed as "Cast Presentations Ltd" (648, 1983: 68). Pat Condell was the Cabaret section's resident poet during 1983–1984 and appears to have been a favourite with its editor, Peter Nichols. There are also more features in the new "caption review" about the circuit's performers. What is also noticeable is the increase in the numbers of benefits for a variety of political causes being listed in both the Cabaret and Agit-prop sections. This wave is also marked by the popularity of ranting poetry on the circuit. Performance poetry had become popular in the late 1970s through the work of John Cooper Clarke and Linton Kwesi Johnson and by 1983, the number of poets on the circuit had increased. Apples and Snakes, a club dedicated to poetry, opened in 1982 in Covent Garden and provided a hub for the Poetry Society, an organization dedicated to the promotion of poetry, which also provided subsidies for performance poetry. Those who were working on the circuit as poets at this time were Mark Miwurdz (Hurst), Little Brother, Joolz, Attila the Stockbroker, and Seething Wells. Enterprising cabaret promoters could apply for funding to pay ranting poets and this may well provide some explanation for their proliferation on the circuit during 1983–1986.

At the beginning of 1983, the circuit was still small, but throughout the course of the year, according to Bob Boyton and Ivor Dembina there would actually be "a shortage of acts" (see Chapter 4). The dearth of talent was due for the most part to the number of performers who had migrated to television to appear in the Comic Strip's productions on Channel 4, *The Young Ones* or other projects. During the latter part of 1982, cabaret courses were established at the Crown and Castle and Jackson's Lane Community Centre to produce the next generation of performers. These courses self-consciously referred to themselves as 'cabaret' rather than 'comedy' courses, which promised to teach novices "cabaret techniques" (McGillivray, 1990: 165).

Taking advantage of the Comedy Store's forced closure, Maria Kempinska and John Davy open Jongleurs at the Cornet in February 1983 in a former roller rink above the Cornet pub, adjacent to Lavender Hill in Battersea, South London. Jongleurs would become the Store's first serious rival, competing on the circuit for the status of flagship club. The choice of the name 'Jongleurs' is significant because it is French for 'jugglers' and implies a circus or, perhaps, carnival atmosphere, and is thus in keeping with the trend for such performers on the circuit. Kempinska's choice of location is equally significant: during the 1980s, Battersea was undergoing rapid gentrification, with its working-class residents in the north of the borough being displaced by a combination of homes being sold cheaply to private developers, Right to Buy, and Wandsworth Council's alleged gerrymandering – the so-called 'homes for votes' scandal. According to Wilmut (1989: 119), Jongleurs tended to market itself to a "relatively well-off audience". Cook (2001: 84) goes further, adding, "To many comics, this Battersea club soon became synonymous with those twenty-something Thatcherites called Yuppies". These views are supported by Mark Kelly (2012 interview) who says, "it very much belonged to the Radio Four, you know, type acts".

Jongleurs positioned itself as a commercial player within the alternative sub-field and thus represented a shift away from the anarchic cabarets of the previous years. By contrast, Jongleurs established itself as something slicker, professional and, more importantly, legitimate in relation to the amateurishness of the rest of the circuit and in this sense, one can see that Jongleurs, like the Store, stands apart from the rest of the circuit because of its positioning. Kempinska's rationale for breaking rank was simple:

> In those days you had people who were politically orientated, who would just get away with being just political on stage – without any intention of being humorous – but the audience accepted it because they were a fringe audience, and it was fun; nobody knew what was going to happen next.
>
> Kempinska, quoted in Wilmut, 1989: 118

Kempinska[11] appears to be saying two things here: first, she complains about "politically orientated" comics and then blames the audiences knowing no better. Yet the audiences attended altcab shows precisely because they were politically engaged and unpredictable. Second, she then admits it was "fun", citing the unpredictable nature of the cabarets. Her rationale for Jongleurs seems to have been constructed from two contradictory positions: the first denigrates the [left-wing] politics of some of the acts and the second finds the randomness – the very essence of the clubs – endearing and yet the model is rejected because it does not appear to be a commercial product. Furthermore, Kempinska's statement can be seen both as a rejection of left-wing politics and as a declaration of war on what remained of the 1970s countercultures. Indeed, when Jongleurs opened, the war in the Falklands was only a few months away and this would provide some of the comics with material and even provide the inspiration for a cabaret act called the Port Stanley Amateur Dramatic Society.[12] However, because of its mainstream positioning on the field, it is unlikely that Jongleurs would have been comfortable with material that opposed the war.

Jongleurs' commercial objectification tends be the object of criticism for many performers I spoke to, and the club's approach to performers could often be patronizing and heavy-handed. Dreenagh Darrell, for example, never played Jongleurs because Kempinska insisted that she wore a dress (2010 interview). In this sense, Jongleurs exhibited the *doxa* of the dominant cultural ideology, which is insistent that women dress and behave in a certain way, lest they be mistaken for men (Garber, 1993). Tony Allen and Mark Kelly (2011 and 2012 interviews, respectively) refer to Jongleurs as a comedy 'McDonalds',[13] because of its insistence on standardization. Here, we see that the commercial eye is incapable of recognizing aesthetic value and can only regard the performer as a source of potential revenue. Indeed, it would be reasonable to argue that Jongleurs had successfully marketed itself as an adjunct to the hospitality industry and produces commodities in the form of comedians, which are graded according to genre, packaged and then sold to whichever corporate client is interested in purchasing their services. We can see that Jongleurs, as a

---

[11] In 2003 Maria Kempinska received an MBE for her work in the entertainment and *hospitality* industry.

[12] Port Stanley is the capital of the Falkland Islands and was later renamed 'Stanley'.

[13] Ironically, McDonald's was one of Jongleurs' corporate customers.

corporate promoter (with an alternative gloss), transformed the sub-field of holiday-camp entertainment, which was originally the extension of the variety-theatre/music-hall circuit until the 1990s. Jongleurs also sells itself as the complete entertainment package for hen and stag parties and this kind of marketing has its obvious drawbacks: the drink, the food, or the dancing may take priority over the comedy and variety in the minds of the punters. In my experience, such audiences tend to like their comedy simple – free of difficult concepts and the kind of wordiness that needs to be comprehended with a sober mind. Therefore, the emphasis on this kind of comedy product matches the food in terms of its predictability and obviousness.

Jongleurs therefore appeals to a certain kind of audience and a certain kind of comedian who is prepared to compromise in order to make a living from their craft. There is nothing wrong with this and there are many performers who are prepared to compromise their principles for the lure of a decent wage. A comedian is self-employed and needs to keep a roof over their head and food in their belly. Yet such compromises demand a philosophical disengagement with the wider world that, in turn, panders to the lowest common denominator. Stewart Lee (2011 interview) suggests that Jongleurs have merely stepped into the void left behind by the diminishing number of working men's (CIU) clubs, with the new comedy styles supplanting the pre-packaged joke-telling of the old guard. The jokes themselves may not be pre-packaged, but they tend to follow roughly similar themes. The punters who make up a Jongleurs audience, like those of the WMCs, therefore know what kind of jokes to expect, and if these are not forthcoming then there can be problems (Kelly, 2012 interview).

Of all the acts that mentioned Jongleurs, Steve Rawlings (2013 questionnaire) was the only one who enjoyed playing there. However, there is an explanation:

> I used to love playing Jongleurs Battersea as I had enough space and height to do my full act there and I used to tear the place apart; Even getting standing ovations sometimes. It was also the place that the TV people used to come to watch acts and I got a lot of good work from that.

The high ceiling at Jongleurs at the Cornet made it an ideal venue for jugglers and other speciality acts that required room to perform, and reminds us of why the name 'Jongleurs' was chosen in the first place. Many clubs did not have the necessary ceiling clearance and therefore did not include jugglers on their bills. This is particularly true of many clubs that opened towards the end of the second wave, some of which occupied small rooms. Steve also reminds us that Jongleurs provided another showcase for television light-entertainment schedulers and producers. For all its faults, Jongleurs can be complimented for its embrace of variety and new circus.

A month after Jongleurs' circuit debut, the Store reopened in a former gay club called the Subway (previously the 400 Club) on Leicester Square. Located in a basement, it had a larger capacity and seated 150 people, but it had awkward sightlines and the facilities for the performers were basic. (The wash basin in the 'dressing room' was used as an *ad hoc* urinal.) Although Ward had taken possession of the Subway, it would remain mainly dark for nearly two years because of the lack of a public licence and the physical condition of the space (Wilmut, 1989; Cook, 2001). This accounts for its omission from *TO's* listings during 1985 (Wilmut, 1989: 117; Cook, 2001: 84). The new location would also begin a new era in terms of the Store's house aesthetic: speciality acts would be phased out from its stage, partly because the ceiling excluded jugglers and others who required the advantage of a high ceiling, and also because there was a change of emphasis on the part of Ward and Kinnie, who wanted to position themselves away from cabaret to stand-up comedy. Indeed, the opening of Jongleurs, which positioned itself explicitly as a cabaret club, has been cited by Cook (2001) as a possible reason for the Store's repositioning on the field. As if to sum this up, Kinnie admitted that "Don doesn't like prop acts" (Cook, 2001: 84). Prop acts, impressionists, jugglers, and other speciality acts would no longer appear on the Store's stage. They would, however, be welcomed at Jongleurs, provided they were willing to conform.

The planned deployment of American cruise missiles on British soil caused a great deal of alarm among anti-war protesters and CND saw its membership rise from around 79,000 to over 100,000 (Stewart, 2013). A march through London in October 1983 attracted over 200,000 demonstrators, while a women's camp was established at Greenham Common in Berkshire, where the missiles were due to be based. However, the Conservatives saw CND and the Labour Party as being in hock to the Soviet Union and regarded CND, in particular, as a Soviet front group that had financial backing from the Kremlin. CND had close ties to the left wing of the Labour Party and had support from a variety of smaller left-wing parties and religious groups like the Quakers. A year earlier, the

Labour left successfully persuaded the party to adopt unilateral nuclear disarmament as a manifesto commitment. Not only would this policy prove apparently disastrous in the forthcoming general election but it led to a violent backlash from the Conservative Party, which sought to destroy both the Labour Party and CND by pursuing it through the courts (Lewis, 2013).

In June, Thatcher went to the polls and the Conservatives won a landslide victory. Her party had seen a rise in popularity in the aftermath of the Falklands War and it is this reason that has always been cited as a major factor in the Tories' 1983 election victory (Evans, 1997). Labour MPs blamed their party's poor results on two things: Foot's leadership and what was seen as the party's *socialist* (*sic*) manifesto, which, *inter alia*, called for further nationalizations and withdrawal from the European Economic Community (later called the European Union). Rather than produce a unique manifesto for the election, the party adapted a policy document and presented it as a manifesto. Former writer for *That Was the Week That Was* (*TW3*) and the MP for Manchester Gorton, Gerald Kaufman, referred to it as "the longest suicide note in history". The divisions in the Labour Party became more public and there was open warfare between the right and left wings of the party, which played into the hands of the Conservative Party and its servants in the mass media. Tony Blair was elected the Labour MP for Sedgefield in a by-election; his rise through party ranks was rapid, being given the job of frontbench Treasury spokesman within a year of winning his seat. Damascene left-winger Tony Benn lost his seat when it was abolished in boundary changes and chose to contest a neighbouring seat, which he also lost. However, he was re-elected in the Chesterfield by-election the following year. Following this defeat, Foot immediately stepped down as Labour leader prompting a leadership election.

Autumn 1983 began with the mass breakout of 38 IRA prisoners from the Maze Prison in September, the largest such breakout from a Northern Ireland prison since the mass escape of 30 prisoners from the same prison – then called Long Kesh – in 1974. This was a major embarrassment for the government, which had taken a hard line against the republicans. At the Labour Party conference in October, Neil Kinnock was elected leader. He was challenged by left-winger Eric Heffer and right-winger Roy Hattersley. Kinnock chose the latter as his deputy but had a hard task ahead of him with the party flagging in the polls and the left wing of the party (including Militant) apparently making life difficult for him. United States forces invaded Grenada, a former British colony in the Caribbean, to overthrow the Revolutionary Military Council which had in turn overthrown the Marxist People's Revolutionary Government months prior to the invasion. The British government was unaware of the invasion and offered a timid criticism of American actions.

New cabaret clubs continued to open in London's suburbs, many of which would vanish before the end of the decade. One of the more successful clubs was Andy Waring's Banana Cabaret, which opened in November 1983 at the Bedford pub in Balham, South London. This large venue has two large rooms that can accommodate a combined audience of 400. The downstairs room is circular with a domed ceiling, while the upstairs room is long and rectangular with a slightly lower ceiling. The Banana is unique for being the only club on the circuit to have no compère; the acts are simply introduced by one of the organizers. Waring eventually retired from promoting the Banana and left the day-to-day running of the club in the hands of Dave Vickers at some point in the early 1990s.

Less than two months later, Malcolm Hardee's Tunnel Palladium opens at the Mitre pub, North Greenwich on New Year's Day, 1984. Hardee, who was one-third of the Greatest Show on Legs, had been involved in the proto-alternative scene of pub entertainment in the years leading up to the opening of the Comedy Store. The Tunnel (as it is better known) was notorious for its colourful hecklers and moments of mindless violence. Steve Gribbin (2011 interview) recalls the opening night:

> the Tunnel opened [...] on January the 1st 1984 and Skint Video did the inaugural, um... gig with Fiasco Job Job and the Greatest Show on Legs... that was the bill, compèred by Malcolm, of course. And, uh... it was an amazing evening... erm... and it was wild and the Tunnel existed for those people to go there... you know... people like Eric Fellowes, Venezuelan... from Venezuela, the worst singer–songwriter in the world...

Unfortunately, the Tunnel attracted some unsavoury elements – which Hardee described as "Rough herberts" and the "Cortina lot" from Eltham (Wilmut, 1989: 120) – some of whom were associated with the BNP, whose headquarters were located in nearby Welling. Unlike many of the clubs on the circuit, the Tunnel Club seemed to consciously appeal to working-class audiences, largely because of Malcolm's working-class roots and his local reputation as a lovable rogue and prankster, but also because of its location in a rather down-at-heel part of Greenwich. Dreenagh Darrell (2010 interview), who worked at the Tunnel, unusually, as a paid open spot, says: "I think the Tunnel [was] probably… of its time… but if you think about it, it was just a big boisterous working men's club". This part of town is now part of the regenerated Greenwich Peninsula but its landscape was once a mix of industrial sites and post-industrial dereliction with few residential areas and poor transport links. Dreenagh's comparison of the Tunnel with a "working men's club" is thus an interesting one, for its clientele seemed to reflect its locale and was the very opposite of the more upmarket Jongleurs.

Jerry Sadowitz was possibly one of the few performers to take on the rough crowd at the Tunnel and win, though it is entirely possible that his Glaswegian accent and confrontational manner actually helped in this situation. While Sadowitz 'faced down' his audience, others were not as fortunate, as Bob Boyton (2010 interview) observed in the case of Jewish comedian Arnold Brown (also from Glasgow).

> Arnold Brown was on stage there once and somebody shouted out "Gas the Jew!" You know, Malcolm should have barred him when he said that, because he knew a lot of people who'd come in… you know and he could have done that… he could have… he could have straightened that out… people had glasses thrown at them and that stuff.

On television, *Spitting Image* began its first series on the ITV network in February and made use of circuit performers like Chris Barrie and Harry Enfield to voice its puppets. *Spitting Image*'s appearance on television in 1984 was remarkable, if only for its timeliness. Aired during a politically turbulent decade, it captured the spirit of defiance to the Thatcher government through its latex puppets, which were instantly recognizable to the millions of viewers. Yet it was little more than a big 'two fingers up' to the establishment and cannot be considered an example of passive resistance, because it did little, if anything, to raise consciousness. It was, however, an effective piece of carnivalesque that helped millions of viewers to identify the politicians who were running the country. Significantly, *Spitting Image*'s innovative use of puppets allowed it to push the boundaries of taste and decency. It was also the first satirical show to lampoon the royal family, who were considered off limits until the 1980s. *Spitting Image*'s puppets seemed to recall the caricatures of Gillray, Rowlandson, and Hogarth, and lampooned politicians from all political parties and other famous figures. The royal family, whom satirists had avoided mocking since Cruikshank was bribed over one hundred years earlier for a pledge not to caricature or depict George IV, made a return to the public sphere of ridicule (Chester, 1986; BBC, 2012). The caricatures of politicians that appeared in *Spitting Image* are particularly instructive: for example, Margaret Thatcher was portrayed as a cross-dressing bully and tyrant; Norman Tebbit[14] was a leather-jacketed thug; Labour leader Neil Kinnock was a tedious windbag; the Queen was a little mad and sported a CND badge; while Pope John Paul II was depicted as a globe-trotting rock star.

In March 1984, the government went ahead with the pit closures that it had planned in 1982, when recently appointed National Coal Board chairman, Ian McGregor (who had previously been the chairman of British Steel), announced the loss of 44,000 jobs and the closure of around 20 pits. While the number of pit closures was fewer than those that had taken place under the previous Labour government, there were no jobs to replace those that were being lost.

In response to pit closures and redundancies, the National Union of Mineworkers (NUM), led by Arthur Scargill, called its members out on strike without a ballot. Unknown to the NUM, the Tories' preparation for a possible miners' strike was made under the terms of the Ridley Report (Conservative Research Department, 1978). Thatcher's government had been building up huge stocks of cheap imported coal for years and had recruited non-unionized lorry drivers to transport coal to the power stations. Scargill and Kinnock were split over the issue of a ballot and this led to tensions between the Labour leadership and the NUM. The Labour Party's support for the strike throughout the twelve months varied from tepid to complete indifference. To compound matters for the NUM, the Thatcher government had passed legislation in 1982 that would allow it to sequestrate a union's assets in the event that a union utilized 'unlawful' actions, like secondary and flying pickets, to persuade non-striking miners to join the strike.

Over the course of the next twelve months, many miners' benefit gigs would appear in *TO*. The strike galvanized the British working classes

---

[14] Tebbit was the MP for Chingford in Essex. He was employment secretary in the first Thatcher government (1979–1983), then trade and industry secretary (1983–1985) and party chairman (1985–1987). Tebbit has a direct and combative style and it was his comments in the aftermath of the Brixton riots that cemented his reputation as a 'hard man' in the public mind. He was referred to as "The Chingford Skinhead".

and those on the political left, who saw an opportunity to roll back the Thatcher government's 'reforms'. Assistance funds were established and food was sent to the families of striking workers, whose only source of income came from the tiny strike fund (the government had passed legislation that denied the families of striking miners access to social security benefits). Notably, CAST was involved in supporting the striking miners and formed Pit Dragon to mobilize comedians to entertain striking workers on picket lines around the country. Some of these entertainers had only recently been politicized by the Falklands War, the rioting in the inner cities, and the continuing situation in Northern Ireland. Although it would be fair to say that many of the performers involved in Pit Dragon had some prior experience of political activity, some like Harry Enfield, who wasn't necessarily known for his political observations, were also involved, thus demonstrating how deeply the strike had affected many sections of British society. Topical song parodists Skint Video were one of many acts to perform at miners' benefits and performed a parody of *The Laughing Policeman*, which satirized the use of police roadblocks to apprehend and detain flying pickets:

> I am a laughing policeman, I travel far and wide
> I look into the backs of cars for pickets hid inside
> And at the Dartford Tunnel, the miners parched and squelched
> They said "What about democracy?" and this is what we felt
> Oh ha ha ha ha ha ha ha… Ha ha ha ha ha ha ha!
>
> Skint Video, *The Laughing Policeman*, 1984
>
> Uploaded by Brian James Mulligan, YouTube, 2013

The *TO* cabaret section barely covers half a page at this juncture and lists little more than a dozen regular shows, most of which are part of CAST's NV circuit. There is an intriguing advertisement in issue 729 for "Time Out presents The Comedy Tapes recorded at Jongleurs, which features, Jenny Eclair, Fiasco Job Job [Arthur Smith and Phil Nice], John Sparks, Rory Bremner, Calypso Beat [later renamed Calypso Twins] and Dusty and Dick [Harry Enfield and Bryan Elsley]" (*TO* 729, 1984: 37). The same issue carries a listing for the "Off the Kerb Roadshow with John Hegley, Roy Hutchins, Podomovsky, Eric the Roadie + Brian Bailey" (1984: 37). Although it looks as though five acts are appearing on this bill, Podomovsky and Eric the Roadie are played by Andrew Bailey, a former street performer and popular comic, who was also a member of the Dialtones with Ronnie Golden and Mac McDonald. At this point, Off the Kerb[15] was an emerging artistes' management agency that was founded by Addison Cresswell[16] in 1981. Cresswell first represented John Hegley when he was working as an events officer at Brighton Polytechnic and gradually signed other acts like Bailey, Skint Video, Mark Steel, and Jeremy Hardy. Off the Kerb's biggest acts are currently Jonathan Ross and Michael McIntyre.

Saturday Live starts its first run on Channel Four in January 1985, with Lenny Henry as host. The launch of *Saturday Live* would prompt repositionings on the circuit, which Cook (2001) suggests led to the politically orientated comedy of Ben Elton and others being semi-legitimated by television light entertainment. In other words, left-wing-orientated stand-up comedy became the new mainstream and, on television, was reduced to little more than a spectacle. Here, contained in the television studios, altcom could do little more than conform. However, it would be fair to say that *Saturday Live* was not solely involved in the commercialization and eventual commodification of altcom as a standalone genre. The Store also played its part in reshaping the aesthetic contours of the cabaret circuit, because according to Cook (2001: 100) "The Store was the club where telly people went to trawl for talent". Through this relationship, it would appear that the idea of altcom as a classification had been mediated by television, because this term had not been widely used, if at all, before 1985; because of its relationship with television and the lucrative promise of regular paid work, the Store became the stand-up comedians' *El Dorado* and it is for this reason that many stand-up comedians will do all they can to secure the coveted 20-minute spot at the club – even if this means having to perform open spots *ad infinitum* and dying each time to achieve this goal.

Cook's (2001) thesis that audiences became bored with political comedy is refracted through the lens of the Comedy Store, while the politics he describes is framed within the narrow discourse of political ideologies and political parties (anti-Thatcherism expressed in its crudest, most misogynistic terms). There is certainly no reason to suggest that identity and other forms of political discourse were absent from the circuit's stages or the Store. It would appear to be the case, however, that some of the performers that Cook (2001) spoke to, no longer felt the need

---

[15] OTK is best known for its massive comedy tours and comedy game shows.
[16] Cresswell died in January 2014.

to include a mention of Thatcher in their routines and this would suggest that the mere mention of her name was seen as an easy way to get a laugh. This would also appear to indicate a lack of serious engagement with political discourses generally on the part of some comics, who now felt they were being constrained by so-called 'political correctness'. Indeed, for my part, there was always an insistence that the word 'politics' was being employed in a much broader context than Cook's (2001) narrow description. Nonetheless, the success of *Saturday Live* had the effect of creating new positions on the field, and the few political acts on the circuit were becoming fewer in number.

We should also consider how different the Store's audiences were in comparison to those in the clubs outside the centre of London. For the most part, the Store's late-night audiences were an often-dangerous mix of clientele who were fuelled by alcohol. The rest of the circuit, as Cook (2001) acknowledges, was very different, and experimentation and political discourse were still welcomed – for the time being. The Tunnel Club was perhaps the only exception and played to its own rules.

Nick Revell (2013 questionnaire) notes the highs and lows of playing the Store and compares this experience to the rest of the circuit:

> At the Comedy Store the audience would be a mix of counter-cultural and very mainstream people who were there for the heckling and the simple fact it served drink till 2am or whatever time it closed. So it was quite a volatile environment. Particularly doing political stuff – some people cheering, others threatening physical violence. Elsewhere, the audiences were much more gentle, and far more consistently 'alternative' – willing to give the benefit of the doubt to the more experimental acts, and willing to overlook the technical deficiencies of inexperienced stand-ups in favour of hearing the ideas. We were all so inexperienced.

However, this volatility could sometimes be reversed. Ronnie Golden (2012 interview) recalled

> seeing a comedian jump offstage and nut somebody in the audience and his nose just burst open into claret – everywhere and, um [laughs]. At other times, somebody would get up onstage and try and attack you 'cos they didn't know they were so drunk or they didn't like what you were saying… och, God, man, it was pretty 'out there'.

This danger was certainly common to the Store and the Tunnel, but there was little chance of anything similar happening at the Earth Exchange, the Meccano Club, or Banana Cabaret, whose audiences were suburban, often left-leaning, middle class, well-behaved, and tolerant.

By February 1985 (755), *TO's* Cabaret section covers two half pages spread over two pages and includes a half page of advertisements. More clubs are starting to open in outer London, one of which is Simon Palmer's Rub a Dub Club at the Greyhound pub in Sydenham. The bill for this show is small and only features two acts: Attila the Stockbroker and Jim Barclay. Elsewhere there is a miners' benefit concert listed at Stoke Newington Town Hall, which includes Bronski Beat and Benjamin Zephaniah. The Fundation continues to play at the Tramshed in Woolwich and this time lists folk singer and comic Richard Dignance and Hale and Pace on the bill (*TO* 755, 1985: 31). The Earth Exchange Cabaret celebrates its fifth anniversary with a special line-up of acts that includes Skint Video, who appear in the caption review. Peter Nichols (*TO* 755, 1985: 3) writes: "Of all the stages to strut and fret an hour upon, none is smaller than *The Earth Exchange*. The auditorium is a living room, centre stage the hearth".

February 1985 also sees a number of shows in support of the Greater London Council (GLC), which was being threatened with abolition in the government's Local Government Bill. The shows are called "GLC Giro Shows" presumably on account of the cheap entry price of £1. The GLC Giro Shows were organized by CAST and toured each of London's 32 boroughs, with the shows taking place at local town halls. Issue 756 (February 1985: 32) lists two of these benefits and what is interesting about these shows is the range of entertainment on offer. The show at Hornsey Town Hall on 15 February has a bill that comprises Northern soul superstar, Geno Washington, Dave Kelly, Lioness Chant, Port Stanley Amateur Dramatic Society, and "rasta comic" Kevin Seisay. The show for the following evening at Crayford Town Hall offers a bill of poets Benjamin Zephaniah and Anne Ziety with comic Kevin Seisay and "indie" bands Eyeless in Gaza and Microdisney (756, 1985: 32).

By March 1985 (*TO* 759), there is evidence of marked growth in the number of clubs on the circuit. There are 21 shows on Friday night and 16 on Saturday. The bills list very few performers who can be described outright as stand-up comedians and the roster of acts tends to consist of poets, bands, and speciality acts. The Jongleurs listing in the same issue makes a point of mentioning the fact that comedy double act Punt and Dennis are "ex-Footlights" (759, 1985: 32), they are supported by another double act, the Flaming Hamsters (Sara Crowe and Ann Bryson) who later appeared as the faces of the Philadelphia Cheese advertisements in the 1990s. This reinforces Mark Kelly's (2012 interview) view that Jongleurs appeals to a Radio Four-listening, middle-class audience.

TO lists another "GLC Giro Show" at Brent Town Hall on 23 March with a bill that comprises George Melly and John Chilton's Feetwarmers, jazz 'hoofer' Will Gaines, and poets Little Brother, Pat Condell, and Don Carroll (*TO* 761, 1985: 31). Again, there is a noticeable absence of stand-up comedians on this or any of the other bills listed in this issue of *TO*. This tells us that altcab was seen as a form of variety entertainment with no single form being more important than any of the others. We must also remember that television had yet to make a successful attempt to capture the essence of a night at a cabaret club. This would happen in the following year.

In April 1985, the Cabaret section had expanded to cover two pages (762). The Fundation had also expanded to two nights (1985: 36). Also listed is Open Heart Cabaret at the George IV in Chiswick (now the home to Headliners). The bill for this evening is not entirely eccentric and features Johnny Immaterial, Gideon Vein (Tony Green), Owen Brennan, Port Stanley Amateur Dramatic Society, and the intriguingly named Jockeys of Norfolk (1985: 36). The Bon Marche in Brixton, a former department store, once part of the John Lewis chain, is also listed but tends to feature street and new circus performers and does not seem to have a name. Up the road on Brixton Hill was Room 16 at the George IV pub, run by Stompy and Flat Hat (Wilding, 2013 questionnaire). These latter two clubs remind us of the enduring popularity of the New Circus field, which overlapped with the street entertainers field.

TO issue 797 (page 7) has a feature on the launch of Red Wedge, a cultural venture organized by the Labour Party that aimed to encourage young people to vote for the party in the forthcoming 1987 general election. At this stage, only musicians like Paul Weller and Billy Bragg had been signed up for the coming tour and comedians would be added towards the final stages of the campaign. Red Wedge, while formed by the opposition Labour Party, cannot be considered as a form of counter-cultural activity and existed solely to attract young voters to support Labour in the general election. Unlike RAR, nearly a decade earlier, the Labour Party was fully in control of Red Wedge, whereas the SWP's association with RAR was a loose one. Indeed, the Labour Party had been largely ineffective in challenging the Thatcher government on a range of policy issues and its support for those people who appeared in the government's sights – travellers, gays, and lesbians, for example – was non-existent. Yet there was a good deal of hope that a Labour government would reverse Thatcher's cuts, privatizations, and council-house sales. Indeed, the Labour leadership hoped that its earlier purge of Militant would attract more voters.

In January 1986, the Gaslight Club opened in Peterborough in the function room of a local sports and social club. It offers "variety including comedians, jugglers and musicians" but adds "No open spots" (McGillivray, 1989: 152). Clubs like this failed to produce local talent and ended up struggling because of their reliance on London performers, some of whom could not be bothered to travel the 100 or so miles to Peterborough for £50.

The Public Order Act 1986 came into effect in April. This gave the police the power to break up convoys of 12 or more motor vehicles/people on the grounds that they were about to commit an offence. Rioting was also defined more rigorously in the act. This part of the act was specifically designed to force new age travellers off the road, but it also spelled the end of the free festivals, which had been part of British cultural life since the first jazz and blues festivals at Beaulieu the late 1950s (BBC, 2010).

September 1986 saw the opening of the Friday Alternative at the South Hill Park Arts Centre in Bracknell, Berkshire. This was a popular out-of-town gig for many comedians and was often included in *TO's* listings along with Cabaret at the Square in Harlow. The South Hill Park Arts Centre had Arts Council funding, but as its entry in the *British Alternative Theatre Directory* (McGillivray, 1990: 168) says, "The Friday Alternative is intended to be self-supporting", reminding us that while the arts centre was supported by the regional arts board, the comedy-cabaret was not. On the other hand, the Square received a subsidy from Essex County Council and paid its acts a modest fee (McGillivray, 1990: 170).

The proposal for the Community Charge, or 'Poll Tax', was included in the Tory Party manifesto for the next general election. The Scottish secretary, Ian Lang, told the press that the tax would be "popular" in Scotland and proposed that it should be introduced in Scotland first. This decision would inadvertently herald the beginning of the party's 25-year decline in Scotland.

By the following year, there was a noticeable change taking place on the circuit and *TO* was now starting to list cabaret bills that were composed entirely of stand-up comedians. There are two possible explanations for this: first, the new clubs were opening in pub rooms with lower ceilings, which precluded the inclusion of jugglers and other acts that require high ceilings. Second, the popularity of *Saturday Live* on Channel 4 had led to a rush of new stand-up comedians. Many of the new clubs that opened in the middle of this wave would survive into the next wave and beyond. Even the Hemingford Arms would return as a cabaret venue – albeit for brief periods each time. In the next section, I discuss how the cabaret circuit became the comedy circuit.

The Third Wave and Transition (1987–1990)

Despite its success, *Saturday Live* was cancelled in April 1987, only to reappear a year later as the short-lived *Friday Night Live*. The programme's cancellation would create a vacuum that would be filled by shows like *Cabaret at the Jongleurs* (1988) on BBC2 and *Paramount City* on BBC1 (1990 to 1992). In 1996, *Saturday Live,* this time hosted by Lee Hurst, was briefly revived by ITV but only lasted for six episodes before being cancelled.

Thatcher won her third term in June 1987 with a slightly reduced majority, while Labour picked up 21 more seats and repelled a challenge from the SDP–Liberal Alliance, who had positioned themselves to replace Labour as the country's main opposition party. The decline in the fortunes of the SDP–Liberal Alliance would eventually lead to the merger of the two parties in 1989. Due to the first-past-the-post voting system, the Conservatives won more seats but their percentage of the vote was less than the anti-Tory votes combined. Under a proportional system, Labour could have theoretically formed a minority government with Alliance support, but there was so much bitterness between Labour and the SDP that the likely outcome of such a pact would have been a short-lived Labour minority administration followed by another general election. The former leader of the SDP, Roy Jenkins, lost his Glasgow Hillhead seat to Labour left-winger, George Galloway. Enoch Powell also lost his seat in South Down to the Social Democratic and Labour Party's Eddie McGrady. The SDP's failure to split the Labour vote led to a repositioning of the Labour Party. This process of so-called 'modernization' would be completed by the time of the 1997 general election. Almost on cue, the second Chapeltown riots took place in Leeds within days of Thatcher's election victory.

In October 1987, millions of pounds were wiped off the value of shares (the largest single fall in shares since 1929) in what would later be termed "Black Monday" (Evans, 1997). The crash began on Wall Street and spread throughout the financial world at a speed that was helped by the Big Bang. The causes of the crash are blamed on the volatility of the value of stocks but the precise cause of the crisis is not known. However, some of the possible causes included over-speculation in the property markets as well as the effect of changing from a paper-based system to a totally electronic one.

In issue 908 (January 1988) Jerry (spelled in *TO* as 'Gerry') Sadowitz appears on the front cover strangling a *Spitting Image* puppet of Robin Day, the host of BBC1's *Question Time*. Sadowitz also has his own regular column on page 25 in which he attacks Lenny Henry and Ruby Wax, but reserves most of his fury for TV presenter Muriel Gray. Sadowitz, an accomplished magician as well as a comedian, had a remarkably rapid rise to fame/infamy. According to Wilmut (1989) he first performed at the Store in 1984. On pages 18 to 23, there is a massive feature on the circuit's burgeoning stand-up field. On page 19, Tony Allen rails against the alternative label:

> I hate that posy word – alternative – a load of rancid oral bolshevik [*sic*] wank to define the difference between Bernard Manning and the bunch of right-on middle class tossers drivelling about their peculiar sex habits, unpleasant bodily functions, their latest trip to the supermarket and other thrilling bullshit like that.

On the same page, Bob Boyton notes the difficulty of doing challenging material, especially when it comes to homophobia, and observes "increasingly threatening attitudes". The backlash against 'political correctness' was, at this point, well underway and the Conservative-supporting press was publishing a steady stream of apocryphal stories about 'political correctness gone mad' on a near-daily basis.

TO's new Cabaret editor, Malcolm Hay (908, 1988: 19), also comments on the increase in the number of women comics and observes:

> There are those like the loud-mouthed Dreenagh Darrell [...] who act like they have more balls than Alexei himself. There are others (Hattie Hayridge, The Sea Monster (Jo Brand)) who base their acts on self-deprecation and playing the role of the victim.

The circuit is a tough place for women, but it is even tougher for – and indeed, harder to find – any Black performers on the circuit, let alone

Black or Asian audience members. There are features on other comedians too: Nick Revell, Kevin Day, Norman Lovett, Mark Miwurdz, Ronnie Golden, Claire Dowie, and Mark Thomas are included.

The Local Government Act (1988) contained the notorious **Section 28**, which outlawed the "promotion of homosexuality" by local authorities. It is not entirely clear what is meant by the word 'promotion'. Section 28 and the Public Order Act, that was passed in the previous year, were aimed squarely at the body and can be read as another in the government's arsenal of weaponry to be used against the 'permissive society', by curbing certain 'lifestyles' that were perceived as degenerate and subversive. The section was indicative of the notionally Victorian sense of morality that dominated Thatcherite thinking on cultural and social issues and was contradicted by the private behaviour of some Conservative MPs. We should also remember that Section 28 was produced at the height of the 1980s AIDS scare and this was used as a convenient stick with which to beat gays.

The Education Reform Act (1988) followed the Local Government Act and introduced Grant Maintained Schools, the National Curriculum, Key Stages, and school league tables and abolished academic tenure for those academics that had started in their posts on or after November 1987. This meant university commissioners could alter their charters and could force redundancy on academics. The Act also paved the way for the abolition of higher-education maintenance grants and essentially tore up the provisions of the **Robbins Report (1961)** and **Education Act (1944)** (also known as the "Butler Act" after its sponsor, the wartime coalition education minister, R.A. 'Rab' Butler, a Conservative), which granted the working-class access to higher education for the first time.

Whose Line is it Anyway? transferred from radio to television in April 1988 and began a run of ten seasons. Hosted by Clive Anderson, it features many of the circuit's best-known improvisers – many of whom performed with the Comedy Store Players and Theatresports at Notting Hill's Gate Theatre. The show was based on Keith Johnstone's concept of Theatresports as outlined in his book, *Impro: Improvisation and the Theatre* (Johnstone, 1989).

In October 1988, the home secretary, Douglas Hurd, announced a broadcast ban on the spoken words of members of organizations that supported terrorism in Northern Ireland. The ban became effective from November and affected republican and loyalist groups alike but it was, for all intents and purposes, directed at Sinn Féin and the Irish Republican

Socialist Party (the political wing of the INLA), whose profile had been raised considerably since the hunger strikes earlier in the decade. The broadcast media found a way to circumvent the ban by dubbing the voice of Gerry Adams or Martin McGuiness with that of an actor. The ban was eventually lifted in 1994 after the announcement of an PIRA ceasefire.

TO 953 (November 1988) carries a disturbing story of Clarence and Joy Pickles, who had plastic beer glasses (some of them full) thrown at them at the Tunnel Club. According to the story, Joy sustained a serious gash on her forehead and her glasses were damaged (1988: 66). In a subsequent issue of *TO* (955), the Tunnel story continues. Performers were urged by Arthur Smith and others to boycott the club until "there's some assurance that the violent behaviour has been contained" (1988: 67). Perhaps feeling threatened by the possible closure of his club, Malcolm Hardee sent a letter to punters warning them against violence but it appeared to have had little effect on them, and in the following year, the Tunnel would close for the final time. A year later, Hardee would open a new club a couple of miles away in Greenwich called Up the Creek, which, while it wasn't as dangerous as the Tunnel, could be just as raucous. Anvil Springstien (Ward, 2013 questionnaire) describes his first and only experience of the club:

> I remember standing at the side of the stage at 'Up the Creek' being introduced by Malcolm Hardy [*sic*]. The crowd were baying. He had his cock out. He said "Can't remember this next fuckers name? Some piece of shit from up North?" I handed my pint to the guy standing next to me: "Hold this for me, mate – I won't be long". It was Jools Holland. I wasn't long.

Malcolm's schtick was to give performers a nonchalant or insulting introduction, thereby forcing the comic into a confrontational situation with the audience. This also depended largely on the act Hardee was introducing. For example, if Malcolm said "This next bloke's an actor", it would be sufficient grounds for the audience to give them a tough time (Gribbin, 2011 interview).

In 1989, the Buzz Club opened at the Southern Hotel in West Chorlton, Manchester. It had a different beginning to most London clubs, as John Marshall/Agraman (2013 questionnaire) explains:

> The Buzz was not opened as a comedy night but as a continuation of the folk club with the addition of world music dance bands, but

it soon became apparent that there were two audiences coming along, one for music and... one for comedy, so I moved all music to Wednesday nights and ran every Wednesday for six whole years, the comedy continued every Thursday and ran for 15 whole years, only closing when I moved out of the area!

In the North of England, clubs tended to be established along the same ethical lines as the early London clubs, with a strong emphasis on non-racism and non-sexism. The Buzz Club was originally a folk club that morphed into a cabaret club. Another folk club that ran cabaret shows around the same time was Phil Ferguson's Streetwise at the Horse and Jockey in Doncaster (McGillivray, 1989, 1990). We must also remember that the folk clubs produced some of the early altcab performers like Jenny Lecoat and Kevin Seisay. Folk clubs were also known for their left-wing sympathies and it was in such clubs that CAST first performed in the 1960s (see Chapter 5).

In February 1989 (issue 962), the long-running Earth Exchange closed its doors following a disagreement between the promoter and compère, Ken Wells, and the owners of the restaurant, who found some of the acts "distasteful" and "rude". In his column, Hay (962, 1989: 62) remarked, "Presumably they've never been to Jongleurs or the Comedy Store". The club would reopen in a month's time under new management, only to close again for good a short time later. The same issue carries a listing for Laugh at the City, a lunchtime comedy show at Fairholt House on Whitechapel High Street. The box advertisement has a stylized graphic of a city gent, which informs the reader what class of punter this show is designed to appeal to. Lunchtime comedy is an unusual idea and the brevity of this club's run reveals that this kind of show did not become fashionable.

In March 1989, the Poll Tax was introduced in Scotland. Anti-Poll Tax unions were established in response and a mass campaign of non-payment was organized. Six suspected members of the IRA were shot dead in Gibraltar by the SAS as part of Operation Flavius. These extra-judicial killings became the subject of a controversial Thames Television documentary titled 'Death on the Rock', as part of its *This Week* current affairs series. The programme won a BAFTA award for television journalism but was condemned by the government. The home secretary, Geoffrey Howe, tried to have the programme banned but the Independent Broadcasting Authority, the ITV network's regulator, rejected his request;

however, the government would eventually get its way and when Thames's licence came up for renewal in 1991, it lost its franchise to Carlton.

A pilot for *The Mary Whitehouse Experience* aired on BBC Radio One on 10 March 1989. The programme's core performers were the pairings of David Baddiel and Rob Newman, and Steve Punt and Hugh Dennis, who were supported by Mark Hurst, Jack Dee, Skint Video, and others. The core performers of this programme would be managed by Avalon, a new talent agency, which was founded at some point in 1989 by Jon Thoday and Richard Allen-Turner, according to its company website. Thoday was a former president of Cambridge Footlights and the son of a Cambridge University academic. Early into his career, Thoday produced a musical called "Nightclub Confidential", which lost £402,000 (Such Small Portions, 2013). Allen-Turner was originally an entertainments officer at Middlesex Polytechnic (now Middlesex University). He was initially 'hired' by Thoday in 1989 and a short time later became his business partner. Their new agency would eventually rival Off the Kerb as a large-scale comedy talent promoter and they would later migrate into television production. The first act signed by Avalon was Steve Brown (of BBC Radio Four's *Radio Active* and ITV's *Spitting Image*). Richard Thomas was the agency's second client and would later co-write music for *Jerry Springer: The Opera* in 2003 with Stewart Lee (Such Small Portions, 2013). David Baddiel was Avalon's first major signing. Avalon's performers at this juncture were mostly drawn from Oxbridge, with a mere handful of non-Oxbridge-educated comics. This is a clear example of how social capital reproduced in these institutions is also used to reproduce social relations and class power within the fields of comedy, light entertainment, and the broadcast media generally.

In 1989, most of the performers listed in the *British Alternative Theatre Directory* (McGillivray, 1989: 99–105) are represented by the New Variety Performers Agency (NVPA). Other agencies include (Charlotte Lang at) Studio Productions, Off the Kerb, Noel Gay, and 20th Century Vixen. Out of these companies only NVPA, Off the Kerb, and Noel Gay survive to this day, with the latter being considered to have greater seniority on account of its longevity (formed in "the late 1950s", according to its website) and having had (and continuing to have) more influence within the legitimated field of light entertainment. It's worth pointing out that the earliest-known agency to emerge in the 1980s was Pranksters, which was run by Ivor Dembina and Jonathan Richards.

There is a final mention of the Earth Exchange in issue 973 (April 1989), which had closed in February and reopened under new management with on the part of the Mean Fiddler to cash in on what is now being called a 'comedy boom'. The Mean Fiddler, owned by Vince Power, began as a live music venue of the same name in Harlesden in 1982 and was part of a growing live music empire that later included the Reading and Leeds festivals. Power's empire would later become embroiled in a bitter 'poster wars' with CAST/New Variety/the Hackney Empire (see Chapter 5).

Jerry Sadowitz appeared again in *TO* and there was much talk about his solo shows. Sadowitz divides audiences; some even walked out of his show, because of his lack of 'political correctness'. There is a small half-page advert on page 66 for his forthcoming show at the Bloomsbury Theatre. Ivor Dembina (2012 interview) remarks on the moment when Sadowitz emerged onto the circuit, which was now beginning to look very different from its countercultural past:

> it got to the point where there was a kind of a thought police around.... [N]o one knew who they were but watch what you say [...] and it did actually hold comedy back – thinking about it now. And this got completely blown to smithereens by Jerry Sadowitz.

This view is supported by Mark Hurst (2012 questionnaire): "the over-policing of language eventually became a piss off for some young comics coming onto the scene. Then Gerry [*sic*] Sadowitz arrived and broke all the rules". It would seem that there was no middle ground and no room for all styles of stand-up, and instead of making accommodations, the circuit swung violently from one extreme to the other. The joke that made Sadowitz popular attacks the iconography of Nelson Mandela as well as the pious hostage, Terry Waite, who had been held captive in Lebanon, while ostensibly on a peace mission on behalf of the Archbishop of Canterbury.

> Nelson Mandela – what a cunt! Terry Waite – fucking bastard! I know, you lend some people a fiver, you never see them again. sort of person, if you lent me a fiver and never saw me again, be worth it.
>
> Jerry Sadowitz, quoted in Wilmut, 1989: 232

…l seemingly allowed the circuit to breathe a sort of …f. The word 'cunt' could now theoretically be used …k of censure, but in reality, it wasn't that simple, …nd performers continued to regard it as a taboo word and avoided its use. What was being referred to as 'political correctness' in the mainstream press was now being held responsible by some performers for the lack of growth on the circuit. This new postmodern attitude to the metanarratives of the 1980s was now coming under sustained assault from a small group of younger comedians who refused tolerance, ostensibly on the grounds that it limited free speech. Mark Hurst (2012 questionnaire) observed, "Then Baddiel & Newman did the 'new lad' thing and that started the backlash against what some saw as the 'right-on' brigade". Here, Mark reminds us of the role *The Mary Whitehouse Experience* played in shaping the new comedy aesthetic, which heralded the arrival of so-called 'lad comedy', and was much less concerned with political and social issues than it was with football, casual sex, and drunkenness. In some ways this seemed like a return to the pre-alternative days when whiteness and male chauvinism held sway, only this time it concealed itself beneath a veneer of ostensible non-racism and non-sexism. While these changes were taking place in 1989, the full effect would not be felt until the massive *Newman and Baddiel in Pieces* Wembley Arena show, which ushered in the stadium comedy era where comedy shows would compete with rock giants like U2 in terms of spectacle and scale. I shall return to the theme of the anti-'right-on' backlash later in this chapter.

In *TO* 984 (June 1989) lists *The Mary Whitehouse Experience* recording of a programme at the BBC's Paris Studios (located on Regent Street) with Jo Brand, Mark Thomas, and Skint Video as guests. *The Mary Whitehouse Experience* is unusual for radio comedy because it aired on Radio One rather than either Radio Two or Radio Four, which tend to carry programmes of this kind. This informs us that the show's target demographic was young people between the ages of 18 and 25. June 1989 also saw the beginning of the regular "Club Sandwich" nights with Ronnie Golden and his band, the Rex, at the Comedy Store with Ivor Dembina and a capella band Draylon Underground providing support.

In the July 1989 issue of *TO*, Massive Stop the Poll Tax Benefit is listed at the Hackney Empire (987, 1989: 64). In the same issue, Malcolm Hay asks:

> Is comedy still capable of creating a few shock waves? Are there any taboos remaining for comedians to trample on? Nine performers take over the Purcell Room on the South Bank (starting Monday) to see what they can achieve in the way of outrage.
>
> *TO* 987, 1989: 61

The show features Steve Edgar, Trevor Stuart (listed as a "Black comedian"), Chris Lynam, Mark Thomas, and Jack Dee. Out of all of these acts, only Thomas and Dee are gaining national recognition. Curiously, the circuit's *enfant terrible*, Jerry Sadowitz, is noticeably absent from the panel. To celebrate the launch of Roger Wilmut's book, *Didn't You Kill My Mother-in-Law?*, a public forum was held at the Institute of Contemporary Arts (ICA) in June 1989 to discuss alternative comedy (altcom). The members of the panel included Wilmut and comedians Jenny Eclair, Simon Fanshawe, Dillie Keane, and Nick Revell. Wilmut opened the discussion by suggesting that the phrase "alternative cabaret" was a problematic (ICA Recording, 15 June 1989). Furthermore, he noted that it was a term that the performers had also rejected and added that the phrase had been coined by the press to describe a form of comedy-cabaret that had rejected the comedy-aesthetic that had gone before it (ICA Recording, 15 June 1989). It's worth remembering that when the New Romantics first emerged, the press first called them 'peacock punks' and 'the cult with no name' – until they settled on a name. Likewise, the press had no name for post-punks and called them 'progressive punks'; the label 'post-punk' was applied retrospectively.

In August 1989, Ben Elton performed a full-length solo show at the Hammersmith Odeon (*TO* 991, 1989: 62). Elton had been performing in larger venues since 1986 and although this kind of show was occasional for other performers, this was an early indication of the direction that altcom was taking. There had been a Comic Strip tour of provincial theatres in 1981 and Alexei Sayle had also toured with rock bands in the earlier part of the decade (Wilmut, 1989). The Odeon is a medium-sized music venue but, at this juncture, it was huge in terms of altcom. There would be more full-length shows of this type by other stand-up comedians in the years leading up to 1993, which were usually promoted by Avalon, Off the Kerb, or Phil McIntyre Entertainments.

In October 1989, Nigel Lawson resigned as Chancellor after discovering Thatcher was taking independent economic advice from her special economic advisor, Sir Alan Walters.[18] Lawson, who had also opposed the introduction of the Poll Tax, believed that he had been overruled by the Prime Minister on the advice of Walters. In the event, Walters also

---

[18] Walters had visited Chile in the late seventies and admired Pinochet's economic model, particularly the privatization programme, which would be adopted by the Thatcher government as one of its central policies.

resigned and Thatcher appointed John Major as Chancellor. The following month, the All-Britain Anti-Poll Tax Union was founded to organize resistance to the Poll Tax.

Disquiet among Tory backbenchers over the Prime Minister's autocratic leadership style (which was now being regarded as a serious liability) continued and she was challenged for leadership by the 'stalking horse' candidate, Sir Anthony Meyer, in December 1989. Meyer stood no chance of winning but his challenge started to weaken Thatcher's position as leader of the party. Although there had been rumblings of discontent within Tory ranks over the Prime Minister's style for some time, the threat to her rule was often brushed aside; but the pressure on her to quit would continue to mount over the course of the following year.

The first Black Comedy night took place at the Albany Empire in Deptford in October (*TO* 999, 1989: 21). These comedy nights usually consisted of a bill of mainly Black comedians, with a famous Black musician as compère. The rationale behind including a musician with a high profile appears to be a strategy for drawing in a mainly Black audience by using someone in the public eye as a magnet. Though I appear at some Black Comedy nights, I approach them with a mixture of apprehension and suspicion because I suspect that these all-Black shows are a way of ghettoizing performers on the basis of their skin colour. As far as I am concerned, this seems to be a retrograde step for the circuit. However, this is brought into sharp relief when one realizes that the number of Black and Asian performers on the circuit was small and that there were few Black or Asian faces in the audiences.

In November 1989, Malcolm Hay (*TO* 1,005, 1989: 71) asked,

> Where did all the odd acts go? In the early days of alternative comedy, we're told, the stand ups would rub shoulders with a rag bag army of eccentric acts and assorted crazies. We live in more professional (that is to say, more tedious) times. Many comedians are so busy being funny that they fail to convey much sense of joy – or any sense of danger. Very few comics allow themselves to be silly...

What's interesting about this quote is how Hay uses the phrase "alternative comedy" rather than "cabaret". There now seems to be a conscious recognition of the changes that are taking place on the circuit generally. The name of *TO's* Cabaret section would not change for another three years and would be subtitled "Comedy and Variety" to reflect this shift. The article also gives a mention to Chris Luby,[19] an eccentric sound impressionist, Randolph the Remarkable, a silly 'stuntman' and oddball musical act, and the Amazing Mr. Smith. Luby continued to perform into the early 1990s but his appearances were often limited to Malcolm Hardee's Tunnel Club and later Up the Creek in Greenwich. Hay's question seems to herald the end of an era. With television taking an increasing interest in the circuit, the clubs and the performers were becoming more professionalized and there was little room for experimentation. To capitalize on the growing demand for stand-up comedians, new comedy courses were beginning to appear to cater for those wanting a career in comedy; the first of these was Jill Edwards' stand-up comedy course, based in Brighton.

In the same issue, the Comedy Store celebrates its tenth birthday and Raging Bull, Eddie Izzard's new club, opens at the Boulevard Theatre, which was once home to the Comic Strip. Izzard seems to have been consciously aware of the historical significance of this location to the extent that they exploit it in the club's publicity (1989: 72). The opening bill includes Skint Video, Mark Thomas, and Izzard as compère (1989: 72). *TO's* Christmas issue (1,009/10) quotes Janet Prince of East Dulwich Cabaret as saying, "The cabaret circuit has developed into a high professional standard. But it's now verging on a conveyor belt style of comedy. Wouldn't it be nice if there was more room for acts to relax and for more experimentation?" (1989: 77). Interestingly, a "conveyor belt" was how Don Ward described the Comedy Store in its early days (Cook, 2001: 77) and its advertisements always used this word to describe itself. The "conveyor belt" is analogous with the industrial process and the dominant cultural industries' fetish for the standardized product. In some respects, the circuit was now becoming the Comedy Store's – and by extension, television's – feeder: this is where newer comics played before they felt ready to play for the bear-pit of a late slot at the Store.

The change from cottage industry of amateurs to a professional circuit is lamented by other promoters like Pete Harris (Screaming Blue Murder) and Peter Grahame (Downstairs at the Kings Head). In issue 1,009/10 Harris says, "Audiences have become more demanding and acts have become safer, less experimental" (1990: 77). It is likely that with the television exposure of the stand-up comedy element of altcab, the audiences expected the same thing when they entered the cabaret clubs

---

[19] Chris Luby died in February 2014.

(Gordillo, 2012 questionnaire; Clayton, 2013 questionnaire). Harris's quote reminds us how important a role television played in shaping the audience's view of comedy. The more experimental performers tended to come from the field of street performance and these acts were becoming rarer. It is worth remembering that Eddie Izzard, Harris's partner at Screaming Blue Murder, started as a street performer and only developed a recognizable 'indoor' act when the former became compère of the club.

The Poll Tax was introduced in England and Wales in January 1990. This was a flat tax, which meant that everyone paid the same rate regardless of their income. Flat taxes are often claimed by right-wing economists to be 'fair' because they allow people (the wealthy) to keep more of their income. The Poll Tax was arrogantly defended by Sir Nicholas Ridley, the minister responsible for it. Despite its defenders' claims of fairness, for those people at the bottom of the income scale this meant paying more in taxation, which thus subsidized those at the top end. The All-Britain Anti-Poll Tax Federation was set up by Militant and mobilized a campaign of non-payment, which was supported by the SWP and other community and left groups. The Labour Party, on the other hand, refused to support this initiative and advised people to pay the tax. Indeed, Labour effectively offered no alternative to the Poll Tax and very little opposition to it. The tax cost much more to collect than the government had predicted and this led to further local authority budget cuts. The reasons for this are obvious since councils would have to spend considerable amounts of money to pursue and prosecute cases of non-payment. The Poll Tax also criminalized large sections of society, who had already suffered from redundancies and unemployment caused by the privatization of state industries and cuts to public services.

Banana Cabaret was threatened with closure when pubco[20] Grand Metropolitan put the Bedford pub up for sale (*TO* 1,020, 1990: 61). The Banana's predicament reminds us of the often-precarious relationship between club promoter and owner–proprietor of the venue, which relies on nothing more than goodwill between the two parties. Even successful

---

[20] A pubco is a large pub chain that is often owned by a much larger company involved in other activities in the hospitality and leisure sector. Since the pubs were 'liberated' in the last years of the Thatcher government, large combines have bought former tied houses. One of the largest pubcos during this period was Grand Metropolitan, which also owned Wimpy and Burger King. The Bedford pub had previously been tied to Truman's Brewery, which Grand Metropolitan had purchased in 1972.

clubs can be cancelled at a moment's notice, often at the whim of the manager or landlord, who may have decided to book a wedding party in the same room. Yet this is also a period of expansion that is exemplified by a move towards creating chains of clubs, for at some point in early 1990, Andy Waring of Banana Cabaret opened venues in Acton and Barnet, though by 1993 both of these outposts had closed, while the Bedford, once free from the threat of closure, continued to thrive. Another example of this orientation toward club chains is the Punchline Comedy Club, which expanded to include the Boston Arms pub in Dartmouth Park, North London – the only venue, apart from the Comedy Store, that explicitly referred to comedy in its name.

March 1990 ended with a mass protest organized against the Poll Tax, which escalated into a riot; this event unsettled the government and led to the resignation of Nicholas Ridley. He was soon replaced by the party's rising right-wing star, Michael Portillo. The Poll Tax riot was condemned by many Labour MPs, but it marked the beginning of Thatcher's decline, with many more backbenchers now regarding her as an electoral liability.

The Crown and Castle in Dalston reopened as Backyard 2 in April (*TO* 1,024, 1990: 66). The original Backyard Comedy Club was located a few miles away in Whitechapel, organized by Lee Hurst, who compères under the name 'Douglas Douglas'. Hurst had yet to appear on television and in time he would move his club to Bethnal Green, where it remained until he decided to "close [the] club and raze it to the ground". "In its place", according to his website (Hurst, 2013), Hurst developed "a seven-storey hotel" with the Backyard Comedy Club on the ground floor.

In issue 1,026 (April/May 1990) there is a single column advert for the *City Limits*-supported Black Comedy Special at the Hackney Empire. Black and Asian people were still poorly represented on the circuit as performers or as members of the audience. Part of the drive to promote Black comedy is to search for Black talent, and to this end, a number of talent competitions and quests were held. The latter was a creation of CAST/New Variety and there is a specific reason why the word 'quest' was chosen over the word 'competition', which I will discuss in Chapter 5.

The Cabaret section now straddles six pages and includes a greater number of advertisements from the larger comedy clubs. The Store no longer dominates the advertisements; it is now joined by the Comedy Cafe (run by former mainstream comic Mike McCabe, whose brother, Dave, was given the role of resident compère) and Up the Creek, Malcolm

Hardee's new venue. Significantly, there is also an advert for "Holstein Pils Stand Up, America!" with a roster of acts that featured, among others, Bill Hicks, whose bill matter reads "Whose mean and sarcastic style is fashioned for the age of the psycho" (*TO* 1,057, 1990: 71). This was Hicks' first appearance in Britain and he would go on to influence many comedians – myself included. Dennis Leary, who was once accused by Hicks of stealing the latter's material, has an advertisement for his 'No Cure for Cancer' (which he performed at the Edinburgh Fringe in August) tour and is clearly the bigger name of the two. Eddie Izzard's Raging Bull club appears on page 68, and the club is typical of the newer kind of clubs because there are no open spots for new performers, which seems to be a trend, with fewer clubs now offering such spots.

In November, Geoffrey Howe resigned as Deputy Prime Minister. He made the following comments in his speech to the Commons:

> It is rather like sending your opening batsmen to the crease only for them to find the moment that the first balls are bowled that their bats have been broken before the game by the team captain.
>
> Howe, 1990

The following day, Thatcher was challenged for the leadership by Michael Heseltine. She won the first ballot but Heseltine's significant numbers forced a second ballot, which she subsequently lost. She resigned as Prime Minister with immediate effect, prompting a leadership election. John Major, the Chancellor of the Exchequer, seen as a safe pair of hands and Thatcher's anointed successor, won the subsequent leadership election by beating Heseltine and late entrant, Douglas Hurd, the Foreign Secretary. The Thatcher years were over, and although Major would eventually abolish the Poll Tax and steer his party to an unexpected election victory in 1992, his party's time in power was also near its end. Dogged by a combination of sex scandals (which the press dubbed "sleaze") and internal divisions over the European Union, the party's poll ratings continued to decline. In 1997, he and the Conservatives would be defeated by Tony Blair's New Labour Party by a landslide.

Issue 1,058 carries an advertisement for the Hackney Empire's "Big 89th Birthday Benefit" (1990: 81). Elsewhere, Bob Boyton was performing his one-man show, 'Bob Boyton: Puts the Boot In', at the Canal Cafe Theatre in Little Venice. 'Comedians for Justice at the Red Rose' was a benefit for the Tottenham Three, who had been arrested and charged in

1987 for the murder of PC Keith Blakelock during the 1985 Broadwater Farm riots in Tottenham. Appearing on the bill were Jeremy Hardy, Mark Thomas, Mark Steel, Mark Hurst, Kit Hollerbach, musician Neil Robert Herd, and "a speaker" (1990: 82). The three young men arrested were Winston Silcott, Engin Raghip, and Mark Braithwaite, who were later cleared on appeal in 1991.

A "Black Variety Night" at the Albany Empire appears in issue 1,059 (1990: 73) and the 291 Club at the Hackney Empire advertises for the first time on page 72. I played the former along with Curtis and Ishmael, Angie Le Mar, the Men from C&A (a mime troupe), Short, Sharp and Shocking (a comedy trio), jazz 'hoofer' Will Gaines (a favourite of the New Variety circuit), and singer Jacqui Maxwell, with Leo Chester as MC.

The Death of Alternative Cabaret (1991–1992)

The first issue of *TO* (1,063) in the final year of altcab carries a box advertisement for the Comedy Cafe on page 59 that reads "Tuesdays 'Variety open spot' and Wednesdays 'Open spot'". *Prima facie*, there appears to be little difference in the two kinds of open spot but this was an attempt on the part of the Comedy Cafe to find new variety acts, of which there were still a few remaining on the circuit. Ultimately this was a fruitless search because the vast majority of the new acts on the circuit were stand-up comedians, with the remaining performers working as character comics. Following on from this, *TO* issue 1,064 (January 1991) carries a Cabaret Preview on page 26 in which Malcolm Hay interviews a number of oddball acts, who are quickly becoming a rarity on the circuit. Of Andrew Bailey, Hay (1991: 26) writes:

> Bailey is a clown who deals in the dark side of things. Characters include Podomovsky (i), Eric the incompetent roadie and Frederick Benson, an imposing figure, reminiscent of Herman Munster.

Randolph the Remarkable, on the other hand, "adopts a less disturbing and frankly sillier approach. His act involves feats of skill and daring involving fire and a blue bowl of lukewarm water". Randolph also appeared on Julian Clary's television show *Sticky Moments* (Channel 4, 1989–1990) as the character "Hugh Jelly". Also mentioned is Marcel Steiner of "The World's Smallest Theatre". A proto-alternative act, Steiner's theatre was a motorcycle sidecar that had a seating capacity of two, while Steve Rawlings is described as

> a juggler, who sets fire to his head. "When it went wrong" he says "it used to put the fear of God in me. You could hear the hair crackling. There's a very distinctive smell too".

Seemingly, the point of this review was to try and promote what was left of the true alternative showmen on the circuit, but this was futile and within the next three years, all of the oddball acts would disappear from the circuit completely.

With the First Gulf War underway in January 1991, Malcolm Hay's 'Cabaret Preview' in *TO* 1,064 (199: 29) comments on "Gulf Humour" and notices a lack of political and philosophical engagement with the conflict. He further notes the numbers of performers who have dropped out of the "No to the War in the Gulf Benefit". I am one of the few (though unmentioned in this article) who was performing anti-Gulf War material. Mark Steel was another and was quoted as saying:

> I was at a show the night Thatcher resigned and the first comedian on stage didn't mention it. He talked about toothpaste tubes instead. If a bomb exploded in a club, there are some comics who'd stick to their prepared set about rubber plants.
>
> Steel, quoted in *TO* 1,064, 1991

This was one of the more worrying developments on the circuit, caused mainly by the lack of comedians coming from countercultural formations. The philosophical and political disinterest among comics would eventually lead to a situation in which comedians rarely, if ever, mentioned politics of any kind onstage. The countercultural spirit that once defined the circuit had faded and had been replaced with something altogether more commercial and ready-made for television. This seemed indicative of a general mood of defeat caused by Thatcher's election victory in 1987 but also the collapse of the Berlin Wall, the ongoing press attacks on 'political correctness', and the rise of celebrity culture. History, left-wing political ideologies, anti-racism, and anti-sexism would be dismissed as 'politically correct' and 'outmoded' by those on the political Right as well as people who would claim to be 'apolitical'. Within a year of this article's publication, Steel would leave the circuit for radio. The circuit, it seems, no longer had room for anything politically engaged or aesthetically challenging.

The same issue (1,064) carries another article by Hay, this time in the Cabaret section on page 59, in which he expresses concern about the lack of opportunities for new performers. He writes, "a healthy circuit can only be maintained through a continual supply of new acts. It's here that the fundamental problem lies. The number of clubs that offer new and untried performers 'open spots' (short slots, generally unpaid) on their weekly bills has shrunk considerably in the past two or three years" (1991: 59). Hay then notes that the Hackney Empire New Act of the Year, the Guilty Pea, and the Comedy Pit are exceptions, observing "The catch is that, in this prevailing climate, it can take a very long time for new acts to gain the experience that will enable them to get better". This problem would become more acute as the professionalization of the industry gathered pace throughout the 1990s, eventually leading to the formation of a separate open spot circuit from which few performers would escape. The influence of television on the cabaret field, conferred by the success of *Saturday Live* and other such programmes, could be discerned in the circuit's apparent repositioning as a proving ground for future television hosts. As if to reinforce this new trend, Every Other Thursday, a club for established performers to try new material, had opened in the previous week and its second show is listed (*TO* 1,068, 1991). This reveals to us that at this point there was less room on the circuit for experimentation, and that comics felt the need to create a space for themselves in which they would be free to develop and test new comedy material. This is reflected in an article titled "Waving Magic Wand Awards", which asks a few of the circuit's figures what changes they would like to see on the circuit (*TO* 1,069, 1991: 56). Magician John Lenahan makes an interesting point about clubs having to rely on the goodwill of pub landlords and notes that the Chuckle Club has been a recent victim of this when it was forced out of the Stag on Bressenden Place in Victoria. Pete Harris of Screaming Blue Murder echoes Hay's concerns and complains that audiences are "too demanding, which discourages experimentation". Harris's erstwhile partner, Eddie Izzard, facetiously offers "more dressing rooms" and John Gordillo, of the Crisis Twins and London Theatresports, criticizes the industrialized nature of the new circuit.

> There's often the feeling that shows are like conveyor belts – the audience knows what to expect and many skilled comedians provide them with just that – and only that. No one is doing anything very special.
>
> Gordillo, quoted in *TO* 1,069, 1991: 56

This reads like a description of the WMCs from which the early alt comedians had distanced themselves. Within two years, the entire circuit would produce similar, standardized products, which were mostly disinterested comics who took no position on anything other than to comment on the mundane. Around this time, I was party to dressing-room discussions with other comics regarding the state of the circuit. We were concerned that the circuit was heading for the same fate as its American counterpart, which had witnessed a creeping stylistic conservatism that had been brought about by greater television exposure. This led to a proliferation of what are described in the business as 'hacks', who use what are referred to as 'dick jokes' or 'knob gags', for example, to get easy laughs.

In March 1991 American comedy chain, Coconuts, opened a branch in Larry's Baa beneath a hotel in Covent Garden. In issue 1,072, there is an advertisement but no listing (1991: 57). I was given the role of resident MC (on account of my American-sounding accent) but what the American comedians told me is rather disturbing: all of the comedians who appeared at Coconuts were flown over by the company but were paid as little as £30 for each appearance. The Comedy Store, Jongleurs, and Banana Cabaret, for example, paid considerably more and at the Banana it was easy for a headline act to earn over £200 on a good night when both rooms were open. No British performers ever appeared as paid acts at Coconuts and the club failed to attract large audiences and folded within a couple of months.

On the same page, Up the Creek has its "Anniversary Show" listed. It is only a year old. On the following page there is an advertisement for Roy 'Chubby' Brown, which reads, "Britain's Naughtiest Comedian. If easily offended please stay away" (*TO* 1,072, 1991: 56). Although the circuit was still ostensibly *alternative*, the presence of this advertisement appears to indicate a collapse of the boundary between 'alternative' and mainstream. Indeed, it was now actually possible to argue that the old-school circuit had become the *new* alternative because comedians in the ever-decreasing numbers of WMCs were mainly hidden from the public glare of television.

Altcab officially comes to an end in the pages of *TO* in late November 1991 (issue 1,110). The Cabaret section, which has been in existence for less than nine years, is renamed "Comedy". Interestingly, it is now subtitled "Stand-up and Variety", though the variety element would soon fade away as more stand-up comedians joined the ever-swelling ranks of circuit comedians. The change of title is not announced in the previous week's issue (1,109) nor is it mentioned by Malcolm Hay in issue 1,110. Altcab disappears without a mention, but performers noticed the change and commented on it. I should explain that *City Limits*, which had split from *TO* over ten years earlier and threatened the very existence of *TO*, folded over a year later in 1993 after going through a period during which ownership of the magazine changed hands several times. By this stage, *City Limits* had lost any of the influence it once had and in 1990, as if to signify this decline, its back pages began to carry advertisements for sex shops and 'personal services'. A combination of falling advertising revenue and a shrinking readership ultimately conspired in its demise. Now *TO*, alone, held a monopoly on London's listings and its role in legitimating and consecrating the field's new comedians would continue until the end of the 1990s, when it would come under attack from the new medium of the Internet and be forced to reduce its activity on the field. *TO* then became a free magazine that was only available from London Underground stations. In July 2022, it went entirely online.

Chapter 3

The Outsider

"I'd lived in a certain way and I could just as well have lived in a different way. I'd done this and I hadn't done that. I hadn't done one thing whereas I had done another. So what?"

Albert Camus, *The Outsider*

"I am an invisible man. No I am not a spook like those who haunted Edgar Allen Poe: Nor am I one of your Hollywood movie ectoplasms. I am a man of substance of flesh and bone, fiber and liquids, and I might even be said to possess a mind. I am invisible, simply because people refuse to see me."

Ralph Ellson, *Invisible Man*

Introduction

There is a reason why this chapter is called 'The Outsider'. I have often seen myself as an outsider, a stranger, and this began in my childhood. I'm a child of a military family and we moved frequently, but there was one constant amid this change: we were the only mixed family on the bases on which we lived. In 1960s Germany, we were the only family of colour living among the local population of Hof/Saale in Bavaria, a city that was almost entirely white. This is one moment out of many that helped to shape my outsider status. Not only do I see myself as an outsider, but I sense that others also see me in this way.

In his book for beginner comedians, Murray (2007: 59) states that an outsider is "a very powerful energy to play as a comic". Comedy outsiders can be foreigners remarking on the foibles of the country in which they're playing, or they can be social misfits. In my case, I wasn't a foreigner, I had been enculturated into British popular culture from an early age; I had spent periods of my childhood in Liverpool; I knew what *The Woodentops* and *Andy Pandy* were. Relatives would send us British cultural products like selection boxes and comic annuals for Christmas. I am, however, an outsider: I am a Black man of mixed-heritage who's lived in Britain for most of his life; a dual citizen of the United States and United Kingdom, but who was born in the former West Germany. Comedy often relies on handy stereotypes to make it easier for the audience to apprehend the humour. However, the complexities of my background defy the easy application of classification. What am I? In Situationist terms, at least, I can say that I am the physical embodiment of détournement, and it is easy enough: I appear to be one thing when I am another.

Being an outsider meant that I often felt I didn't fit in; that I often didn't *belong*. If the post-punk era taught us anything, it was to consciously reject notions of what is supposedly 'natural' or 'obvious'. This is perhaps why I was so attracted to post-punk, because unlike punk, it came from everywhere; it wasn't one thing or the other. It was, to partly coin the title of a recent BBC4 (31 March 2021) documentary on Indie music, "music for misfits".[1] As a young man, I was part of a group that felt we were too old to be punks and too young to be hippies, so we called ourselves 'freaks', and we occupied a sort of liminal space between the two subcultures/countercultures. To this end, I was drawn to underground movements. Altcab had an underground feel to it: it was a space that attracted eccentrics, oddballs, and people who seemingly didn't fit in with the official spaces for legitimated entertainment. In other words, people like me.

The two quotations at the top of this chapter come from two writers who helped to shape me as a comedian, as a researcher, and as a Black man. I read Camus' (1963) absurdist book *The Outsider* (*L'étranger*) in 1997, shortly after my mother's death in December 1996, an event that coincided with my epiphany as a comedian. Although Meursault's opening line, "Maman died today or maybe it was yesterday. I can't be sure" appeared cold and detached, the lesson I took from *The Outsider*

---

[1] Full title: *Music for Misfits: The Story of Indie*.

impelled me to be courageous, to take more risks onstage, and to be *me*. Moreover, Meursault also defies expectations: he doesn't think or behave as he is expected to by society-at-large; he is nobody's man but his own and similarly, in Ellison's (1963) *Invisible Man*, the unnamed Black narrator also resists having an identity thrust upon him by others and has to navigate the pressures placed upon him in the form of race, social class, and political ideologies. Ellison's book also addresses the geographical differences and competing social and cultural narratives within Black America and the African diaspora. Like Meursault, the narrator is an outsider, but in his case, it is because of his race, his social class, and his status as a Southern Black man, who throws himself into the unfamiliar world of New York City, a place where there is no segregation. I, too, have had to negotiate many of the same issues as Ellison's *Invisible Man* but I was also metaphorically invisible: I hardly appeared on broadcast media, I was never reviewed, and few people outside the comedy circuit knew who I was. Indeed, as Black people, generally, we are visible but paradoxically, we are also invisible in wider society. We cannot be seen in the boardrooms of FTSE 100 companies nor as university vice-chancellors, and we make up only one per cent of professors.

Writing this autoethnography has been a difficult process that has demanded two things from me: first, I had to confront my past, my memories, and my emotions. Second, I had to step back from my personal story and adopt the role of researcher. At times this process has been celebratory and, at other moments, it has been akin to stripping away the epidermis and exposing the dermis beneath. Long buried emotions have been exposed and addressed. The pain lingers but is duller. When I first embarked on this project, there were many questions: how much of my personal history do I need to reveal? Surely, it is important to tell the complete story; one that included my comedy influences and how and when I first learned to imitate other people's voices? The most important question of all was "how do I avoid sounding bitter?" I was also concerned about those people – promoters, punters, and so on – who Othered me. How would they respond? It's reasonable to say that they would have never experienced refusals because of their skin colour. They may have been refused for other reasons, but not because they were people of colour.

Critics may question this research method and dismiss it as self-indulgent and overly emotional, but I would argue that autoethnography provides the reader with a richer account of the phenomena that occurred, as well as the writer's responses to them. It produces what Geertz (1973) called a "thick" description of culture. For those people, the punters, who have only seen the outside walls of the comedy world – the end process of performance and the interior of a comedy club – the use of autoethnography places the researcher in the role of chief witness; someone who is able to provide first-hand testimony of the events that shaped altcom and altcab.

This chapter makes use of my diaries, notebooks, and even the mix tapes that I listened to before gigs. I only have some of the diaries from the 1990s: these cover 1990 and 1996–2000. The diaries from 1991 to 1995 were lost in a house move in 1995. The 1990 diary contains entries that tell how I felt about the gigs I played but, for whatever reason, I didn't write detailed entries in subsequent diaries. This means that I have had to draw on my memories, which are not entirely reliable. Conscious of this problem, I have triangulated my memories with these objects of ephemera and conversations with my erstwhile contemporaries. In some cases, the set lists have no dates attached to them, but I can make sense of these by seeing what kind of material I was writing and performing, which anchors them to specific moments of my comedy career.

There are three stages to my main comedy career: the early period (1986–1990), the middle period (1991–1995), and the late period (1996–2000). Each period represents a stage in my development as a performer and is marked by changes of direction that were brought about by new influences and insights. Because this book deals with the altcab era, which ended in 1992, this chapter mostly covers my early period and part of my middle period. However, the final part of this chapter briefly discusses my final years on the comedy circuit and my reasons for leaving it behind.

My adventure in stand-up comedy began with a brief performance at the BA (Hons) Creative Arts Christmas party in December 1986, when I was asked to perform a short routine on the basis that I was a 'funny guy'. I had no experience of performing stand-up because at this juncture it was still my intention to become an actor or join a rock band. There were no cabaret courses in Newcastle-upon-Tyne, where I was student, as there were in London, and no 'teach yourself stand-up comedy' books. According to Double (2005: 3), early alt comedians had some performance experience prior to performing comedy. For me, this included a brief dalliance with punk poetry (1977–1979), a spell as a pirate radio DJ (1980–1985), and a couple of years in amateur dramatics (1984–1986) but there was no experienced comedian to guide me and I relied entirely on my own inventiveness. This was Newcastle in the 1980s – the ripple effect from altcab's explosion had yet to touch the city or the Tyne and Wear region. I didn't consider performing as an occupation until I began an A-Level Theatre Studies course in 1983, initially with the aim of becoming an actor.

However, I was always aware that roles in theatre, film, and television for Black people in Britain had been traditionally limited to stereotypical depictions as victims or criminals. In light entertainment, the situation was equally dire and, inspired by the example of Paul Robeson, I refused to perform to white expectations of Blackness. Working as a cabaret performer appeared to offer a way around that dilemma, because it not only offered me a chance to write and perform my own material; it also allowed me the opportunity to work in an entertainment space that was ostensibly non-racist and non-sexist. I was further encouraged by the presence of Felix Dexter, who, along with Sheila Hyde and Simon Clayton (of the Crisis Twins), was one of a small cadre of stand-ups of colour on the circuit in the late 1980s. What was refreshing about Felix was the way he avoided the trap that had ensnared so many Black performers, like Lenny Henry or Charlie Williams in the official world. He didn't perform to expectations and presented himself as authoritative and erudite, and spoke in a home counties accent rather than patois. For me, this was a refreshing change from British light entertainment, in which Black performers operated within the limits imposed on them by the industry's mandarins. Yet if there were few Black people in the entertainment industry, then it's worth considering that before the 1990s, British Asian people were completely invisible on television, save for characters like the head-wobbling base wallahs in sitcoms like the BBC's *It Ain't Half Hot Mum*.

This chapter is divided into four subsections: the first deals with my social and cultural background and the events that shaped me. The second deals with my comedy and how I approached devising material, while the third looks at how I navigated the issue of difference, marked by race. The chapter ends with what happened next.

Acquiring My Cultural Capital

According to Bourdieu (2003), inculturation takes place through early socialization: the family, the school, and so on, and it is through these institutions that one becomes familiar with cultural products and their uses. Our most elemental tastes, like those for music and food, are physiological and deeply embedded in our bodies. Therefore, because comedy produces a physical response in the form of laughter, it too is deeply rooted in the body. My cultural experiences differ from those of many of my former circuit colleagues, because I mostly attended schools for the children of American military personnel and was exposed to a great deal of American popular and mass culture from an early age. Yet, through my British mother, I also inherited much of her cultural capital.

For me, the dominant culture was represented by the United States Air Force and its rules and regulations, to which all – dependents included – were bound. Subversiveness within such a social environment was never particularly difficult; even the slightest deviation from what was expected of dependents could be considered 'dangerous' and could reflect badly on my dad.

My first act of resistance happened in kindergarten when the teacher instructed us to 'salute the flag' and recite the 'Pledge of Allegiance'. This nationalistic ritual took place before class at the start of each school day, but I refused to recite it until the day I left school. I believe this ritual served to remind us that we were Americans and made the unstated claim that we were 'chosen people'; part of what Anderson (1989) calls an "imagined community". Avoiding the Pledge was instinctual and the impulse to resist it came from within my countercultural habitus. I seem to have been born rebellious and could recognize subversive possibilities from an early age. My kindergarten teacher never provided a reason for saluting the flag; it was considered axiomatic that young children would obey her request unquestioningly. We were just children, so why would we not do as we were told? My tactic for avoiding the Pledge involved what De Certeau (1988) calls a "ruse": I would mouth the words to it, and whichever national hymn the teacher had selected for the day. Each member of the class was also required to take turns to 'lead the class' in the Pledge. So, when it was my turn to lead the class, I would perform a variation of the ruse by saying the first three words "I pledge allegiance…" and then mouth the rest of it.

Another event that helped to shape my habitus occurred at the age of five when my white Liverpudlian mother explained 'race' to me. I sat horrified as she explained how she and my father had different skin colours. Yet, before being told this, I'd never noticed my parents' skin pigmentation; these were my parents and not people of different 'races' who had a 'mixed-race' child. Indeed, one may ask why the job of telling me about race fell to my mum. In my early years, I rarely saw my dad except briefly when he came home from work or at weekends. During the Cuban Missile Crisis, I didn't see him for over a month, which at the age of four, seemed like an incredibly long time. My mother also told me there were some people who hated people with different coloured skin. Alarmed by this, I questioned why anyone would behave this way. She shrugged and said that some people are horrible and that I would have to deal with it. Race is a serious and difficult concept to relate to a five-year-old child and I suspect her reason for doing so was to prepare me for our eventual stay in Liverpool, when Dad went to Vietnam and there was a possibility of him not returning.

I decided there and then to resist any attempt to be caged within my brown skin and that I would fight this 'melanism', because even at such a young age one could immediately see, not only the injustice, but also the absurdity of 'race' as a social determinant. I also seemed to have understood that racism was closely associated with American nationalism and institutionalized at every level of society, including film and television. Where were the Black Americans in the national stories that were being imparted to me in school? Were all of them slaves? We were told about slavery, but the slave rebellions were never mentioned, apart from John Brown's raid on Harper's Ferry. Why were American Indians depicted as savages in B-movie Hollywood Westerns, while white men seemed to shoot them for sport? Who spoke for them? Questions like these impelled me to keep a wary eye on authority and resist or subvert it wherever possible, and I did this through humour. This involved changing the words of national hymns or mocking folk heroes like slave-owners Davy Crockett and Daniel Boone. In this sense, my school years are redolent of the hackneyed backstory of the stand-up comedian, who was the 'class clown' who created mischief and enjoyed making people laugh.

My introduction to stand-up comedy happened at school and came via Bill Cosby's 'Chicken Heart' and Bob Newhart's 'The Driving Instructor'. Yet I don't recall finding either one particularly funny. Their material was inoffensive and clean, and this is likely the reason why teachers deemed their humour to be suitable for young ears. Introducing stand-up comedy into the classroom seemed to be a way of filling time or as a treat and wasn't directly connected to the curriculum. Although, in hindsight, this was an introduction to the world of American popular culture. At home, my parents owned no stand-up albums and comedy was experienced through Hollywood films or television situation comedies. From an early age, I loved the sick–silly comedy of Jonathan Winters, who appeared on American television and in films like *It's a Mad, Mad, Mad, Mad World* (dir. Kramer, 1963), and enjoyed the slapstick of the Three Stooges; and like the participants in my original study, I appreciated the Marx Brothers' films but mainly for Groucho's quickfire wit. In my early teens I heard a recording of African-American comedian Dick Gregory and was impressed by his social consciousness – his *négritude*. I had read interviews with him in *Jet*,[2] in which he spoke out on civil rights, feminism, and the Vietnam War. Gregory's style differed greatly from that of Cosby because he talked about being Black, whereas Cosby avoided it. At this stage, I hadn't seen Richard Pryor, who followed Gregory onto television shows like the *Tonight Show with Johnny Carson*. Gregory was the only Black comedian of his kind because he was also a committed activist, and this lent gravitas to his words and made him appear more 'authentic'.

My father was an African-American airman from Brooklyn and my mother came from a working-class Scottish-Irish Liverpool family. It seemed fortuitous that the cities from whence my parents came have rich comedy traditions, and Liverpool and Brooklyn have produced two of my favourite comedians: Woody Allen and Alexei Sayle. I inherited my parents' senses of humour: my dad was especially adept at sarcastic one-liners and clever put downs, while my mum enjoyed malapropisms, puns, and spoonerisms, and had a very Scouse turn of phrase. However, unlike them, I displayed an early talent for mimicking voices, and I would perform impressions of my teachers and others to amuse my classmates.

When my dad was sent to Vietnam in 1963, my mother, my siblings, and I had to relocate from base housing on Selfridge Air Force Base in Michigan to my grandparents' house on the Norris Green estate. The reason being that, should my father be killed, we couldn't live on Selfridge; our relationship with the USAF would end. Liverpool in the early 1960s was still visibly bomb-damaged and was a completely different world to the one I'd left behind in Michigan. Everything in England seemed fusty and decayed. There were no Black people living in Norris Green and the only other person of colour I saw was the local general practitioner, a Dr Pereira, who I presume was Sri Lankan or Goan. In the 1960s, many people of colour lived in Toxteth (or Liverpool 8) in the south of the city, but even

---

[2] Along with *Ebony*, *Jet* was one of two periodicals for African-Americans and published by a Black-owned company based in Chicago. *Jet* focussed more on political and social issues, while *Ebony* concentrated on Black celebrities and fashion.

when we ventured into the city centre, I don't recall seeing many Black people. When we crossed the Mersey by ferry to Birkenhead, where my aunt, uncle, and cousins lived, there seemed to be no people of colour at all.

While we were in Liverpool, I attended the local primary school, where I was the only brown-skinned kid out of a cohort of around 300. I tend to make friends easily and this ability made moving home frequently much easier. My friends came from a cross section of cultures and ethnicities, and even transcended the enlisted–officer class divide. This imperative to make friends quickly is fairly typical of life in the military, because you're always the 'new kid' at school. However, the Liverpool experience of 1963–1964 was an exception. It was a culture shock: I had gone from a kindergarten where I was well-liked and had many friends to a school where my attempts to form friendships were rebuffed, solely because of my colour. Perhaps this was the reason why my mum explained 'race' to me: she realized that I would have to deal with it in Liverpool. Desperate to fit in and realizing that I had a talent for mimicry, I asked my mum to teach me to do a Scouse accent, but she'd always refused to speak in her native accent (dialect was another matter and her speech was littered with 'Scouse-isms'), and directed me to my Aunt Alex, who simply said "use your teeth". I eventually mastered the accent, but this failed to win me any friends and the racist name-calling and taunts continued. The most frequent chant was "Nigger, nigger, pull the trigger. Bang! Bang! Bang!" Craig Charles, who is several years younger than me and who lived in a different part of Liverpool, recalled the same chant in an interview in the *Guardian* (29 May 2015). When we eventually returned to Michigan in 1964, none of my classmates could understand what I was saying, so I had to quickly revert to a generic American accent.

Children of American military personnel are called 'military brats', and as such, I was expected to follow in my father's footsteps and join the USAF – or if not the USAF, then another branch of the military. However, I had other ideas: I wanted to become either a physician, a journalist, or a political cartoonist. The thought of being a comedian never occurred to me. I liked the idea of being a political cartoonist and drew some of my own cartoons and often looked at those drawn by American editorial cartoonists like Oliphant, whose name is the only one I can remember – perhaps because it sounded like 'elephant'. Oliphant's cartoons were syndicated and appeared in the *Stars and Stripes*[3] and the *New York Times*,

---

[3] The *Stars and Stripes* is the daily newspaper for American service personnel and contains syndicated articles and commentary.

which my dad bought religiously. I later dropped any idea of becoming a physician when I realized that cutting people open was a possibility, but also because I'd only managed to get a 'C' in Algebra and failed Physics. American medical schools insist on better grades in mathematics, so this route was closed off.

My comedy tastes matured while I was at London Central High School in High Wycombe, Buckinghamshire, a day and boarding school for military dependents, where I was introduced to Cheech and Chong, whose drug-referencing humour I found hilarious. My roommate, Ed, also had a cassette copy of the Firesign Theatre's 'The Continuing Adventures of Nick Danger', which was a contrast to Cheech and Chong and had a 'stream of consciousness' feel to it. The Firesign Theatre was an American absurdist comedy company which had its own radio show and had been associated with the 1960s counterculture. Influenced by the *Goon Show*, their comedy was clever and made oblique references to philosophy, popular culture (especially the Beatles), and Carlos Castaneda's *Tales of Power*. Sometime later, I discovered George Carlin's *Toledo Window Box* and *Occupation: Foole*. One of Carlin's main themes was the peculiarities of the English language, and he influenced some of my earliest routines, especially my pieces that dealt with the power of words. Also influential was Richard Pryor's (1979) video, *Live in Concert*, which was a revelation, and again showed how far advanced African-American comedians were in comparison to their British counterparts – represented at this time by the likes of Lenny Henry and Charlie Williams.

In terms of British comedians, I liked Ken Dodd, Tommy Cooper, and Stanley Baxter, but also enjoyed the work of Irish comedian Dave Allen, whose *Dave Allen at Large* and *The Dave Allen Show* were on BBC1. Allen was probably closest to the American comedians in terms of material and style, and moreover, he had something to say. Cooper was effortlessly funny but my mum hated him, while Baxter often cross-dressed and played all kinds of absurd characters. My appreciation for Dodd comes with being half-Scouse and I related to him being a Liverpudlian, but he was also a master joke-teller who could reel off gags without pausing for breath.

Television comedy viewing in our family consisted mainly of sitcoms like *Nearest and Dearest*, with Hylda Baker and Jimmy Jewel, and *Are You Being Served?* My parents were fans of *Till Death Us Do Part*, but this show was always on television after my bedtime. I was allowed to watch *The Goodies*, but not *Monty Python's Flying Circus*, which was *verboten* on the grounds that my mum thought it "wasn't funny". Curiously, old-fashioned comedy shows like *The Comedians* were deemed family viewing by my parents. I found *The Comedians* rather strange because it consisted of mainly white middle-aged men telling what I thought were playground jokes, but what was perhaps most noticeable about the show was the preponderance of racist and sexist humour. I'd never heard American stand-ups tell traditional jokes and I found the aesthetic rather old-fashioned; it seemed to serve as a metaphor for the fustiness and nostalgia that gripped the country during those post-war years. Indeed, this kind of stand-up seemed to be at least 20 years behind American stand-up. The only exception to *The Comedians*' conveyor belt of politically and socially disinterested comedians and their perfectly formed jokes was Norman Collier, who performed a hilarious broken-microphone routine. Collier wasn't a stand-up comedian; rather, he was a comedy absurdist who also performed a chicken walk that wasn't as funny.

In all the light-entertainment programmes we watched on television in the early 1970s, there were very few Black people of any significance, save for Charlie Williams and Kenny Lynch (Lenny Henry came later). Williams was a mixed-heritage Black Yorkshireman who had been a footballer and miner, and who was a regular on *The Comedians*. What was interesting about Williams was how he used the same joke-butts as white comedians. These were: the Irish (Paddies), the Welsh (Taffies), Scots (Jocks), Black people (Williams oddly referring to Black men as 'coloured chaps'), and South Asians (the catch-all term for which was 'pakis'). I would argue that he understood the *doxa* of the dominant comedy field and operated within its limits by relying on a form of self-deprecation to appeal to his overwhelmingly white Northern audiences (Ilott, 2019). Positionally, therefore, he assumed the role of low-status Black man in relation to his high-status white audience. When I first saw Kenny Lynch on television, he was paired with Liverpudlian comic, Jimmy Tarbuck, who used Lynch as a butt for racist banter. I found this disappointing, because it was only a few years after the Black Power salute at the 1968 Summer Olympics, yet here was a Black man playing up to the white audience's postcolonial/colonialist expectations of Black people. By contrast, African-American entertainers possessed more self-respect. This was the era of Black consciousness and taking pride in being Black. Thus, in my eyes, Williams and Lynch had no self-respect and appeared to be erasing their Blackness to play up to their white audiences' expectations of Black people. My father expressed his displeasure with Lynch in the most explicit manner: he was that "goddamned Uncle Tom", while Williams seemed to get a free pass. Yet wasn't Williams also an 'Uncle Tom'? Wasn't he also playing the white game? Yes, he was. However, it is ironic that, for all its apparent social progress in comedy terms at least, the United States in the 1970s remained deeply divided along racial lines in terms of housing, job opportunities, and representation. For example, if a Black character appeared in a Hollywood action film – Jim Brown's character in *The Dirty Dozen* (dir. Aldrich, 1967), for example – they were usually killed off before the end of the film.

I left school in 1975 and went through a series of undemanding, menial jobs, while I made up my mind about my future. In 1978, inspired by Linton Kwesi Johnson and John Cooper Clarke, I began writing poetry and lyrics. Each of them spoke to me in different ways: Johnson wrote socially conscious poems – delivered in patois – that were mixed with Dennis Bovell's dub beats. He was Black Britain's answer to the Last Poets in terms of his *négritude*. Cooper Clarke, on the other hand, had a spiky wit and sneering delivery; the *New Musical Express* referred to him variously as "Bob Dylan on acid" and a "punk poet". I found the surreal prose of Captain Beefheart similarly appealing; I loved his work on *Trout Mask Replica* and the semi-live album *Bongo Fury* with Frank Zappa and the Mothers of Invention, and I would occasionally perform renditions of Beefheart's 'Sam with the Showing Scalp Flat Top' or 'The Old Fart at Play' alongside my poetry and prose *impromptu* at pubs around Hitchin. However, for all my poetic efforts, I would happily admit that most of my poetry was terrible, and my readings did not always meet with my unwilling audience's approval.

In 1980, I began working as a disc jockey for a land-based pirate station called Radio Fiona, under the name of 'Bob Stone'. Radio Fiona broadcast on the medium-wave band on Sunday afternoons to North Hertfordshire and East Bedfordshire. I played a mix of punk, post-punk, rockabilly, R 'n' B, jazz, pop, psychedelia, and easy listening on my weekly 'Hot Valves' radio show. I had always had an interest in radio, having spent many hours listening to the Armed Forces Network (AFN) and Radio Caroline, the latter of which played album tracks rather than singles. I had ambitions to work in radio after running a small pirate station with Ed at boarding school. Given that there were only a small number of *legal* radio stations[4]

---

[4] There were several land-based pirate radio stations in England, many of which were concentrated in the south. From memory, I can recall a station called Radio

in Britain, getting work as a disc jockey was never going to be easy or straightforward. Hospital radio has been a traditional route to the airwaves for many DJs and announcers, but I was impatient, and I didn't want to play records I found dull. There was also another reason: in the 1970s and 1980s, the talent on the BBC consisted mostly of middle-class white men like Tony Blackburn. This was an unspoken message to anyone from a minority background that in order to work for a national broadcaster, you had to be white. The arrival of Chiltern Radio (now called Heart Dunstable) in the Bedfordshire and Hertfordshire area in 1981 merely confirmed this suspicion. There was no glamour in land-based pirate radio in the provinces: it was a lonely and, in the winter, a cold job, as you set up the broadcast site, and then stood around in a copse or a spinney in a frozen farmer's field for a few hours, quickly flipping over cassette tapes to ensure the best possible continuity, while looking out for British Telecom (later Department of Trade and Industry) enforcement agents. You also spent long hours recording a programme on a cassette tape, trying to dub a jingle or station 'ident' between the music. I hated jingles: I found them pointless and old-fashioned; they were the kind of thing that Radio One DJ, Dave Lee Travis, would have overused, and I only submitted to their inclusion under pressure from Jonny, the station owner.

Around this time, I was working as a buyer for a small manufacturer of electro-mechanical gauges in Hitchin, Hertfordshire. My role was to buy a variety of consumable items from cap screws and valves to circuit boards and reams of photocopier paper, but I saw no future in this job and left it in March 1983. I had thought of going into teaching but realized that, to teach, I needed to gain qualifications. In early September of the same year, I made a snap decision to go to Hitchin College (now called North Herts College) to take some A-Levels in Theatre Studies and English, with the intention of going to drama school and becoming an actor. However, I failed to get accepted by the two drama schools for which I auditioned and, in 1986, I was offered a place on the BA (Hons) Creative Arts course (Drama major) at Newcastle Polytechnic, which was orientated towards community arts practice. Many of the lecturers on the course had been involved in community arts organizations or agit-prop theatre companies. My second-year tutor, Richard Stourac, was a founding member of Red

City in North London, which played rock 'n' roll and rockabilly; Radio Jackie, a community station based in Tolworth in South London; and Alice's Restaurant and Dread Broadcasting Corporation in West London.

Ladder and Broadside Mobile Workers Theatre and had worked with the prestigious Berliner Ensemble theatre company, which had been co-founded by Bertolt Brecht and his wife, Helene Weigel. Course leader Baz Kershaw had worked with Welfare State International, a company that specialized in large-scale celebratory spectacles. Initially, I found the Creative Arts course disappointing because there was little in the way of actor training, but I soon had my rather narrow ideas about the theatre challenged, particularly by the compulsory Arts Society and Culture (ASC) module, which provided the theoretical basis to our work and was essentially an introduction to cultural studies. It was ASC that provided me with the sociological tools to deconstruct the world around me and would provide the theoretical basis for my political satire, eventually leading to me taking a PhD.

Making Comedy

In 1980s Newcastle, there was no one to tell you how to be a stand-up comedian or how to write material. This had to be done from scratch. There were no stand-up comedy courses like those in Trevor Griffiths' play, *Comedians* (1975). There were, however, cabaret courses in London where the scene was more developed, but not in the North of England or Scotland. To create the first and subsequent sets in the early period, I learned by observing comedians in live settings and on television and video, and by using trial and error. This approach produces comedy that is not formulaic, but which was highly risky because of its use of bricolage and its 'work-in-progress' feel. Avant-garde artists will often experiment using bricolage and will sometimes produce a product that's hybridized. Alternatively, they will strip the form down to its basic components and build 'from the bottom up' (Wollen, 1975; Campbell, 2017). It seemed immediately obvious to me that alt comedians must have constructed their comedy performances from bricolage, because like me, they had no previous experience of performing stand-up comedy, therefore they would need to draw from whatever cultural/counter*cultural* capital they possessed. This seemed to be the most logical approach, and yet I also realized that it would take years to become a good comedian. I also drew inspiration from my favourite American comedians and from making use of my physicality, personal obsessions, facial expressions, and talent for impressions. George Carlin was probably my biggest influence, and

The Outsider

Figure 1: Cabaret A Go Go, first poster

I loved his discourses on the power of language. 'Some Werds', on his album *Toledo Windowbox* (Little David, 1974), provided inspiration for material about the foibles of the English language, of which the following is an example: "Disgruntled? You never meet anyone who is gruntled". This joke of mine, unbeknown to me, was similar to an anonymous joke, which may have been told by a variety artist in the 1940s or 1950s:

Disgruntled is such a strange word.

I mean have you ever been a gruntled worker?

I only told the disgruntled joke once or twice and then dropped it. As for the rest of the material I'd written for that night, this has been lost in the mists of time. My memory of the first gig is hazy, but I remember finding the experience exhilarating and wanting to repeat it. However, there were no regular cabaret clubs in Newcastle where I could try out my material and develop as a performer. For that to happen, I would need to create a cabaret club from scratch. This meant bringing in like-minded people in from the Creative Arts course. However, it would take another year before this idea could be realized. So, in late October 1987, I put the idea of a cabaret club to fellow student Clive Lyttle, at the Barley Mow pub on the Quayside. We looked at the Bridge Hotel, which had a cellar room, and the Broken Doll, which had an upstairs room with its own bar. We chose the Broken Doll because the landlord was enthusiastic about the idea and the room suited our immediate needs. We created a collective called the Fun Committee, named the club Cabaret A Go Go (CAGG), and arranged to put on a show every two weeks on a Thursday – though the first show actually took place on a Friday (Campbell, 2022).

Throughout my comedy career, I performed under the stage name 'Buddy Hell' and this name needs some explanation. In the 1980s, stage names were common and, as I point out in Chapter 5, many comedians chose to use stage names because they couldn't afford to go professional and had to live on unemployment benefit (which became Jobseeker's Allowance in the 1990s). My choice of stage name is tied to an idea of distancing my off-stage self from my onstage persona. Many comedians often say their onstage persona is either unlike them in real life or an exaggerated version of themselves. Indeed, history is also full of examples of those who chose a name other than their own for professional reasons. For example, 'Issur Danielovitch' does not sound as impressive as 'Kirk Douglas', and Kirk would have been unlikely to have had the success he had by using his real name. Before settling on a permanent stage name, I went through a number of aliases. When I began performing in December 1987, I called myself 'Johnny Boiler'; I have no idea why I chose this name, and it would appear that I did it for no other reason than avoiding using my real name. In January 1987, I changed my name to 'Ray Burns' before realizing that this was the real name of the Damned's bassist, Captain Sensible, and deciding to drop it for that reason. A month or so later, while walking down a street in Newcastle city centre, I can remember looking at the sign for Alfred Marks, a now defunct employment agency, and thinking that if I deleted the first three letters from the first name, I could call myself 'Red Marks'. This suited my politics but was too obvious, so I dropped it after using it once. Then, one Sunday lunchtime in late February 1987, while watching a local band play downstairs in the Broken Doll, my mind began to wander and I found myself asking, what happened to Richard Hell of New York punk band the Voidoids? And for reasons that I am unable to explain, I also thought of Buddy Guy, the American blues musician. Then it occurred to me that if I joined the latter's first name with the former's surname, I had 'Buddy Hell'. It was at once a

Figure 2: Cabaret A Go Go, first mention of Buddy Hell

pun on the expletive 'bloody hell' and a punk-sounding name. The first mention of that name appeared on the poster below (Figure 2).

Like many people of my generation, I had been affected by punk; thus the name seemed a natural choice. I kept this name until sometime in 1992, when Paul Jay (Eugene Cheese), the promoter of the Chuckle Club, offered to manage me and insisted that I change my name. I had performed the obligatory open spot for him in 1990 and he always refused to book me because of my stage name. His club paid well and getting regular paid spots at the Chuckle was something to aim for. So, thinking that he could get me more work, I agreed to change my name to 'Buddy Wells'. I merely took the surname of the blues musician Junior Wells (who had played harmonica with Buddy Guy) to replace the 'Hell'. Jay managed to get me one gig in the time it took me to get ten, but he never booked me for the Chuckle. Growing impatient, I gave up and reverted to Buddy Hell a short time later. I concede that this name change may have confused promoters and may have possibly set my career back by two years.

I initially experienced difficulty in writing material. How is one supposed to go about it when there is no one and nothing to guide you? I spent ages staring at blank sheets of A4 paper, hoping the words would magically appear on the page. Was this how stand-ups went about devising material? How do I know this is funny? It is well known that Frankie Howerd used to perform a shambolic, almost rambling set that belied its tight scripting; even the asides and the comments to the audience were scripted. Yet he made it *seem* so spontaneous and off-the-cuff. Many American comedians also seemed to improvise but Carlin, who inspired much of my early routine, also performed to a script. Pryor, on the other hand, freewheeled his set – or at least, that's how it seemed. His first performance after recovering in hospital from self-inflicted burns has an entirely improvised feel to it. Thinking that I could do the same, I spent the first couple of months trying to improvise in front of our audiences but with little success. But how does one know what material works if one doesn't experiment? Having one's own club helped a great deal in that regard.

I was resident compère at CAGG for three years and without this regular practice, I would not have been able to develop as a performer. So by the second year of my career, I had created an observational piece about insects called 'Flies and Wasps', for instance, which came from a fascination with insects and made use of my physicality. Here is an excerpt from that piece:

> People use expressions like "I'd loved to have been a fly on the wall", but I wouldn't want to be one; they're filthy and carry 49 different diseases on their bodies. But when flies see us, they see us in slow motion.
>
> [Moving and speaking in slow motion] "I'm going to get you, you filthy bastard!"
>
> The fly sees this and says "fuck off" [sticks two fingers up]... and flies straight into the sticky flypaper.

This piece relies on audience recognition and many people have had experiences of dealing with flies in their homes, either through trying to encourage them to leave through an open window or otherwise attempting kill them with a rolled-up newspaper. The punchline is weak and the piece is carried by physicality alone. Ten years later, I recycled part of the opening of this piece and used it in a piece about General Pinochet taking tea with Thatcher. 'Flies and Wasps' was a popular piece, but it was less than two minutes long, and I knew that I would have to devise more material if I wanted to fill a twenty-minute set. At this point, I only had a little over five minutes' worth of material, some of which was topical. This would have to change.

The moment of change occurred in the summer of 1988 as I was watching actor and playwright Roy Smiles, who was performing a one-man play in which he played all the characters at the Earth Exchange Cabaret in Highgate. Afterwards, I created a cinematically themed routine that included a film trailer parody, a British Pathé newsreel parody, and a 1950s sci-fi horror film spoof called 'The Shopping Centre that Ate the World' in which I played all the characters. These included a Nazi scientist that was modelled on Werner von Braun, a useless president, and romantic male and female leads. If I'm honest, some of the characters in 'Shopping Centre' were facsimiles of characters in *Dr Strangelove* (dir. Kubrick, 1962), but it was also partly inspired by the sci-fi horror film *It Conquered the World* (dir. Corman, 1956) and the preamble to the song 'Cheepnis', from the partially live album *Roxy and Elsewhere* by Frank Zappa and the Mothers of Invention (DiscReet, 1974). Unfortunately, the only copies of the original scripts for 'Newsreel' and 'Shopping Centre' were in the appendix of my undergraduate dissertation, which I have since lost, thus I am unable to reproduce extracts. 'Film Trailer', on the other hand, was committed to memory.

The idea for 'Shopping Centre' came to me on a bus journey as I was riding past the ever-expanding Eldon Square Shopping Centre in Newcastle City Centre, but the recent completion of the Metro Centre in Dunston near Gateshead was also a contributing factor to this piece. I imagined these places as monsters that not only devoured public spaces, but also functioned as predators that were feeding upon gullible humans by entrancing and draining them of their money and humanity. It also seemed to me that the retail sector and certain sections of the media were complicit in diverting people's attention away from Britain's structural issues and towards the objectification of designer labels that were being deployed as status symbols. Here, aspects of the sixties countercultures, like notions of individualism, were used to sell 'ideal' lifestyles (Desmond et al., 2000: 251–272). Thus, the consumption of luxury items, aided by the availability of cheap credit, became paramount and little mattered beyond what signs and symbols one could consume. This was encapsulated in Thatcher's phrase, though decontextualized, that there was "no such thing as society, only individuals and families" (quoted in Keay, 1987), which appeared to sum up the atomization of British society. 'Shopping

Centre', therefore, served as the alchemical means of transmuting the base metal of my disgust with consumerism into comedy gold. Yet 'Shopping Centre' didn't allow for updates, and thus was a prisoner of its scripting. Its geographical specificity also meant that it was difficult for audiences outside of Tyne and Wear to comprehend, and I needed material that could be transported anywhere.

The same was true for 'Newsreel', which was a very short piece that was delivered in the style of an announcer of the period and satirized the departure of troops bound for another pointless war. 'Newsreel' was based mainly on my memories of seeing newsreels before the features at the ABC cinema in Liverpool in the early 1960s, but it was weaker than the rest of the material. 'Shopping Centre' and 'Newsreel' were jettisoned after my first stage death at Sheffield University in May 1989, which although a crushing experience, was a valuable lesson in writing and performing comedy. When a performer dies, they can either reflect on the reasons for their death and produce stronger material or leave the profession. I chose to do the former. In hindsight, it might have been better to adapt 'Shopping Centre' to Sheffield and use the recently completed Meadowhall Shopping Centre as a substitute.

Removing 'Shopping Centre' and 'Newsreel' from my set left a gap that needed filling and I went through a number of pieces. According to my diary from 1990, one of these was called 'Tories' but I am unable to recall anything about it, apart from the fact that it used the voices of several government ministers. 'Film Trailer' remained in my set and became my signature piece. Although it was scripted, it had an inbuilt flexibility that allowed me to update the voices and sections of the piece, as required. Its voices were drawn from a constantly updated master list of some thirty-odd personalities that I could impersonate. Here, it's worth mentioning how I choose the voices to impersonate. The art of selecting voices for impressions is the product of years of training one's ear to identify how the voice is being produced. Is it nasal or adenoidal? Is the speaker producing the voice from the chest or throat? How are the organs of speech – the tongue, the teeth, the lips, and the hard and soft palates – being used? I usually know instinctively if the speaker's voice is within my vocal range, and the ability to tune into people's voices and imitate them can be likened to playing music 'by ear', where one picks up an unfamiliar instrument and plays a tune on it for the first time. However, the voice is only half an impression, because without the mannerisms of the subject the impression is less convincing. In this respect an impressionist is like a caricaturist: they both have an eye for detail and distort a person's physical attributes or voice for comic effect. In caricatures, physical characteristics are seized upon and exaggerated for emphasis. Exaggeration is a necessary component of the caricature because it magnifies the difference between a person and a thing (Hillier, 1970; Bal et al., 2009).

Updating the voices in 'Film Trailer' kept it fresh, and I would argue that performing the voices of figures who no longer have a public profile demonstrates laziness on the part of the impressionist. Television impressionists, like Mike Yarwood, had become complacent and continued to imitate the same personalities long after they disappeared from the public eye. Although the voices in 'Film Trailer' were changed fairly frequently, two impressions would remain constant: one was Marlon Brando, who would take a tissue or handkerchief from his pocket, look at it, begin to speak, change his mind, wipe his brow, scowl a little, appear anguished, go to speak, hesitate, stare at the tissue, raise his arm in the style of a Shakespearian actor, and deliver a belch or a grunt. This would take around thirty seconds to perform, much longer than the other impressions, which would only last a couple of seconds at most. In this 'scene', I was caricaturing Brando's method acting and, particularly, his mumbling, pause-laden performance as Colonel Kurtz in *Apocalypse Now!* (dir. Coppola, 1979). The second impression was Dr Ian Paisley, the leader of the Democratic Unionist Party. Paisley had been one of my favourites; his oratorical style, his booming voice, and 'fire and brimstone' manner made him an easy target. I had been performing impressions of Paisley for my friends and workmates since the late 1970s. In 'Film Trailer', he was given the phrase, "I am the anti-Christ!", which was a reference to his outburst of "I denounce you as the anti-Christ" when Pope John Paul II spoke to the European Parliament in 1988 and to his Calvinism. Sometimes I would swap this for the words "Never! Never! Never!", which he said in a speech condemning the Anglo-Irish Agreement in 1985 that he and his party had opposed.

After my work placement at the Hackney Empire in 1989, I was inspired to create two new acts: one was a street act called Onemanandabox and the other was a character called Les Bogroll. I created the first act after my work placement at the Hackney Empire, which was inspired by variety performers, such as Otiz Cannelloni and John Hegley as the Brown Paper Bag Bros, and Steve Murray the Teddy Bear Trainer, who I'd seen in London during the holidays. Onemanandabox was a speciality act and I figured that we needed such an act, because up until that point most of our acts were poets and musicians; even stand-up comedians were few in number. For Onemanandabox, I learned to spin plates and to juggle cigar boxes and coloured scarves, the latter of which are used to train jugglers before they progress to balls and other objects. Cigar box juggling or manipulation originated in Japan but was popularized by W.C. Fields and involves flipping cigar boxes to create a visual effect. I never graduated to juggling balls but kept the scarves and used them occasionally throughout the 1990s as an effect for a short piece about being trapped inside a washing machine. I also had a collection of cardboard boxes of various sizes that I used for telling a series of dreadful puns. For example, I would take a medium-sized box and make barking sounds and ask the audience "What's this?" then say, "It's a boxer dog".

Les, on the other hand, was created specifically for the purpose of hosting our Alternative Seaside Specials, of which there were two in 1988 and 1989. Les was a composite of various WMC comedians but was based mostly on Bernard Manning. Les's first name came from Les Dawson. I added the word 'bogroll', the colloquialism for toilet tissue, as his surname. The suggestion being that Les was a failed comedian because he was shit. Like Bernard Manning, Les spoke in a north Mancunian accent that was so convincing that it fooled some people into thinking that I came from Manchester. Les told a series of anti-jokes, none of which I am able to recall, but the idea behind them was to send up the sexist and racist jokes told by trad. comedians. Jon Thompson's Bernard Righton had a similar kind of act but evidently had more success than I did.

The Alternative Seaside Specials were intended to send up the BBC's long-running variety series, *Seaside Special* (1975–1979), and its revival, *Summertime Special* (1981–1988), which featured traditional performers. *Seaside Special* was set in a circus big top while *Summertime Special* was recorded in an 'end-of-the-pier' setting. Like many shows of its kind, *Seaside Special* and *Summertime Special* were rather nostalgic, sentimental, and seemed insulated from the youth cultures in the outside world. It was these three things that I wanted to satirize, along with the entire seaside experience. We dressed the stage to resemble the seaside and I created a temporary piece of art using a drinks tray and some builders sand that I 'liberated' from a nearby building site. Into this, I added some cocktail umbrellas, some water, and detritus. This was a comment on the state of Britain's beaches, many of which had lost their blue flag certification because of litter and sewage outfall being washed back to shore. This was the seaside that one never saw on *Seaside Special*.

Figure 3: Alternative Seaside Special

In December 1989, Martin Kellner of BBC North's *Night Network* asked me to perform some topical impressions on his show. This show also featured Caroline Ahearne, who performed as Sister Mary Immaculate but is perhaps better known for her Mrs Merton character, who also featured on the show. Around the same time, I started to include more topical comedy in my set, but writing this kind of comedy is demanding, because it dates quickly. Therefore, many comedians avoid it and play safe by relying on tried and tested gags. Such concerns did not deter me, because I wanted to avoid becoming stale and have a genuine interest in current affairs. Topical material tends to be political, and I will provide some examples below. Like other comedians of the period, I had a piece about Thatcher:

Anyone here interested in astrology?

I'm a Libran, which means I'm kind, gentle, easy going [pause]. Thatcher's a Libran... [pause]. Astrology's a load of bollocks, isn't it?

Notebook 1, 1989

This kind of material marked a change of direction from pieces that made use of my acting and movement skills to something that more closely resembled stand-up comedy. Here, I make use of astrology's description of the Libran character and counterpose it against the authoritarian personality of Thatcher, while at the same time commenting on the dubious scientific value of astrology in the punchline. The comedy comes from the tension between the notion of Thatcher being gentle because of her star sign, and the media-constructed image of her as the Iron Lady. Therefore, any suggestion of kindness on her part seemed absurd, given the suffering of the communities that were destroyed by her government's evisceration of the traditional industries, and the sense of hopelessness and desperation felt by people living in poverty.

Thatcher was eventually toppled in 1990 by a combination of two things: her autocratic style of leadership and the Community Charge or Poll Tax. Yet the Kinnock-led Labour Party refused to oppose the tax, and so the fight against it was led by Militant, the SWP, and local grassroots groups. During this time, I was playing Anti-Poll Tax League benefits and much of my material was articulated around this theme. The minister with cabinet responsibility for the implementation of the Poll Tax was Nicholas Ridley, who featured in a couple of my pieces. Ridley was a hardcore free-market capitalist and was reviled by the Left, particularly for his role in the privatization of the nationalized industries and his attacks on the miners (q.v. 'The Ridley Report'). In this piece, I cast him as an aspiring comedian:

> I write jokes for politicians… Nicholas Ridley came up to me and said, "Buddy, write us some gags because I'm thinking of moonlighting as a comedian. I hear there's a lot of money in it". So, I said, "Nick, me old mate"… cos we're close, like… [Half aside] I live in Newcastle and he lives in London, which is as about as fucking close as I want to get to him… "Nick, of course I will. How about one about the Community Charge (Poll Tax)?" Anyway, I did… I wrote one that he did at conference… "Why should a duke pay more than a dustman?" [shout] BUT HE FORGOT THE PUNCHLINE! Why should a duke pay more than a dustman? [shout] BECAUSE HE FUCKING CAN!
>
> Notebook 1, 1989

This piece, like the rest of my material about the Poll Tax, was very popular with audiences. The piece works through its use of incongruity and finishes with a hard-hitting line spat out in punk style. This was written in response to Ridley's speech to the 1989 Conservative Party conference in which he attempted to justify the hated tax by asking, "Why should a duke pay more than a dustman?" The piece is framed by announcing to the audience that "I write jokes for politicians" and from there I played with the absurd suggestion that Ridley wasn't a serious politician but a comedian, a very bad comedian. Ridley's question was insulting; the tax was an unfair burden that had been imposed on people who didn't have the economic means to pay, and so by claiming it was 'fair', he was being dishonest. There was also one written for the Labour opposition, which was used alternately.

> I wrote some gags for the Labour Party but I never thought they would end up in a policy document… the wittily titled "Looking to the Future".
>
> Notebook 1, 1989

For me and many others on the left, the Labour Party under Neil Kinnock had been a bitter disappointment; we felt betrayed. Kinnock had initially associated himself with the Labour Left. He was a member of the Anti-Apartheid Movement and the CND. However, as soon as he assumed the leadership, his apparent leftism evaporated. His refusal to support the Miners' Strike and his speech to the 1985 party conference in Bournemouth, in which he denounced the Militant Tendency, signalled the party's further shift to the right. This lack of political courage led me to attack Labour as much as the Tory government. I did this, not for the much vaunted and mythological 'even-handedness' that seems to afflict many BBC political satirists, but because I had a deep loathing for the party's leadership and its eagerness to appear as a 'government-in-waiting'. This seemed to me to compromise its ability to oppose and, moreover, offer socialist policies. Indeed, Labour's historical tendency to face towards parliament rather than turn towards its voters is discussed at some length in Ralph Miliband's book, *Parliamentary Socialism* (1972). The leadership of the party claimed that they were making Labour more electable, but I had grave concerns, especially when Kinnock urged people to pay the Poll Tax regardless of their personal circumstances (Epstein, 1998).[5] Labour's assumed electability was dashed on the rocks of the 1992 general election.

---

[5] The government made no provisions for people who couldn't afford to pay and there was no form of support. Consequently, those without the means to pay were taken to court and, in many cases, imprisoned for non-payment.

Nicholas Ridley was forced to resign in July 1990 over comments he made about the European Union and Germany. Typically, he claimed that he was resigning to spend more time with his family. My response was little more than undisguised venom and the intention was to channel any latent rage in the audience into laughter:

> It's about time he spent some time with his family. His career is hanging by a thread [pause]. He should be hanging from the end of a rope! By the way, his name is an anagram of Nice Shy Old Liar.
>
> Notebook 2, 1990

Ten years of Thatcherism had not produced the promised results of mass home-ownership. This and an item on BBC News about homelessness prompted me to write the following throwaway piece:

> I saw this report on the USSR. Party leaders have country houses while some people have to live three families to a small flat – in this country people have to live in cardboard boxes!
>
> Notebook 2, 1990

As far as I was aware, there was no homelessness in the Soviet Union. However, it wasn't my intention to give praise to the Soviets but to draw attention to the fact that for a highly developed capitalist nation, with its promises of freedom and potential riches, homelessness in Britain had been increasing since 1980 and this was generated, in no small part, by the sale of council houses under Right to Buy (RTB), and the high numbers of repossessions that had taken place in the wake of Black Monday in 1987. Furthermore, the Thatcher government's economic policies were predicated on the notion of 'efficiencies' and local authorities were forbidden to use their capital receipts from RTB to build replacement properties. At least the Soviet Union could get something right, for a country in which there were ostensibly no personal freedoms and food shortages. Such things were also the stuff of television news bulletins, with their images of long queues of people waiting for hours outside a shop with empty shelves. Indeed, the regular airing of such images seemed to be the state's warning to those tempted to embrace 'communism' as a solution.

There was a tacit consensus among comedians that performing material about television shows was lazy. The reason for this was never properly explained to me but it is a certainty that one cannot assume everyone in the audience watches the television show to which one is referring.

However, there was a Findus 'Lean Cuisine' advert that featured a young man inviting his girlfriend around for dinner, only to serve her a frozen ready meal. My response to this was:

> Has anyone seen that Findus Lean Cuisine ad? [sings] Hey good looking, what you got cooking? [spoken] This guy invites his girlfriend around for dinner and instead of cooking her something *special*, he serves her a frozen ready meal! Now if I were that woman, I'd be thinking one of three things: one, do you think I'm fat? Two, can't you cook? Three, don't you like me? BASTARD!
>
> Buddy Hell, *The Late Show*, BBC2, April 1990

This advert mediated the 'perfect' female form to the viewer as well as suggesting that if one were to eat Findus Lean Cuisine, one would be rewarded with rapid weight loss and the company of a handsome young man with a 'six-pack' abdomen. By pointing out the absurdity of the advertisement's premise that consuming mass-produced frozen food leads to a fulfilled life, I was attacking a diet industry that convinces women to hate their bodies, but I was also critiquing the trope of the male who is unable to cook a proper meal. The word 'BASTARD' at the end of the piece was spat out with Alexei Sayle-style venom. This piece would always get plenty of laughs, especially from women in the audience but it was only useful as long as the advert was on television, and so was dropped in late 1991 once the advert was no longer being shown.

I made a brief visit to London in March 1990 and appeared at one of the early Black Comedy shows at the Albany Empire in Deptford that was organized by David Bryan and Jenny Landreth. My diary entry reads:

BLACK COMEDY CLUB @ Albany Empire

Debut of Geordie. Debut proper of new intro. Reintroduced expressions as part of intro. The idea is to get some good laughs in at the beginning. Need more expressions or short bits. Ambulance is starting to drag in the second half. Needs some attention. Need more IMPRESSIONS! More use of facial expressions. The use of a good expression at the end of a weak line can have great comic effect.

Opening one's set with strong material establishes the rhythm for what follows, but why rhythm? Double (2005: 205) writes that "rhythm is probably as important to comedy as it is to music". Part of one's rhythm is timing, which is a much-discussed issue among comedians and comedy aficionados, but Attardo and Pickering (2011) remind us that little has been written about this important element in comic performance. Murray (2007: 109) mentions it but in relation to speeding up one's set and warns the reader that the "timing will be off". This seems fairly obvious because all the pauses will be elided and the rhythm will be mostly absent. Double (2005: 202) argues that no one is particularly clear on what timing actually means and offers a number of meanings from a list of comedians past and present. However, I agree with Attardo and Pickering (2011) that there are structural affinities between music and comedy in terms of their rhythms and timing. When one looks at sheet music, the first thing that one sees is the time signature, which is determined by the number of beats. Common and waltz times are fairly easy to identify: one is 4/4 and the other is 3/4 and both are found in contemporary music. On one level, this seems absurd: how can comedy be determined by a time signature? However, as Double (2005: 202) explains, one is rarely, if ever, aware of timing, and rhythm and timing are more closely bound up with the individual performer. Quirk (2015b), however, sees timing as a form of audience manipulation that comedians engage in when convincing them to laugh. Whatever the case, comedy and music share a use of punctuation, which is most evident in pauses, as well as changes of pitch, speed, tone, and volume. The use of rhythm, for instance, can be identified in the pause before a punchline (Attardo and Pickering, 2011). Indeed, the punchline can be reasonably compared to the crescendo, when the intensity and volume increases towards the end of a piece of orchestral music. Timing can also be seen when comedians allow time for an audience to laugh, because speaking though audience laughter makes the comedian look uninterested in the audience, and allowing them time to laugh helps to reinforce the rapport between comedian and audience. Inexperienced comedians only learn this with practice. Many comedians will start off with an up-tempo rhythm and will move to down tempo before raising the tempo again towards the end of their set, to finish on a laugh.

For me, 'setting the beat', as I called it, initially meant listening to other comedians before a gig, but I soon noticed that I adopted their rhythms, and it wasn't until the beginning of my middle period in late 1991 that I began to experiment with music as an aid, in the same way that a musician uses a metronome. Initially, this included listening to Public Enemy, Stereo MCs, and the Spin Doctors before gigs, because I felt their sonic energy – their rhythms – matched my onstage energy as a physical performer. However, by the time of my epiphany in 1996, the choice of music would tend towards the phased/flanged sounds of Ride or anything with guitarists either playing heavy chords or using a fuzzbox or flanger. This included PJ Harvey's 'Sheila Na Gig' and the Fall's 'Free Range'. It is difficult to describe the deeply personal relationship between my musical choices and how they worked on my sense of timing, because this is an area that requires further study.

The 'Ambulance' mentioned in this diary entry was about the ambulance drivers' strike of 1989–1990 and was jettisoned when the dispute ended. However, the idea that one could use a facial expression to carry a weak gag was naive. I had yet to relax on stage and was more concerned with getting the words in the right order. I also mention the "Debut of Geordie" here; this was my standard introduction until around 1995, when I began to use improvised pieces. Many comedians open their set by telling the audience a little about themselves and this was a way of addressing issues of ethnicity and difference in a city where a majority of the population was white. For a while, this worked but there were times when audiences who had been raised on traditional comedy or who were too 'right-on' would not appreciate the material. For some audiences, I was just a Yank who was mocking the English for cheap laughs.

> As you can tell from the accent, I'm not from around these parts [pause] I'm Geordie! [in a Geordie accent] Why aye, ya bugger, it's canny lush to be here. hadaway and shite, ya soft southern bastard!
>
> Because anyone from south of the River Tyne is a SOFT SOUTHERN BASTARD! Gateshead is just south of Newcastle across the Tyne Bridge… people from Gateshead are called COCKNEYS!
>
> Not many Black people in Newcastle. I was sitting on the bus, it's full, except for one empty seat next to me and there's one guy standing. He's looking at me, looking at the seat (repeat 3 times). I can actually hear this guy thinking "Ah divvent wanna sit next ta him! His Blackness might rub off on wor! Ah might develop a sense o' RHYTHM!"
>
> Notebook 2, 1990

Claiming I am a Geordie when my accent is transatlantic is patently absurd. In this routine I speak the words of a man on a bus in a Geordie accent complete with rising inflection towards the end of the piece. This accent had taken me eighteen months to master, and I was initially worried that my imitation of their accent would irritate the Geordies but as it turned out, they rather liked it. The line, "His Blackness might rub off on wor! Ah might develop a sense of rhythm" was influenced by Dick Gregory, who performed a piece about moving into an all-white neighbourhood. The idea of Black people moving into a hitherto-all-white neighbourhood was often used as a heckle put-down and it's worth remembering that trad. comedian Charlie Williams would tell hecklers, "If you don't shut up, I'll come and move in next door to you!" (quoted in Ilott, 2019: 14). By doing this, he adopted a low-status position in the power relationship between Blacks and whites (Ilott, 2019: 14). Unlike Williams, I adopted a high-status position because my intention here is not to play the victim, which is expected of me, but to comment on middle-class white suburban anxiety about Black people. The media and politicians, for example, will often resort to the language of hygiene and contamination with regard to foreign Others with claims that their culture will 'infect' the supposedly 'indigenous' population. The idea of Blackness as a contagion was discussed by Fanon (2001: 32) in *The Wretched of the Earth*, in which he describes the colonizers' use of Christianity as a form of social decontaminant. However, for all that, Christianized Black people were still seen as foreign bodies in a white world. This piece makes use of repetition, but it also mocks an old trope that Black people make great dancers because they have an innate sense rhythm that may be pathogenic to white bodies. Being a person of ed-heritage, I had grown up hearing claims that we would 'grow onfused' or we would be 'depressed' about our alleged 'condition'. ns like these are rooted in the mythology of racial purity, itself ned by the pseudoscience of social Darwinism, and reinforced by rrative figure of the 'tragic mulatto', a trope of American pulp (McNeil, 2011: 360–376). Even the word 'mulatto' has zoological nd is based on notions of hypodescent, the so-called 'one drop ndstrom, 2001: 285–307). I discuss this in more detail in the on of this chapter.

e' would segue into the 'Cockney Wide Boy' character vignette, levised in May 1990. My diary entry for 17 May 1990 reads:

of 'Cockney' equivalent to 'Geordie' for use in Tyne and ough it may be good to use <u>both</u> in London…

The Outsider

This was a largely improvised piece that utilized a variety of Cockney clichés and examples of rhyming slang, and was, frankly, derivative of Alexei Sayle's preamble to his single, 'Hullo John, Got A New Motor', which he performed on *OTT* (Central Television, 1982). 'Cockney Wide Boy' always ended with

> Gawd bless the Queen Mum! Gawd bless 'er! She's a game old bird... I'd still do 'er, like... you know what I mean? [half aside] Bag and all! But at the end of the day, right? At the end of the bleedin' day, right? It's night!

This piece comments on unthinking deference to royalty and is an attack on those who live vicariously through the royal family. I took the idea of the 'Cockney Wide Boy' character's mannerisms from a security guard that I met at the Barbican Centre while working there during the summer holidays. Unfortunately, and unbeknown to me at the time, the last line bore a resemblance to one of Phil Cornwell's lines, "At the end of the day, it gets dark" (*The Cabaret Upstairs*, BBC2, 1988). This piece was eventually dropped in 1994, because I was bored with it, but also because it was unoriginal. One of the problems of working on a live circuit with hundreds of other comedians is the possibility that others may have the same idea, and there seems to be no way around this problem. 'Cockney Wide Boy' was often well-received almost anywhere I went, except for NV gigs, where it would be met with complete silence, and I suspect the reason for this was due to it being read as a slur on working-class Londoners.

I appeared as part of a Black Comedy Special at the Electric Cinema in Notting Hill on 24 April 1990, which was recorded for BBC2's cultural programme, *The Late Show*. This was my third appearance for Black Comedy.

> What a corker! Certainly one of the best audiences yet. Relaxed and friendly. "Late Show" video'ed [*sic*] me and "Paramount City" made an approach. Asked back for inaugural gig on 1/6/90...

Personal diary, 1990

After the show, the programme's producers interviewed the comedians. However, in the final edit of the segment, I'd noticed that the interview with Kevin Seisay and I had been cut. I suspected this was because we both questioned the idea of Black comedy as a standalone genre, when the interviewer asked the crass question, "What do you think is more important? Being Black or being funny?" I recall looking at Kevin and him looking back at me and thinking, "What kind of question is this?" For me, the question was predicated on a knowledge of the Other, but it also seemed quite insulting. Would white comedians be asked this question? In any case, our replies to this question must have defied their expectations. The "inaugural gig" mentioned here referred to a new comedy gig at the Electric Cinema, run by Jane McMorrow, who had, up until this point, been working for the Hackney Empire. I also mention how *Paramount City* expressed an interest in me hosting the show. *Paramount City* was a relatively new stand-up comedy programme that had been airing since 1989 with Arthur Smith as host. However, the producers never made any further contact and the next thing I heard was that Curtis and Ishmael, who were compères for the Black Comedy gig, had been chosen as the show's hosts instead. Television producers have very specific ideas about what kinds of faces they want to see on their programmes, and my face and accent defied all their expectations. Presumably, I wasn't quite Black, but I wasn't white either. I wasn't quite American, but I did not sound British. I didn't fit; I was an outsider.

During this period, I had yet to settle on a persona. It is fair to say that when I began, the idea of having a persona never occurred to me and I went onstage as myself. In late 1988 or early 1989, I settled on a deadpan persona, which I believed suited me; it felt right, but then I heard of a comedian called Jack Dee, who had a similar persona. Worried that I'd be accused of stealing Dee's identity or even his act, I dropped it and spent the next three years going from being a highly energetic act to having a sort of neutral or even *ad hoc* persona. I was still experimenting on a circuit that increasingly regarded experimentation and danger as contrary to its unstated commercial aims. In many cases, I couldn't remember how I'd performed at the previous gig. What was my persona? How did I deliver this material? Double (2005) argues that persona is tied up with how a performer delivers their material; it helps the audience to make a connection. Quirk (2015b) explores this idea further and argues that the persona, *inter alia*, is part of the process of manipulation that the performer engages in with his/her audiences; it is the way in which audiences relate to the performers; thus, it can be regarded as the vehicle by which the gags or material are delivered. What determined my high-energy persona was the fact that, for the first three years on the London circuit, I was an opener,[6]

---

[6] The first act of the night.

which is a difficult position on the bill for any performer. Having a highly energetic act was the only way I believed I could survive and win over the audience. It was only much later, when I stopped worrying about the audience liking me, that I freed myself from this self-imposed straitjacket and became myself. Yet I also had to resist having a persona imposed on me that was based on audience and promoter expectations of Blackness. The high-energy persona was eventually discarded in 1993 as I began to move up the bill.

I played the Edinburgh Fringe for the first time in August 1990. The Fringe was, at times, a bizarre and terrifying experience: our venue was in a notorious dive bar called the Phoenix Club on Cowgate, beneath the George IV Bridge, that was frequented by elements of Edinburgh's criminal underworld. The week before the Fringe, someone had been stabbed in the gents' toilet, and this did not augur well for our time in Edinburgh. The show that I was involved in was a joint venture between CAGG and Arnold Kuenzler-Byrt's Salamander Club (Lyttle, 2011 interview), and began a week before the official opening of the Fringe. On 8 August, the unofficial first day of our run, I wrote: "Had trouble settling in". The next day was no better: "Performed a pissed [drunk] set. Spent most of the time dealing with hecklers and battling the constant chatter" (Diary entry, 9 August 1990). The entry for the first official night, on 12 August, simply reads "Don't remember much". It would seem that a great deal of time was spent during these days drinking too much beer and trying to organize the space and promote the show.

A few days later, I played Malcolm Hardee's 'Arrrrrgh! It's the Tunnel Club' for the first time at the Pleasance. I wrote:

> Won through, though dipped in the middle. Interviewed by R4 Kaleidoscope. Learned to relax on stage again.
>
> Diary entry, 15 August 1990

Learning to relax onstage was a constant theme during this period. The next diary entry is on 27 August 1990 and reads, "Introduced strip pine Cortina to set. One of my better performances". 'Strip Pine Cortina' referred to a contemporary interior design trend for stripped pine furniture, in the late 1980s and early 1990s, that I associated with a kind of middle-class, left-liberal metropolitanism and its separation from the dire social conditions created by Thatcher. 'Strip Pine Cortina' was a kind of *homage* to one of Alexei Sayle's rants about Stoke Newington residents knitting jumpers out of muesli.

What I noticed about the Edinburgh Fringe was how stratified the comedy cohort was. On the London circuit, the hierarchy was mostly concealed, whereas in Edinburgh it was patently obvious. If you weren't playing the 'golden triangle' of venues – the Assembly Rooms, the Pleasance, and the Gilded Balloon – you had a sense of your place in the hierarchy, and I was at the bottom. Such venues were out of reach for those of us at the start of our careers, and were booked by the new management agencies like Off the Kerb and Avalon, who had the financial resources to promote shows or even, in the case of Avalon, offer their stars an advance that would then be deducted from ticket sales.

My next diary entry, of 29 August 1990, reads:

TUNNEL CLUB

Followed Emo Philips! Malcolm (tell us a joke, show us your dick/bollocks) Hardee made things even more difficult by giving me a shite introduction and heckling me from offstage. Went for it anyway. I used the time honoured "I don't give a fuck, nothing can ruffle me approach". Won through in the end with Trailer. Quite a learning experience this one.

A few minutes before I was due onstage, Malcolm came up and said "I bumped into Emo Philips in the courtyard. You don't mind if he goes on before you, do you?" I wasn't in a position to say 'no'. Malcolm had a habit of setting performers up – especially if they were unknown to him – and I had to take this in my stride. He knew that following Emo Philips would be tough, but after a difficult start I managed to stay the course and went off to laughter and a round of applause. I talk about a "don't give a fuck" attitude but I only seemed to have had this attitude occasionally, because again I seem to have been worrying too much about the words, rather than relaxing and engaging with the audience. At this juncture, I still behaved like an actor who performed comedy, and this was evident in my reluctance to break the fourth wall and address the audience directly. This is because I was frightened of hecklers and was worried that I would not be able to summon up a clever putdown. Again, this comes with practice: few comedians are good at the beginning of their careers, and most take a long time to find their voice and relax on stage.

Shortly after the Fringe, I moved to London to take up more work on the burgeoning circuit. In the North of England there was no circuit and it made sense to move to where I would obtain regular bookings. My first gig in London after moving from Newcastle was on 15 September at Hackney Cabaret. The diary entry reads: "I was dead tired and stoned (and poor!). Played cool relaxed set. Stormed it! My first ever headliner". Moving to London had cost me a lot of money and work was scarce for the first few months. There was a gap between this gig and the next one, with the ones in between either having been cancelled or missed because of a housemate's mistake when taking a call for me (this is how I lost my gig at the Cartoon, Clapham on 22 September 1990). I was booked to appear at Downstairs at the Kings Head (DATKH) on 29 September and my diary entry reads:

DOWNSTAIRS AT THE KINGS HEAD

Quite nearly died. Another one of those "cursed by Hurst" gigs -------
----- did learn something, though, like putting BNP Anti-Social elsewhere and getting quick laughs in early

DATKH is a favourite gig with many comics, but I don't recall having a good time at this venue and I always suspected that the rather middle-class and white audience preferred to see a man of colour who performed to their expectations of Blackness, especially American Blackness – a trope-laden, Stepin Fetchit[7] kind of Blackness that was ultimately lacking in erudition and self-respect. However, there may be a more prosaic reason: I never took myself to a space where I could 'psych' myself up for the gig and would stay downstairs in the club. Murray (2007) says that comedians need to make time for themselves before the gig, even if that means locking oneself in a toilet cubicle. I wrote "cursed by Hurst" because it seemed as though every gig at which Mark Hurst and I were on the same bill, I would die (we were on the same bill at Sheffield University where I had my first stage death). This is an entirely irrational thought based on superstition, a relic from my

---

[7] Stepin Fetchit was a stock 'negro' character in Hollywood comedy films of the 1930s and 1940s. Along with Sleep 'n' Eat (Willie Best), Stepin Fetchit, whose real name was Lincoln Theodore Monroe Andrew Perry, reinforced white audience's views of Black people. Fetchit's popularity began to wane in the 1940s and by the 1950s, his star had fallen as African-Americans saw Stepin Fetchit as a harmful stereotype (Regester, 1994). My dad would use the name 'Stepin Fetchit' interchangeably with 'Uncle Tom' as a term of abuse for Black people who adopted a subservient role to Caucasians.

acting days, and it is likely that I was suffering from imposter syndrome, which became a self-fulfilling prophecy that would have been avoided if I had relaxed more on stage and worried less about the audience's expectations. The 'BNP Anti-Social' mentioned here is an in-joke about the commercial nature of the new comedy industry, that saw talent agents send comedians to gigs that they themselves had not researched; it was thus actually a veiled dig at Avalon Management, who promoted many college and university comedy shows, but who often knew very little about the audiences or the dynamics and quality of the performance space. The 'anti-social' part of the joke is a play on political party social gatherings and relates to my perception of the BNP's anti-social nature. I followed this joke with a one-liner:

> Fascists [pause] don't they just kill you?

Depending on the circumstances, I would change this to "Americans [pause] don't they just kill you?" This joke is an example of a paraprosdokian, a form of speech that uses double meanings or an anti-climax to surprise the listener. Henny Youngman, for example, was a master of this kind of joke. His most famous one was "Take my wife [pause] please!" The idea behind this one-line joke was to summarize the violence of fascists and the futility of engaging them in debate.

A hint of my future direction occurred at the time of the First Gulf War, the preparations for which began during the Edinburgh Fringe of 1990. I spent the next few months until the war's end devising related material, while many comedians ignored it. In February 1991, there were reports in the news about carpet bombing and these provided me with an opportunity to engage in some rather light-hearted word play:

> I see B52s are carpet-bombing Iraqi positions – they'll be shelling them with cushions next! Firing cuddly toys from the barrels of howitzers… ping!
>
> Notebook 3, 1991

My Gulf War material wasn't entirely light-hearted. I concentrated a great deal of my fire on government ministers who were responsible for beating the war drum the loudest. Norman Lamont, the Chancellor of the Exchequer, was tasked with travelling around Europe to gather support for the First Gulf War. Part of his task was to raise money for the war effort.

> This war's costing a few quid isn't it?
>
> The Chancellor, Norman Lamont (he's the one that looks like Dracula) is going around Europe asking for money (for the war effort).
>
> Things must be getting really bad… I saw him at [insert name] tube station asking for spare change.
>
> So I said to him, "Why don't you fuck off and get a proper job?"
>
> Notebook 3, 1991

Here, the Conservatives' 'scrounger' narrative is stood on its head by casting Lamont as a beggar outside a tube station asking for money from passers-by to support the war effort. Many of these jokes were delivered with a great deal of punk-style anger and there were times that I compared my feelings about the oppressive politics of the dominant culture as a form of psychic pain. Thus, at times, my comedy became a form of catharsis. Double (2007: 2) cites Richard Pryor as an exponent of this kind of humour. Pryor took the pain of his upbringing in a brothel, the beatings he received as a child, his cocaine addiction, and setting himself on fire, and turned it into comedy. My pain and anguish come from the frustration of being an ordinary citizen who is beset by grasping and symbolically violent political leaders who I am physically unable to stop. My only recourse was to lash out verbally through the medium of political satire; this thus subscribes at once to De Certeau's (1988: 37) 'tactic as the art of the weak' and Baktinian (1984) carnivalesque. For me, political humour was a tactic for dealing with the frustrations and anger caused by the political system and megalomaniacal politicians, but also it was an attempt to passively resist the government's symbolic violence (Gramsci, 2003).

My transatlantic accent, thought by many people to be a 'strong' American or Canadian accent, concealed my complicated backstory, and sometimes I was read by audiences as another American. One way I dealt with this was through the following piece:

> Yeah, I'm half-American but I'm not like a lot of Americans, I have a good sense of geography. [Breaks into character:] "Hi, could you tell me where Lee-i-sester Square is? Is Scotland Welsh? Is France in England? Can I have a glass of water?"
>
> The great thing about being American is that I get to be first off the plane. OK, so the plane is 35,000 feet in the air and has been hijacked by Abu Nidal! [Makes whistling noise] Splat!

This piece uses a combination of self-deprecation and incongruity, the latter of which is provided by the line "Can I have a glass of water?", which actually came from the many American tourists visiting the Barbican Centre while I was working there. It is an incongruity and an absurdity but it is also surreal in the strictest sense of the word, because the order of things is disrupted by an object that doesn't fit the arrangement.

The first part of the joke relies on the common trope that Americans have poor geographical knowledge and an awkward pronunciation of foreign place names. It was partly inspired by our neighbour at Selfridge Air Force Base in Michigan, who asked my mother if England was in France. Many comedians use self-deprecation to endear themselves to the audience and some use it as part of their persona. In this case, I use my anxiety of being seen as another American abroad by using a plane hijacking as a scenario. Abu Nidal appears because his organization, the Abu Nidal Organization, was accused of being behind the bombing of Pan Am Flight 73 in 1986. This piece was performed infrequently from 1991 to 1992 and was effectively an effort to ingratiate myself with the audience by pandering to possible anti-American sentiments among them. Having an American accent is one thing, but having brown skin *and* an American accent is another matter, as I discuss in the next section of this chapter.

The Wrong Kind of Black Man?

As a man of colour, a discussion of race, identity, and difference is germane because my identity is inextricably wrapped up with these issues; they touched nearly every aspect of my working life. Yet despite the apparent non-racism and non-sexism of the cabaret circuit, and the comedy circuit that succeeded it, old attitudes to difference, be they racial or sexual, persisted in the space, particularly among some audiences and some promoters. Often this was casually expressed; sometimes it was more overt. By contrast, the field of dominant production remained much as it had for decades and postcolonial attitudes to difference were resistant to change. This was brought home to me in 1991, when I first signed up with Crawford's Commercials, a talent agency specializing in placing performers with castings for advertisements. One agent, Nick Young, noticing my brown skin, told me straight away that I was unlikely to get any work and I remember thinking, "Why have me on your books if I'm unlikely to get work?" I went to the occasional casting but was unsuccessful in obtaining work, thus proving him correct. Perhaps it was a failure on his part to appropriately categorize me according to some internalized taxonomy of racial archetypes, which was exercised as a form of discrimination that led to frustration and exasperation. I will never know for certain. It is worth remembering that throughout the 1980s and into the 1990s, Black, Asian, and mixed-heritage people were noticeable by their near invisibility on television. I would argue that there was a lack of imagination among talent and casting agencies, who only saw Black people as suitable for certain roles: as a victim or a criminal. Indeed, I had written a joke about this:

> I've been on television. Yes, I have. I was on Crimewatch [pause] I'm the guy in the balaclava.

In 1990, there were less than a handful of performers of colour working on the London circuit or on television and radio, and there were even fewer comics from a mixed background: singer–guitarist Kevin Seisay, Simon Clayton, and I were the only three such comics working on the circuit and in the early Black comedy clubs. Not only did I feel that I wasn't seen as Black enough, but I also felt at times that I was being judged for not being American enough. Yet wasn't the point of altcom to defy expectations, to détourn, and to subvert? I am not saying that the circuit was entirely racist. In fact, much of it wasn't; but there were people running gigs or sitting in the audiences who held views that were entirely consistent with a postcolonial mindset, one that refused to come to terms with the collapse of the British Empire and Britain's place in the post-war world.

Race is part of a system of human typologies that has its origins in the scientific racism of the nineteenth century, whose chief proponent, Francis Galton, cousin of Charles Darwin, used it to justify a 'natural' order that placed white (often English) people at the top of a social and racial hierarchy, and to rationalize imperialism and the exceptionalism that underpins the peculiarly British strain of racism (Gilroy, 2002: 2–6; Zack, 2010: 877). The implication of Galton's ideas is that the British had an empire because they are a 'chosen people'. I have always refused to be classified or categorized as one thing or another; this often tends to be the impulse of white people, who will read me according to an internalized taxonomy of races, which is based on a cursory and often unconscious knowledge of zoological classifications. To quote Fanon (1986: 116), "I am given no chance, I am overdetermined from without. I am the slave not of the 'idea' that others have of me but of my own appearance". Thus, I often became the product of a gazer's eye that saw me as an Other from one of the former colonies, but not as an equal; not as a person with something to say.

When I was a child in the 1960s and early 1970s, the most popular term in Britain to refer to someone of mixed-heritage was 'half-caste'. I never liked it, but I turned it into a joke.

> I hate that term 'half-caste': it makes it sound as though I'm a semi-formed piece of metal! [Character voice:] "We couldn't afford to finish it, just leave it over there".

This joke, as weak as it is, and to my surprise, actually got laughs. 'Half-caste' was supplanted by the marginally less insulting term 'mixed-race' by the 1980s. This has been recently succeeded by terms like 'mixed-parentage' or 'mixed-heritage'. By the 1980s, census and other official forms began including mixed-race categories. However, these new ways of classifying people of mixed-heritage are not without their problems. According to Gilbert (2005), the category of mixed-race is problematic because there are too many varieties, too many ways for people to self-identify. This creates problems with the classifying practices of the state, which offers a small range of 'mixed-race' options on its official forms that are insufficient to cover all forms of self-identification. Furthermore, Gilbert (2005: 59) argues that "terminology can shift from racial essentialism through cultural absolutism to an implicit genetic determinism". Gilroy (2002) goes further and notes that the construction of the term 'mixed-parentage' (or mixed-race) implies that one 'race' within a racial equation is superior to the other racial fraction. Indeed, the dominant culture still cleaves to the notion of hypodescent: the fractionalization of people according to how much of one 'alien' race they have in relation to the 'white part'. Many mixed-heritage, and some Black and white people, have internalized hypodescent and accepted it as real. For what it's worth, I am not permitted to reject these constructions and write in 'human' on official forms. Nevertheless, there is a tendency on the part of the dominant culture to see only crude stereotypes, and those of mixed-heritage often defy an expectation of racial identity that is projected onto them through what Haritaworn (2009) calls "the scopophilic act of gazing".

I have never considered myself to be any race other than human, although for the sake of expediency, I identify as 'Black', and this brings with it certain problems: namely that some Black people may not regard me as Black. However, I do not like the term 'mixed-race' either and it is only marginally preferable to the bestial-sounding 'mulatto'.[8] For the record, I reject the label of 'mixed-race' and, like other social scientists, I regard race as a social construct, because to even use this term is to acknowledge race as biological reality. However, for the purpose of clarity, I use the terms 'mixed-heritage' or 'mixed parentage', though, frankly, I'm not happy with either. I also use the term 'person of colour' out of solidarity with other non-white people. In any case, in the official world of entertainment, negative racial stereotypes lingered on well past their sell-by date. Thus, for many people, stereotypes are the only way in which they can apprehend difference, and this is something that I believed altcom had supposedly rejected.

When one considers that *The Black and White Minstrel Show* only ceased its twenty-years-long run in 1978, then it becomes clear how difficult it was to effect change on Britain's cultural landscape. *The Black and White Minstrel Show* had its origins in the blackface or 'nigger' minstrelsy of the nineteenth century and was regarded by many as a legitimate form of family entertainment. It helped to crystallize the image of the 'happy-go-lucky', childlike negro, who was also at once a simpleton and a beast, in the public mind. Yet for all its apparent social problems, no one 'blacked up' on American television for the purpose of entertainment. What I also found interesting about *The Black and White Minstrel Show* was how only the men blacked up, but the women didn't. This is not to say that white women never 'blacked up' in the history of popular entertainment; they did, but in fewer numbers.

British attitudes to difference are deeply rooted in colonial and postcolonial discourses on difference and national identity: who is British and who is not; who passes Norman Tebbit's 'cricket test'[9] and who does not. This attitude can be summed up in the music-hall song 'Cockney Coon'.

---

[8] The word 'mulatto' (female 'mulatta') come from the Spanish for 'little mule'. The suggestion being that a person of mixed-heritage shares characteristics with the offspring of a horse and a donkey: the mule. This informs us how people of colour were seen by the colonizers: as animals, in relation to their human masters.

[9] The 'cricket test' refers to a controversial claim by government minister Norman Tebbit that the loyalty of people from the Caribbean and the Indian subcontinent could be measured by which national cricket team they supported.

You heard about the coon who sings about the moon
Well there's a coon I know
Just as big a mouth as a nigger from the South
Just as short of rhino
He thinks that Allybama is as far off as the moon
He knows more of Ally Sloper
For he's a cockney coon!

Quoted in Mullen, 2012: 70–71

The writer of this song implies that Black people, whether they were born here or have lived here for years, are still regarded as alien Others, and any attempt on their part to integrate and become British is risible and ripe for mockery. A Cockney Black man? How absurd! The long effect of empire on the national psyche and the refusal to face up to its legacy continue to colour the way in which many white Britons see people of colour. As Hall (2003: 230) says, "It is much harder for Black people, wherever they were born, to be accepted as British". Black Britons, I would suggest, continue to be marginalized on the dominant cultural field, with only token gestures made on the part of culture industry mandarins. However, British-born Black people have, like their American counterparts, created their own cultural spaces and zones in opposition to the dominant or 'white' culture. By 1989, this had finally happened in the field of comedy production with the creation of Black comedy clubs, and I shall return to this later in the chapter.

My life as a mixed-heritage adult in Britain has been dominated by a single question: "where are you from?" More often than not, this is followed by "you sound American/Canadian". There are two identities being suggested in these questions. One presumes that my skin colour and other physical features denote a foreign Other, while the other is predicated on my accent, which is seen as a signifier of belonging to one country or another. I have this accent because I went to school with Americans until the age of 18. For the occasional punter, a truthful explanation of my background wasn't enough to convince them, and I have been accused of lying or have been told that I was 'West Indian', sometimes 'Indian' or even 'Arab'. The implication is that I am a foreign body; that I'm 'not from around here'. Drawing on Fanon's (1986) concept of dissection, Haritaworn explains how the gaze is used as a racializing technique that is supported by the gazer's sense of entitlement:

In this, the visual is privileged as the technology which extracts knowledge about the body's interior from the body's surface, by looking, examining and classifying. This scopophilic process of knowledge production is a skewed one: the subject of dissection is white, its object, who is fixed, caught in the gaze and arrested thereby in its agency, is Black. The encounter thus reproduces unequal relations of looking and recognizing, which entitle some to gaze at, touch, reach into and define others.

Haritaworn, 2009: 121

I accept this proposition, but I would add to this a Bourdieusian analysis and argue that the gazer's habitus possesses unconscious knowledge of zoological classificatory systems as a form of embodied cultural capital, which is then projected onto the object of the scopophilic gaze. Thus, a judgement is made that I am not who I say I am, but, rather, the product of the gazer's eye. Hence, the tendency on the part of some promoters was to regard me as 'Black' but not quite Black; a conclusion based on a few random signifiers of *typically* Black physical features: the broad nose, the skin colour, the hair texture, and so on. Indubitably, the question "where are you from?" would certainly not be asked of me if I looked white or had two white parents and spoke with a regional accent. Conversely, the same would not have been true if both my parents had been Black. I don't always think about the colour of my skin, but then I'm always dragged back to a place where I have no choice but to be conscious of it, sometimes to the extent that I'm over-conscious of it. Fanon (1986) argues that Black, as a category, was created by Europeans. Thus, the same holds true for 'White', but this is a category that was constructed by white people themselves to declare themselves superior and cleaner in relation to the 'dirty' Others of the world.

Some people of mixed-heritage have sought to magically cleanse themselves of their Blackness. For example, the concert pianist, anti-Communist, and ultra-conservative Philippa Schuyler, a mixed-heritage woman, believed her Blackness was a stigma; something of which to be ashamed; something to be erased through the act of magically becoming white (McNeil, 2011: 360–376). In this sense, Schuyler became the living embodiment of the tragic mulatto trope: the mixed-heritage woman who 'passes' for white but who suffers because of it. Unlike Schuyler, I am proud of my African heritage as much as I'm proud of my Scottish and Irish heritage. It is only racial absolutists who stigmatize and problematize my background, and I say this about some Black people as well as white.

The altcab and later, the comedy circuit of the 1990s has always been dominated by white people, who make up most of the performers, promoters, and journalists. Early in my career, I spoke to Felix Dexter on the phone and asked him if he had experienced racism on the circuit. Felix was polite and diplomatic, and tried to deflect the question. I have no idea why he didn't want to be honest about what he'd experienced, because he'd talked about instances of audience racism in an interview he gave to Cabaret editor, Malcolm Hay in *TO* (908, 1988: 20). Hay described him as "currently the only Black male stand-up performing the London circuit". In the interview, Dexter (908, 1988: 20) said:

> Even 'alternative' audiences can be racist and heterosexist. One recent heckle went "Did you come over here on an oil slick?" Alternative comedy is very much a white middle class world.

When you're a person of colour living in a white world, you become highly attuned to racism and other injustices, and for this reason, I was politicized at an early age. The alternative was to play the game and wear the clothing sewn for me by the white establishment. In response to a question about racism on the circuit, Simon Clayton told me:

> i was never really racially abused, or not that i was aware of, i think i wasn't Black enough for white audiences and later i discovered i was too white for Black audiences, as a solo act at Black comedy gigs, (that might be something you can relate to)…

Clayton questionnaire, 2013

Like Simon, I often thought that some Black audiences didn't see me as being Black enough; but what does it mean to be Black? What are the cultural markers of Blackness? Are there any cultural markers? What is Black? What is white? When I played Black comedy clubs, there were times when I suspected that I wasn't read as Black because of my accent, the way I looked, and the themes in my set, all of which are products of my social and cultural capital. In any case, I didn't perform or even sound like a stereotypical African-American and I couldn't bluff my way through a set by talking about cricket, a subject close to many Caribbean men's hearts and a sport of which I know very little. Jeff Mirza, a fellow comedian of Pakistani heritage, once suggested that I create a Caribbean character. I told him that I wasn't African-Caribbean and that creating a character of this kind would be wrong for two reasons: first, it would be insulting to people of Caribbean heritage and second, it wouldn't be truthful. I saw my role as a truth-teller and I didn't want to simulate someone else's heritage for comedic purposes, because my lack of African-Caribbean cultural capital would have been immediately exposed through my use or misuse of language, terminology, and a lack of familiarity with certain cultural products. Moreover, I found the idea of character comedy limiting. My previous characters had been created for specific purposes and I had no desire to be pigeonholed or typecast.

Unlike Simon, I was often aware of being racially abused by white audience members and early in my career there was an incident in Wallsend, North Tyneside that stands out: it took place during a benefit for striking ambulance workers in 1989. Anvil Springstien (Paul Ward), who organized the benefit, recalled what happened.

> As I walked off the stage one of the striking Ambulance workers, his daughter on his knee, said to me, *"Fuckin' hell, who booked the fuckin' Darkie?"* I went back on stage and called them all a bunch of cunts.
>
> Ward, 2013 questionnaire

Other notable incidents include having coins thrown at me by members of an all-white audience at a gig in Erith in southeast London in 1990 and being booed off stage by a Black audience at Miles Crawford's Cabarave[10] gig at Comedy Cafe before I could open my mouth. In the latter case, it was either possible that I was seen as not being Black enough for the Black audience or, perhaps, I was read as gay because of my attire, which consisted of a leather biker's jacket, black t-shirt, black jeans, black military beret, and black steel-toe-capped boots (my style was actually influenced by the Black Panthers). Indeed, I had been called a 'batty boy'[11] while walking through Brixton by young Black men on more than one occasion. One has always been well aware of the existence of deeply ingrained homophobic attitudes within the African diaspora, which

---

[10] Cabarave was a sort of 291 Club in miniature. The 291 Club, which was based at the Hackney Empire, was shown on ITV as a sort of 'Live at the Harlem Apollo'. The audience had a reputation for rowdiness and given to booing people off stage if they didn't like the look of them.

[11] A common Jamaican slur for a gay man.

themselves are informed by Christian teachings. It's worth recalling that this was at a time when dancehall artists like Buju Banton were releasing songs with titles like 'Boom Bye', which expressed the desire to kill gay men (Chin, 1997).

Racist attitudes also extended to some bookings or, rather, the lack of them: in 1995, the promoter of the Glee Club in Birmingham refused to rebook me on the grounds that I had "died" when, in fact, I had stormed the gig, receiving not only laughs but a few rounds of applause throughout my set. I reminded the promoter that he had actually been absent on the night, but this failed to register and he kept repeating himself. Sensing that pursuing the conversation any further was pointless, I hung up on him. In another example, I travelled from London to Birmingham to play 'Stand Up Heroes' at the Bear Tavern in Smethwick, only to be told that I hadn't been booked, nor were there any future available bookings, and even when I produced the details in my diary this failed to convince him. Perhaps, the promoter heard my accent and pictured an image of a white American man in his mind's eye and was disgusted when a Black man with the same accent appeared before him. I couldn't report this matter to Equity because there was no written contract, thus there was no evidence. I could have told my mostly white counterparts about this incident, but it is unlikely that they would have boycotted the club out of solidarity. Yet would they have believed me if I told them that I had experienced racism from a promoter? I always felt that any complaint would have been met with "you're imagining it" or "how do you know?" We can regard such responses as an exercise of 'white privilege'. Indeed, the very fact that white comedians don't face such problems is indicative of white privilege. They may be refused bookings on the back of dying onstage, but they would not be refused on the basis of their skin colour or be told that they'd died when they hadn't.

On another occasion, I was waiting to go onstage at a club in North London, when, after registering the disbelief on my face at a Black performer playing the Black stereotype, the organizer asked, "You don't play the nigger, do you?" Perhaps what he meant was that I didn't perform to a white person's expectations of 'Black'. Whatever the case, I was annoyed and upset that he felt entitled to use that word in front of me when *I don't even use the word myself*, but the question that he posed was also predicated on a knowledge of the Other. I was stunned by this question and, although I could feel the anger building inside of me, the only reply I could muster was to stare silently at him. This clearly wasn't the reply he was expecting – perhaps he had thought I would chuckle or nod in agreement. Then he sputtered out, "I think that came out wrong". Yet it was too late; the damage had already been done. As for the gig, I died; my confidence had been eroded by this question. The promoter never booked me again.

Incidents like those described above have a powerfully negative effect on one's self-worth and confidence, but that is the point of symbolic violence: you are made to feel bad about yourself through a constant process of marginalization, stigmatization, discrimination, and Othering. In extreme cases, this can destroy one's mental and physical health. In this iteration, symbolic violence exercised in this way can be described as a form of 'soft racism'. Yet for liberal white audiences, the issue is not so much to do with overt racism but a subtly exercised form of racism, which is no less symbolic, and is expressed as incredulity at persons of colour who are erudite. In the parlance of American racists, I would be considered an 'uppity nigger' for daring to speak up about injustices but also for daring to satirically critique the Westminster strain of parliamentary politics and its democratic shortcomings. Arguably, working-class white comedians have a similar problem, because they are not expected to have read books, let alone appreciate the specialized intellectual nature of political satire. This is despite the fact that there has always been a cadre of working-class intellectuals and autodidacts (I come from such a family); I would argue that Thatcher's attacks on working-class institutions like WMCs, mechanics institutes, and more recently, the closure of public libraries under the rubric of 'efficiencies' have left today's working class with few resources, bar the Internet, for self-guided learning. The educated working class, perhaps seen as a threat by the right-wing press and polemical sites like *Spiked Online*, have effectively been erased and replaced with an image of white, flag-waving, heavy-drinking, thuggish lumpens as the 'authentic' or 'traditional' working class, who take no interest in politics and are allegedly nostalgic for the days of empire. For these people, politics isn't something that they engage with daily; it's something that's done *to* them.

In Britain, the production of political satire on television and radio has been historically concentrated in the hands of a small number of former public schoolboys and Oxbridge graduates, who are, without exception, white, male, and middle class. These are people from the same class they're mocking. I would argue that a Black person who performs political satire is seen as a threat by the establishment because first, a considerable amount of intellectual effort goes into the writing of satire; this defies the colonialist beliefs that Black people are predisposed to occupations that require physical activity. Second, as Fanon (2001: 19–26) argues, this attitude to Black erudition is situated in the eugenicist belief that Black people have lower IQs. The problem is especially acute when Black or mixed-heritage performers defy expectations and speak in standard English, possibly with an impeccable home counties accent, rather than patois or Creole (Fanon calls this 'pidgin'). This is best illustrated in Eric Chapple's popular 1970s sitcom, *Rising Damp*, in which Don Warrington plays the Black character, Philip Smith, who speaks in an impeccable English RP accent and is mocked for it by the landlord, Rigsby, played by Leonard Rossiter. On the other hand, there is a refusal to acknowledge the cultural peculiarities that produced patois and its function in African-Caribbean/Black British communities as an essential part of their identity. Even though I speak in what could broadly be described as a transatlantic accent, I am occasionally misinterpreted or misunderstood, despite the fact that my diction is clear.

I would also argue that the satirist of colour, but especially a Black satirist, could be regarded as a threat in much the same way that an educated working-class white person is seen as potentially subversive by the ruling class, or a female comedian is regarded as 'unfunny' by male chauvinists (there are equally very few women involved in the production of political satire). One promoter would often advise me to "give up the political stuff and just do the voices", adding that I was trying to be "like a Black Mark Thomas". The suggestion that I was trying to be a "Black Mark Thomas" is based on two assumptions: the first is that political satire, as signified by Thomas, who was seen by this promoter as the archetypal political comedian, was restricted to certain performers, all of whom were white. This reveals a lack of familiarity with other political comedians – Lenny Bruce, George Carlin, and Dick Gregory, for example. Second, the word 'Black' had been attached to the sign of 'Mark Thomas', suggesting that a Black person should not perform political satire and stick to being a politically disinterested 'happy-go-lucky negro' who makes people laugh. However, the promoter's suggestion that I should not comment on politics annoyed me. After all, his small audiences liked what I was doing, and his problem seemed to stem from his mainstream comedy aesthetics (he had started as a mainstream comedian), with its insistence on an imagined separation between entertainment and politics.

When I first started playing the London circuit, some of my white colleagues would urge me to play the Black comedy clubs. My response to them was always, "Are you trying to get rid of me?" In the United States, a form of entertainment apartheid had existed for decades, and I was concerned that a similar form of segregation was beginning to develop on this side of the Atlantic. In response to discrimination, Black and Jewish people created their own entertainment spaces. First, there was the Chitlin Circuit, which was constructed as a circuit of venues for African-American performers who were colour-barred from playing the mainstream white circuit. The Chitlin Circuit spawned top Black comedians like Moms Mabley, Red Foxx, and Dick Gregory, who would play the same bills as jazz bands and doo wop groups. Second, there was the Borscht Belt, a circuit of venues and resorts for Jewish performers and guests, located mainly in the Catskill mountains of upstate New York. Such clubs provided a launch pad for acts like Jack Benny, Lenny Bruce, Milton Berle, and Woody Allen. Jewish performers and guests, like their African-American counterparts, had also been refused entry at white-owned hotels and clubs. Despite my initial anxiety over whether I would be seen as 'authentically' Black, I began playing Black Comedy nights organized by David Bryan and Jenny Landreth in February 1989 and never had any problems. Most Black London audiences liked me, but some of the out-of-town audiences, like those in Reading, didn't respond particularly well. As Carrington (2008) observes in his ethnography of the African-Caribbean diaspora in Britain, there are differences in tastes and attitudes among Black people across the country, just as there are among any social group. However, it is entirely possible that I was read as not being either Black enough or American enough for the Reading audience's tastes, who probably preferred something more traditional; something that met the expectations of how a comedian should perform.

As far as I am aware, I have never experienced racism from fellow comedians on the main circuit, but there was an isolated incident that I recall, which occurred at a Black comedy night organized by John Simmit's Upfront Comedy[12] at the Comedy Store in 1996. I was about to leave the club while a Black comedian, who was reminiscent of the character Ras the Exhorter in Ellison's *Invisible Man*, was starting his set. This particular comedian, who often projects himself as a Garveyite defender of Black culture, told the audience how he "hated mixed-race people" and how

---

[12] John Simmit started Upfront Comedy in 1992 as David Bryan and Jenny Landreth's Black Comedy was starting to wane. Simmit started Upfront at a venue in Balshall Heath and gradually moved into other towns and cities across England.

"they" were "confused". In this regard, he was being no different to any traditional comic who uses 'race' to get a laugh, but here, he also shared the white supremacist's deterministic and absolutist view that people who are mixed are "confused" about their "heritage". The word 'heritage' is based on the deterministic notion that skin colour is analogous to culture and attitudes. Furthermore, if anyone is going to mock mixed-heritage people, then it should be us mixed-heritage comedians, not Black or white comedians. Otherwise, it sounds racist – and he was being racist. However, the idea that one should be 'confused' because of one's parentage is never applied to those people whose parents are either white or Black but from different countries. Moreover, the very idea that someone would want to identify as 'mixed-race' is seen as not only tragic but misguided and absurd. Hypodescent, which had been posited by European scientific racists had seemingly been internalized by this comedian. Ironically, if he had been a white comic playing to a predominantly white audience on the circuit, he would have been shouted down for being racist. Instead, his diatribe was rewarded with applause and approbation, which confused and upset me because I had appeared on stage before him on the bill and I had done rather well; even 'storming it'. Yet even this wasn't enough for Don Ward, the owner of the Comedy Store, who gave me a curt shake of the head before I could even speak a word. Maybe he did not see me as 'Black enough' or 'American enough'; I will never know. I went home not long after that. In any case, this comedian's words angered me and I also felt hurt, because I had been regarded as an Other, a fraud by a Black man who was using me and people like me to get cheap laughs. Ironically, if both of us were to be seen together on the same street, a racist thug would make no distinction between us. Furthermore, African diasporic communities living in the Caribbean or North America tend to have complicated ancestries, partly due to slavery and partly due to other factors: intermarriage between indentured labourers from South Asia or China and Africans, for example.

At this juncture, it's perhaps worth pointing out that the audiences and comedians at the Black Comedy clubs of the early days (1989–1992) were drawn almost entirely from the large African-Caribbean communities in London. Indeed, according to Bryan (2012 interview), many of the early Black comedians came from churches or theatre companies, like Black Mime Theatre. There were few, if any, Africans in the audience. This was possibly due to the tensions between West Africans, especially, and African-Caribbeans, with the latter deeply affected by the legacy of chattel slavery. Yet even within these communities of Black people there exist cultural divisions, and any attempt to homogenize the African diaspora also wilfully elides the cultural differences that exist between white people in diverse locations like Newcastle and London to advance a notion of comparative white cultural homogeneity.[13] Carrington (2008: 435–436) observes how 'Black British' as a signifier is "internally struggled over" between Black people living in Britain. Some Black people are happy to identify as Black British, while others are not so keen. In my case, despite being half-British (if that's possible), I will probably never be seen as Black British on the basis of a single signifier: my accent. Indeed, I continue to be seen as American rather than British, if I'm seen as anything at all.

It's important to note that many of the Black comedians who played the Black Comedy circuit didn't play the main circuit, which many of them referred to as the 'white circuit'. Yet work on the small Black Comedy circuit in the early 1990s was infrequent, usually monthly, and the shows were held in arts centres, theatres, and other venues but never in the upstairs rooms of pubs where one would find many of the 'white' comedy clubs. In these spaces, particularly those out of town or in the outer London suburbs, it was rare to find any Black people in the audience. Even in clubs like the Store, Jongleurs, or even Banana Cabaret in Balham, Black people were often noticeable by their absence. The reason for this is open to speculation. Maria Kempinska, co-owner of Jongleurs, believed she had an explanation:

> We rarely get Blacks in the audience – there are some but most of them don't go to any venue. I've asked why and they're just not interested; they're out doing their own thing – nor do they want whites to go to their things either… they've got their own brand of humour anyway.
>
> Kempinska in Wilmut, 1989: 274

Here, Kempinska appears to Other Black people by implying that "Blacks", rather than *Black people*, are a homogeneous cultural group that has a single sense of humour. Yet many Black British people watched the same comedy programmes as their white counterparts and although there were few Black people on television, those who were visible, as I pointed

---

[13] For example, within Nigeria alone there are at least 66 different languages and ethnic groups.

out earlier, tended to play up to white expectations. This is, therefore, an evident projection of a constructed form of Blackness onto Black people, who were already marginalized by the dominant culture and who were also being marginalized in the clubs and in the entertainment field generally. However, there is also another reason why few Black punters were seen in clubs like Jongleurs or even those clubs located in pubs. As Small and Solomos (2006) point out, this is due to memories of an unofficial colour bar that operated in many pubs and WMCs in London and the regions from the 1950s to the late 1970s. Therefore, it is reasonable to assume that clubs like Jongleurs and even the Comedy Store were seen as bastions of whiteness. In response to the colour bar that operated in many pubs and in WMCs, British Black people created their own spaces for drinking and socializing. It is perhaps no surprise that Black comedy clubs were created in response to a perceived exclusivity in the 'white' comedy clubs.

Today there are more people of colour on the circuit, but within the exclusive fields of broadcasting, there is still a paucity of Black faces. The tendency on the part of the main broadcasters to ghettoize performers still exists, with many Black comedians, like Gina Yashere, looking to the United States for work. In an interview with the *Guardian* on 15 May 2008, she said:

> Britain is still 15 or 20 years behind America as far as Black performers are concerned; there is still a very tokenistic attitude. You get new white comedians coming through all the time – Russell Brand, Alan Carr, Jimmy Carr – and we've had Lenny Henry for 35 years. It's like a nightclub policy: one Black comedian comes in as one goes out. I'm mid-30s.
>
> I can't wait for Lenny Henry to die just so I can get a TV show.
>
> *Guardian*, 15 May 2008

On the interlinked fields of light entertainment and broadcasting, the tokenistic attitude towards difference remains stubbornly persistent. In a more recent interview in the same paper (Hattenstone, 2021), Yashere discusses how she felt she had no choice but to move to the United States to seek work, after repeatedly hitting glass ceilings. I can relate to this, because I sometimes felt that I would have stood a better chance of regular work and, ultimately, success if I had moved to the United States and restarted my comedy career there; but at the age of 43, I felt that I was probably too old to start again and stayed in Britain. I also toyed with the idea of solo shows, but these required finance – something I didn't have. Here, then, is a reminder of how the world of art and entertainment works in relation to social class. Those people from middle-class backgrounds, who have attended independent schools and Oxbridge, have considerable cultural and social capital to draw upon. Their relationship to capital means that they can afford to work on the circuit for nothing until their talent is spotted, usually by one of their own. If they leave the circuit, even for brief periods, they can always return and pick up where they left off. However, someone like me, who is from a working-class background and who is, perhaps, the 'wrong kind' of Black man, who went to a polytechnic rather than the august institutions of Oxbridge or the red-brick universities and public school, cannot afford to do unpaid work until an opening arrives. If one did, one would surely starve to death before being posthumously recognized.

Finding My Voice but Losing Gigs

Throughout the early 1990s, the circuit was changing and becoming more conformist in order to meet the increasing demands of television. What had started as a loose circuit of venues offering an alternative to the 'straightness' of the official entertainment world was now beginning to resemble the very thing that it had once challenged. Even so, my career lasted for another eight years and, after much inconsistency and struggle, I finally discovered my voice and felt that I was developing as a comedian; but without regular work, it was difficult to continue the momentum. How did this development occur? First, my mother died in December 1996 after a struggle with cancer and to deal with the bereavement, I began to speak truthfully about my pain and attack the nakedly political move to marketize the National Health Service. Second, Bill Hicks and, to a lesser extent, Sam Kinison had begun to have an influence on me from around 1991. Hicks was dark and, like Carlin and Pryor, he talked openly about recreational drug use (a subject that I also adopted) and political hypocrisy. Kinison, on the other hand, was rather politically incorrect, but also talked about drugs. What I liked about Kinison was his anger and his machine-gun rhythm; he was more abrasive than Alexei Sayle (another early influence) and very bitter. What Hicks and Kinison were doing was more free-form and not bound by a script, and I wanted to get back to that style of performing, where I relaxed more and took the audience on a journey. I had done this only rarely; the first time was in Edinburgh in 1990, when I felt there was no pressure on me. I wrote in my diary:

> One of these days [indicating with an arrow to the previous days] I adlibbed for about 30 mins. Most of which I can't remember. A lot of it was site-specific. Out of this came 'Shoplifting' which needs to be hammered into shape. SWP/RCP made a brief appearance [in the set] [...] These 30 mins provided me with a blueprint for future performances...
>
> Personal Diary, 24 August 1990

Whatever happened on that night had somehow been lost in the intervening years, but now, at this moment in my career, it had suddenly returned. I began to assume an attitude of not caring what audiences thought of me; I took the view that if I started to improvise, I would have to follow it through and live with the consequences of my actions. This took a great deal of courage – to paraphrase Meursault (Camus, 1982), this was a path that I chose for myself; I could have chosen another, but I chose *this* one.

Previously, I was afraid to break away from the page; now I felt that I was free from fear. From 1997 onwards, most of my material was created from improvisations. If the improvisation failed to ignite laughter – which it rarely did – the established material was there as a backup, or I could continue until laughs were forthcoming. Improvisations that worked, those that were not specific to a time or place, would be developed into regular pieces. I began to refer to my comedy performance as 'singing my song', which seemed appropriate because I had adopted a new rock 'n' roll attitude to my performances: that is to say, I performed my comedy like the frontman of an invisible rock group; there was more emotion and more *soul* to what I was doing. This was manifested in my use of rock rhythms, attitude, and stage wear. Risks were no longer avoided and heckling was welcomed; even encouraged. I was no longer trying to please the crowd, and pieces that relied on impressions were eventually edged out and replaced with character vignettes and philosophical dialogues. One thing that cripples a performer is pandering to what he or she thinks the audience wants, and not what they, the comedian, feels inside. It is only by projecting one's inner space outward that one can break the chains of non-stop gag-telling and start telling the truth and talking about their pain. Professionally, I felt that I was finally turning the corner.

In 1998, I wrote a manifesto (see below) and sent it to Malcolm Hay at *TO*. He contacted me shortly afterward and said that he would redouble his efforts to see me. (I had never been reviewed, though my photo appeared in *TO* in 1997.) He never did.

1. No 'Uncle Tom' style humour
2. Absolutely no knob gags
3. No gags about making tea or the phone ringing while you're in the bath
4. No gags about girlfriends that are simply thinly disguised 'mother-in-law/my wife' jokes
5. No average drug observation material
6. No pandering to the lowest common denominator
7. No racist/sexist material
8. No cheap jokes at the expense of the dispossessed.

I wrote this bulleted manifesto in response to what I saw as the increasing banalization of stand-up comedy, so-called 'lad' comedy and the reappearance of lazy joke-telling. The phrase, "'Uncle Tom' style humour" is a reference to playing to white expectations of Blackness, something which I categorically refused to do. During the late 1990s, I had noticed a tendency on the part of the new breed of observational comedians to talk about their girlfriends and mock the Welsh or people with red hair in so-called 'ginger' jokes. I felt this was swapping one lazy butt for another. Indeed, one could no longer get away with telling jokes about the Irish, and this offered comedians, perhaps, the next best thing.

By the middle of 1998, much of my work was starting to dry up and many of the out-of-town venues in which I regularly performed, like the Clip Joint in Southampton and the Buzz Club in Manchester, were starting to close as the larger comedy chains, like the Comedy Store and Jongleurs, began to move into those cities. There were also more comedians on the circuit. Once, there had been a couple of hundred working regularly at any given time; now there were a couple thousand chasing roughly the same number of gigs and this had an effect on the number of bookings I was given. On the one hand, some promoters were starting to tell me to "call back in a year's time". On the other, promoters, who were new to comedy and unaware of the circuit's history, refused to take recommendations from other comedians they had booked – acts that I had appeared on the same bill with for years – and demanded that I do an open spot. Looking at my 1998 diary, there's an average of four bookings a month; compared to the previous year where there was an average of six per month. In that year, I was also running a regular monthly gig called RibTicklers at the Clocktower Arts Centre in Croydon. I ran this show on a very tight budget, which meant that, although the acts were paid, I worked for free. This was not sustainable.

After 13 years in the business, I felt that I had already 'paid my dues' and performing unpaid for five minutes for a club that could easily close in a few months' time did not appeal to me. In fact, it was a slap in the face. One innovation that occurred towards the end of the twentieth century was the appearance of a separate open-spot circuit, which grew up in response to the dwindling number of established clubs booking novice comedians for unpaid five-minute spots. I feared that I might end up in this liminal world for the rest of my career, working for nothing or £5 at most.

So, in 1999, faced with these changes, I took the very difficult decision not to pursue any more bookings and let my comedy career fade away. I played what I believed to be my final gig on 13 January 2000 at the Buzz Club. I had effectively turned my back on the world of stand-up comedy and even refused to watch it on television. I was hurt, upset, and angry. Then, in January 2005, while I was attending Malcolm Hardee's funeral, my friend, Andy Foster, persuaded me to return to comedy. I agreed but only on the condition that he help me set up and run a club. A year later, we set up a club called the Cake Shop at various locations over the next six years, until Andy decided that he had had enough of it and moved on. I still enjoy performing, because once you have been onstage, you never lose the 'bug', the urge to get back on that stage and do it again. To some extent, teaching satisfies this need, because I am the centre of attention, and I can include humorous remarks and stories in my lectures and seminars. I still run a comedy club and I can't walk past a pub without glancing up to see if it has a room suitable for comedy. Some habits never die.

Chapter 4

An Ethnography of Alternative Cabaret

*"Your denial is beneath you,
and thanks to the use of hallucinogenic drugs.
I see through you."*

Bill Hicks

Each participant I questioned regarding their influences and inspirations cited anyone from rock musicians and American comedians to philosophers and critical theorists. Such influences are arguably absent from the habituses of traditional comedians, who shunned displays of erudition and learning. Alexei Sayle's embodied cultural capital, for example, reveals itself symbolically through the name-dropping of artists and philosophers. His habitus was shaped by his family's membership of the Communist Party and its emphasis on working-class self-improvement through autodidacticism. For others, their counter*cultural* capital was deployed symbolically through attitude, an air of 'authenticity' or 'coolness' (Thornton, 1997; Revell and Ward, 2013 questionnaires). Alt performers refused to pay their respects to the performers who went before them and, like the punks, mocked them instead. Youthful rebellion was played out through altcom, but it often went beyond gentle ribbing of mannerisms or the mocking of accents and offered some analysis.

Participants also described the early space as small, and this intimacy was sometimes expressed in familial or micro-global terms. Phil Herbert (2013 questionnaire), who performed as Randolph the Remarkable, told me "we had a family of comics with genuine support and care for each other", while Ivor Dembina described it as a "very small world" that was characterized by the social relations between acts, journalists, and promoters. The supportive nature of the space was also highlighted by those who attended the cabaret courses to learn the art of alternative performance (Balloo, 2012 interview). Many performers described the clubs themselves as small and some, like the Earth Exchange in Highgate, were tiny (Darrell, 2010, Dembina, 2012, and Kelly, 2012 interviews; Herbert, Rawlings, Saville, and Thompson, 2013 questionnaires). The size of the early alt-space (1979–1985) also meant that it was easy to pick up gigs, because the population within it was similarly small and there was perceived to be a shortage of acts (Boyton, 2010 and Kelly, 2012 interviews; Smart, 2013 questionnaire). Performers knew that it wasn't possible to make a living by performing because of the lack of gigs and either worked part-time or existed on benefits (much like the up-and-coming bands of the time). This contributed to the space's amateurism. Once the space became larger and more professionalized, it became less close-knit and, ultimately, less countercultural. Many acts began to abandon their day jobs and worked full-time by 1987. Others, including me, made use of the government's Enterprise Allowance Scheme to support themselves and launch their careers, some more successfully than others.

In the following sections I discuss the main themes within the data and present case studies of alt performers in the final section.

Performers' Habituses

The aesthetic disposition of an individual or social group can be attributed to the amount and kind of cultural capital they possess (Bourdieu, 2003). For altcab performers and promoters, their dispositions came from their knowledge of counter*cultural* practices, participation in political activities, artistic (or performance) training, and their tastes, which can be identified by who influenced them. Participants' tastes were shaped by their education and their acquisition of objectified forms of cultural and counter*cultural* capital. Some participants named rock musicians as influences (Saville, Thompson, and Wilding, 2013 questionnaires); while others cited non-comedy figures like Sigmund Freud, Bertolt Brecht, Francois Rabelais, and Karl Marx (Kelly, 2012 interview; Revell, Saville, Thompson, and Ward, 2013 questionnaires). Bob Boyton (2014 Facebook conversation) claimed that he wasn't influenced by rock and was more interested in jazz, folk, and Irish music, which he says, "were a big part of left culture", though he admits to liking Bruce Springsteen and Tom Waits. Martin Soan (2013 telephone conversation), on the other hand, offered Buddy Holly and Duane Eddy as influences, alongside his Uncle Vic. Dave Thompson (questionnaire) offered the most eclectic range of influences:

> Body functions, drugs, and artistes such as George Orwell, Jack Kerouac, Aldous Huxley, Samuel Beckett, Allen Ginsburg, The Beatles, The Rolling Stones, David Bowie, Iggy Pop, and Lou Reed. And The Sex Pistols.

As if to reinforce this, Dave also admits that "Most of my role models were rock stars, actors, and writers with reputations for being rebels". Thus, Dave's view of himself is that of a rebel, an outsider. His inclusion of names like Kerouac and Ginsburg suggests a particular knowledge of the Beat Generation and the sixties countercultures into which they converged. Knowledge of drugs and key historical countercultural figures reveals a particular kind of aesthetic disposition that is geared towards unusual tastes for avant-garde art and its production. The Sex Pistols, who can be thought of as avant-gardists, are offered at the last moment, almost as an afterthought, and this bookends a countercultural period that begins in the 1950s and ostensibly ends for Dave in the late 1970s. Punk has been cited by some writers (Lidington, 1987; Double, 1991; Craig, 2000; Cook, 2001; Murray, 2007) as an influence on altcom/altcab, but this was disputed by some of the performers, who enjoyed the energy of punk but whose performances were not influenced by it (Darrell, W. Lee, and Rawlings, 2013 questionnaires; Soan, 2013 telephone conversation). Only Ivor Dembina (2012 interview), Stewart Lee (2011 interview), and Anvil Springstien (Ward, 2013 questionnaire) directly mentioned post-punk, although the former was also dismissive of any suggestion that punk influenced altcab. This seemed to confirm my hypothesis that altcab was post-punk because, although it contained elements of punk, for example in its use of DIY and use of shock, it drew from other influences, from Brechtian epic theatre and Artaud's Theatre of Cruelty to the chansons of the cabaret-artistique and paintings. Much of altcom's language comes from the rock world, from whence many of its loan words like 'gig' originate. Despite the assumption that the space was dominated by left-wing politics, Anvil Springstien (Ward, 2013 questionnaire) was the only participant to admit that he had been influenced by "anger and Marxism". It is well-known, however, that some comedians who weren't interviewed for this book were political activists – Mark Steel and Jeremy Hardy, for example; the former was a member of the SWP, while the latter supported the Socialist Alliance in the early 2000s.

American comedians like Richard Pryor, Lenny Bruce, and Bill Hicks were popular and influential with many comedians (Muldoon, 2010, and Allen, 2011 interviews; Clayton, Revell, Smart, and Thompson, 2013 questionnaires). Traditional American comedians like Bob Hope and the Marx Brothers were also mentioned by a small number (Revell, Smart, and Thompson, 2013 questionnaires), which would suggest a taste for verbal and visual or 'sight' gags. Traditional American joke-tellers like Hope differed from their English counterparts in the sense that they avoided racist humour, and, in this sense, they were modern – even if they were considered passé or déclassé in the United States. Hope was a wisecracker; a court jester who had the ear of several presidents, represented the show business establishment, and was rather conservative. The Marx Brothers' subversiveness came from two locations: their collective silliness and the rapier wit of Groucho, which combined to intellectually undermine authority's serious image of itself. For those who were not comedians, their performance styles were reflected in other kinds of performers. John Cooper Clarke was cited as an influence on the early performers, particularly the poets, like Mark Hurst (2012 questionnaire) who, as Mark Miwurdz, was also inspired by contemporary ranting poets like Attila the Stockbroker and Little Brother; while Mark Kelly (2012 interview) was influenced by the Merseyside poets and GRIMMS. Juggler Steve Rawlings (2013 questionnaire), on the other hand, was influenced by fellow performers Mr Adams and Mr Dandridge and American vaudevillian George Carl. In each case we can see how influences, which are indicative of cultural capital, were matched to performance styles.

Performers were divided over traditional British comics and some participants like Andy Smart, Phil Herbert (2013 questionnaires), and Ronnie Golden (2012 interview) saw them as old-fashioned, while the traditional comedians who were cited as being influential were the more unusual or 'wordy' comics like Tommy Cooper and Les Dawson (Hurst, 2012 questionnaire; Clayton, W. Lee, Revell, Thompson, Toczek, and Ward, 2013 questionnaires; Soan, 2014 telephone conversation). Bob Boyton (2014 Facebook conversation), on the other hand, said:

I was much influenced by radio comedy e.g. *Round the Horne* and Hancock on BBC TV. I'd probably also have to own up to being influenced by trad. comics, i.e. the guys in dinner jackets, not for their content but their form, I've always liked jokes although they were looked down upon a bit during the '80s.

Demob comedy like *Hancock's Half Hour* (BBC) occupied a sort of middle ground between traditional comedy and Oxbridge humour, its comedy coming from the humorous use of language and ridiculous situations rather than joke-telling *per se*. During the 1980s, alt comedians regarded jokes as old-fashioned and refrained from telling them in their accepted form. This often meant breaking or subverting the so-called 'rule of three'. However, like many comedians, Bob possessed a secret admiration for the joke-form. In any case, alt comedians generally preferred British comedians who had something to say for themselves rather than the gag merchants of the WMCs. Irish comedian Dave Allen was an American-style comedian in the sense that he avoided the sexist and racist pre-packed jokes of club comics and spoke directly to the audience about his views on religion. Thus, he was frequently cited by other comedians as an influence (Hurst, 2012 questionnaire; W. Lee, Revell, Thompson, Toczek, and Ward 2013 questionnaires). I would argue that Allen represented a bridge between the so-called satire boom of the early sixties and altcom in 1979. His eponymously titled show on BBC1 mocked religion and political hypocrisy, but when viewed within the context rest of television's light-entertainment output, Allen was atypical, and his show was a rarity on television. Oxbridge humour, although rejected by the early alt comedians (Triesman, 1983), was represented in the shape of *Monty Python's Flying Circus*, Derek and Clive (Peter Cook and Dudley Moore), and a solo Peter Cook (W. Lee, Revell, Thompson, and Wilding, 2013 questionnaires). These tastes indicate a preference for subversive forms of humour, which in turn influences the choices of the performer regarding the shape of the individual's approach to artistic production and performance style.

Left-wing Politics as Embodied Counter*cultural* Capital

The number of participants that were members of left-wing parties was small, given the assumptions made about the space by many observers. Only three of my participants came from families in which one or both parents were members of the Communist Party of Great Britain (CPGB), and two had been members of political parties; this is a fraction of the agents operating in the space (Boyton, 2010, Darrell, 2010, and Kelly, 2012 interviews; Gordillo, 2012, and Ward, 2013 questionnaires). However, it is reasonable to argue that the overall political orientation of the space was left-libertarian rather than being tied to one left-wing group or another. Only one, Tony Allen, identified as an anarchist. It is also fair to argue that not everyone subscribed to a political ideology and there were performers who took no position on politics or kept their views to themselves. Some participants (Mulligan and Smart, 2013 questionnaires) – including me – had acquired their counter*cultural* capital through participation in demonstrations and protests or had been members of campaign groups like CND and the Anti-Apartheid Movement. This is especially true of those participants who entered the alt entertainment space between 1979 and 1986. This was the circuit's most counter*cultural* period in terms of experimentation, innovation, and political consciousness.

Political education within the context of small left-wing parties and anarchist federations usually takes the form of seminars, meetings, or discussions and is uncertificated, standing in opposition to the formal *capitalist* method of education of the dominant culture. Bob Boyton, who joined the circuit in 1983, was a member of the Young Communist League and later the CPGB. He admits sardonically:

> I'm one of the few people in Western Europe who joined the Communist Party in 1968. I drifted away about '82, '83, but having been a very active member for most of those 15 years.
>
> Bob Boyton, 2010 interview

By claiming to be "one of the few people in Western Europe who joined the Communist Party", Bob admits that joining the Young Communists in 1968 was seen as unfashionable, and possibly 'uncool' because the student and worker protests, strikes, and sit-ins of that year were led by anarchists, libertarian Marxists, and Trotskyists (Horn, 2007). This is because the CPGB, like its sister parties in France and Germany, was opposed to the so-called New Left in 1968 and, in the case of the French Communist Party, had urged workers to abandon their strikes and return to work (Horn, 2007). Bob (2010 interview) was also involved with a fringe theatre company prior to joining the circuit; for many who were politically active, the fringe theatre companies were often attractive because they acted as a cultural carrier of political messages. Bob's comedy was often political, and as a trade-union activist, his cultural capital provided a foundation for his routines and gave them a form of counter-*cultural* gravitas.

Another performer who used his political education to construct his material was Anvil Springstien (real name Paul Ward), who was a member of the Militant Tendency in the early to mid-1980s (Ward, 2013 questionnaire). Originally from Liverpool, Anvil began as a street performer with an act called 'The Human Anvil' that played at local festivals and Militant's branch events on Tyneside. His interest in Marxism was acquired autodidactically through reading while he was a youth worker in Liverpool, and this shaped his political-aesthetic disposition and thus his choices. Importantly, his self-guided study of Marx gave him the tools with which to transform an ordinary street spectacle into a political speech that *made use* of street performance skills (Ward, 2013 questionnaire). He explains:

> I stayed awake all night and wrote a forty minute show where the hammer represents the cultural and industrial might of the masses which, when given the correct leadership, would smash through the stranglehold of international finance capital, as represented by the brick... Eight hours later I shuffled the handwritten A4 pages together and, after putting a staple in the top left hand corner, penned the title 'The Human Anvil'.
>
> Ward, 2013 questionnaire

This street spectacle reminds us of early street theatre companies like Red Ladder, who favoured strong visual imagery to carry their political messages (Itzin, 1986; Stourac and McCreery, 1986). In the carnivalesque performance of the Human Anvil one could delight in the rousing socialist speech and cheer as the socialist hero arose from the debris of capitalism, represented by the smashed brick and paving slab. However, such an act was physically demanding and after suffering a couple of broken collarbones and some cracked ribs, Anvil moved into stand-up comedy in 1989. He continued to use his counter*cultural* capital to write material that contained a great deal of social and political comment from a left perspective (Ward, 2013 questionnaire).

Counter*cultural* capital was also produced through other forms of activism. Tony Allen, for example, was "a squatting activist" based in the

Ladbroke Grove area of West London (Wilmut, 1989). The Elgin pub, in Allen's words, became "a hub of sort of lefty and anarchist, sort of, activity" (Allen, 2011 interview). Allen's experiences were used practically and in two ways: first, the practice of squatting was embodied and projected outwardly as symbolic counter*cultural* capital through his comedy routine. Second, the location of Alternative Cabaret was selected precisely because the Elgin was a meeting place of local activists (Allen, 2011 interview). Moreover, it was located in Ladbroke Grove, a counter*cultural* hub in the 1970s whose residents included bands like Hawkwind, Mick Farren's band the [Social] Deviants, and the Pink Fairies, all of which were associated with the free festival movement and other counter*cultural* events and 'happenings' of the period. The Clash were formed nearby at the Westway and CAST based themselves up the road at Chippenham Mews in Kensal Green. Thus, we can regard free festivals and other unofficial meeting places as facilitators for the circulation of counter*cultural* capital. Such events and meeting places provided platforms for the dissemination of ideas and sites for the circulation of counter*cultural* capital. It is also possible to argue that the Elgin functioned as a counter*cultural* space because it was a place to meet and discuss tactics over a pint or two.

For my part, I had been active in the Hunt Saboteurs, the Eastern Animal Liberation League, CND, and my local Anti-Apartheid Movement branch in Hitchin, Hertfordshire. I had also been a member of Friends of the Earth from 1977 to 1979. However, compared to my participants, my background was unusual for the fact that neither of my parents were left-wing or socialists, although I identified with the Left. However, before 1979 I lacked a political education, and a chance conversation with a work colleague convinced me to become a socialist. Yet I saw the Labour Party as too reactionary for my tastes and increasingly detached from its roots as a trade-union movement; and the Labour government of the late 1970s had also failed to check the rise of the far right. For his part, the Prime Minister, James Callaghan, had nothing to say about far-right violence on Britain's streets, which led to the murder of Altab Ali by white nationalists in Tower Hamlets in 1978. Aside from token efforts like the Race Relations Acts (1965, 1968, and 1976), Labour governments and many of the party's backbenchers were hostile to people of colour – the Labour right's reaction to the flight of Asian people from Kenya in the 1960s being a notable example.[1] Furthermore,

---

[1] It was Callaghan, as Home Secretary, who was responsible for the Commonwealth

people of colour within the Labour Party were marginalized and their efforts to organize Black sections within the party during the 1980s were stymied by the leadership. Such things made the Labour Party unattractive to me as a man of colour. However, at this stage I wasn't aware of other left-wing parties apart from the SWP, whose 'Stuff the Jubilee' stickers could be found on lamp posts around the country in 1977. Therefore, my politics were shaped more by the number of single-issue campaigns in which I was involved rather than by a political party. My political education has been self-guided and is therefore full of gaps; I could not, for example, pass myself off as a Communist or Trotskyist because I lacked intellectual anchorage in those ideologies. I later adopted a position that I describe as either 'libertarian socialist' or anarcho-syndicalist and, like many of the post-punk generation, I was opposed to the Conservative Party as much as 'capitalist Labour' (Reynolds, 2005: i–ix). It would also be reasonable to argue that my view of the world had been partly shaped by the events of May 1968 and the strikes and sit-ins in Paris and Munich (I was living in Bavaria at that time). Furthermore, the images of the Black Power salute at the 1968 Olympics and the Black Panthers, looking sharp and cool in their all-Black attire and berets, were also etched on my memory. Thus, it could also be argued that the media played some role in shaping my countercultural experiences. Bourdieu (2003) is insistent on the crucial role of education in the production and reproduction of cultural capital, and it is no less important in terms of education within countercultural formations.

Although membership of political parties among performers was negligible, the influence of left-libertarianism on the space was considerable and had an unconscious effect on many performers. We see in altcab not a homology with vanguardist politics but, rather, a structural affinity with post-punk and the libertarian Marxist praxis of the Situationist International, the work of the Frankfurt School, especially Adorno and Horkheimer, and the young Marx of the *Theses on Feuerbach* and the *18me Brumaire de Louis Bonaparte* (Marx, 2002). Levels of education also played their part in shaping the political-aesthetic dispositions of the participants and guiding their choices in relation to performance styles and material.

Immigrants Act (1968), which limited the migration of Commonwealth citizens to Britain.

Higher Education, Previous Occupations, and Cultural Capital

In the questionnaires and interviews, I wanted to determine the extent to which participants' prior occupations and education played a role in their selection of performance styles. From 1979 to 1985, many participants possessed prior performance experience, while others had presentational or creative skills that were a crucial component of their former occupations. Teaching was mentioned by three participants (Korn, 2012 questionnaire; James, 2011, and Dembina, 2012 interviews), while advertising was mentioned by one (W. Lee, 2013 questionnaire). The remainder had been involved in some form of alternative theatre (Boyton, 2010, Muldoon, 2010 and 2011, Allen, 2011, Gribbin, 2011, and Sneddon, 2012 interviews; Saville and Smart, 2013 questionnaires) and others had performance experiences that were unrelated to alternative theatre, which included dance (Balloo, 2012 interview), commercial theatre (Herbert, 2013 questionnaire), and, in Dave Thompson's case (2013 questionnaire), drama therapy. Dreenagh Darrell (2010 interview) had performed in cabarets and burlesques in Sydney, while Martin Soan (2013 interview) had begun performing Punch and Judy shows at the seaside. Mark Hurst (2012 questionnaire) was the only punk poet among the participants and began supporting local bands at the Broadfield pub in Sheffield. Ronnie Golden (2012 interview) and Mark Kelly (2012 interview) were the only two participants who had been in rock bands. Steve Rawlings' previous occupations bore no relation to his work as a juggler.

> Before I got onto the circuit I went through a bunch of dead end jobs, including milkman, security guard, horticultural apprentice and lifeguard and finally when I had learnt a few skills I became a street performer.
>
> Rawlings, 2013 questionnaire

Steve saw his route out of "dead end jobs" by becoming a street performer, whereas in the 1960s, many British youths would have aspired to become rock musicians or footballers, depending upon their social and cultural capital. Yet it is interesting that Steve did not want to become a stand-up comedian either.

Higher education (university, polytechnic, or drama school) also figured prominently in the backgrounds of many of the performer cohort of participants. In some cases, it was at these institutes that the participants gained early experiences of performing. In other cases, higher education (HE) provided performers with the tools to deconstruct the world around them (Lidington, 1987; Friedman, 2009). Some performers attended performing arts or similar courses at degree level (Gribbin, 2011 interview; Sneddon, 2012 interview; Mulligan and Thompson, 2013 questionnaires), while Dreenagh Darrell (2010 interview) had attended drama school. Others were graduates of more traditional subjects like English literature or physics (James, 2011, S. Lee, 2011, and Kelly, 2012 interviews; Revell, 2013 questionnaire), English and drama (Saville, 2013 questionnaire), or unspecified humanities subjects (Dembina, 2012 interview), while some had taken degrees in sociology or film studies (Gordillo, 2012, and Ward, 2013 questionnaires). Only two participants had attended Oxbridge (S. Lee, 2011 interview [Oxford]; Revell, 2013 questionnaire [Cambridge]), while a small number did not attend institutions of HE (Boyton, 2010 interview; Hurst, 2012 questionnaire; Clayton, W. Lee, and Rawlings, 2013 questionnaires). Out of those who did not attend university, Martin Soan (2013 interview), Bob Boyton (2010 interview), and Mark Hurst (2012 questionnaire) came from working-class backgrounds. Boyton's political education came through his membership of the CPGB and role as a union activist. However, he says that he completed "a one-year diploma in trades union studies for which there were no academic entry qualifications, but you had to be a trades union activist". Thus, Bob's education was a specific kind that was directly related to his work.

I would submit that the numbers of performers who came from working-class backgrounds but had attained a degree at university is masked by the claim that alt comedians in particular were middle-class simply because they were university graduates. Like me, there were participants who came from working-class backgrounds but had been to university (Gribbin, 2011 and 2012, and Kelly, 2012 interviews; Ward, 2013 questionnaire). In these instances, we were the first in our families to go into HE, thanks to the **Education Act (1944)**,[2] which Itzin (1986) cites as a contributing

---

[2] The provisions set out in the Robbins Report of 1963 also contributed to greater working-class participation in HE by providing students with an education free of tuition fees as well as a maintenance grant. The polytechnics, many of which originated in the nineteenth century as art schools and mechanics institutes, were introduced in 1965; these also contributed to higher working-class entry into HE. However, the increase in these new HE institutions also led to the so-called binary divide in the

factor in the emergence of alternative theatre. Indeed, the trajectories of those who entered alternative theatre are similar to those who entered the alt-space. If rock 'n' roll and Marx (1998, 2002) influenced the alternative theatre generation, then punk and a vaguely defined left-libertarianism influenced the altcab and post-punk generations.

Disrupting the Spectacle

If spaces are practised places as De Certeau (1988) argues, then the alt-space was counter*cultural* in the sense that its agents used practices taken from their work in theatre, their love of rock music, and their instinctive rebelliousness. To this end, it was imperative to understand what cultural influences shaped this world. Given the claims that altcom was influenced by punk, I wanted to interrogate this idea further. Hebdige's (1993) thesis that punk was simultaneously a subculture and a political culture suggests that it was also a counter*cultural* formation. Politically, punk was orientated towards anarchism, but this is not to suggest that individual punks were not politically disinterested or subscribed to conservatism (for example, John Lydon has recently revealed himself to be reactionary in his older years). There was, as Hebdige (1993) observes, the phenomenon of the so-called weekend punk, whose political inclinations may have been harder to identify. Indeed, punk tends to be cited as an important influence on early altcom by other writers of the genre (Double, 1991; Ritchie, 1997; Craig, 2000; Cook, 2001; Murray, 2007; Giappone, 2012, 2018). This influence extends to the establishment of cabaret clubs too, but it is likely that any direct association between punk and altcab has been overstated. Certainly, its raw energy and artistic honesty impressed the participants, and this is evident when they were asked to comment about punk. In terms of its influence on writing and performing, punk's value was often non-existent. Wendy Lee (2013 questionnaire) explains: "I loved a lot of that music, and the excitement that went with it, but I'm not sure it influenced anything specific". This is repeated by Steve Rawlings (2013 questionnaire): "I was heavily into the

---

HE sector. Polys, as they were called, didn't award their own degrees, a body called the Council for National Academic Awards having been created for this purpose. Thus, polys were seen as the second-class relations of the more established universities, including the so-called 'plate glass' universities that were introduced in the early 1960s.

punk scene and still am to a certain degree but performance wise I don't think it influenced me much." In both these cases, it's possible that the respondents misunderstood the question. Where punk influenced altcab/altcom was in its attitude, enthusiasm, and spirit of amateurism. Dave Thompson (2013 questionnaire), who performed as Igor Thompson, takes a different view:

> There was a similar mood to punk at many venues. A feeling that people were just getting on stage and being spontaneous and it didn't matter if things were a bit shambolic. Anyone could get on stage.

The idea that anyone could get on stage and perform comedy is analogous with *Sniffin' Glue*'s exhortation to young punk rockers: "Here are three chords, now form a band". Yet this comparison of comedy style with punk seems to be limited to a few aspects of the subculture: notably its confrontational positioning, its swearing, and amateurism. Punk's shockwaves would be felt across the cultural industries and had far-reaching effects (Wilmut, 1989; Murray, 2007). When prompted, Andy Smart (2013 questionnaire) offered the following:

> I loved the fact that anyone could be in a band, that you could just get up and do it. Also that there was no failure, any performance was good no matter how bad.

This extract highlights the space's amateurism and the agency of its actors; anyone could do it and all one needed was the gumption and the guts. Andy states that "there was no failure" and even bad performances were good. Many audiences went to gigs cognizant that they would see something unusual or unpolished, but their reasons for going to see these kinds of shows had little to do with an appreciation for a finished product and had more to do with the space's unpredictability (Friedman, 2009; Myers and Lockyer, 2011). This is the reason why cabaret was so popular in the 1980s. One of the characteristics of the amateur performer wasn't just their love for what they were doing, but also their courage and willingness to create something from bricolage, and this was appreciated by audiences. Traditional audiences had yet to be enculturated in alternative performance and would baulk at displays of amateurism or unfinished and unpolished performances.

Mark Kelly (2012 interview) observes the effect of punk on the cultural industries and suggests that it possibly influenced later events:

when punk had blown everything open and the record industry had appeared to be in some disarray... quite... quite worried and appeared to be a kind of crack in the culture... an opening, which alternative cabaret was another one later...

Mark refers to a "crack in the culture" and this recalls the words of Debord (2005) and Vaneigem (1967) with regard to the creation of 'situations' to disrupt the all-encompassing spectacle that pervades all aspects of life (Wollen, 1975: 69). When the first wave of punk was recuperated in 1978, it opened up a space that was filled by a DIY culture that was epitomized by small independent record labels and bands that eschewed commercialism and, to borrow from Bourdieu (2003, 2016), played music for music's sake. Punk needed its own spaces for bands to ply their trades and for appreciative audiences to assemble to see them. McKay (1996: 7) argues that "the way cultures of resistance define themselves against the culture of the majority is through the construction of their own zones". What took place within the alt-space was defined by its counter*cultural* elements of bricolage, amateurism, its political engagement, and its democratized social relations. Their amateurism was opposed to the traditionalists' professionalism and commercial objectives, but was it like punk or influenced by its self-reliance and agency?

Another aspect to punk was its disdain for whatever went before it (Marcus, 1989). In this, it resembles the historical avant-garde. Steve Gribbin (2011 interview) told me:

Year Zero of 1977 and punk, you weren't allowed to like anything, but then that also meant that you weren't allowed to like brilliant things like Lou Reed or Neil Young or you know, so gradually you go back and people that were good before then, in comedy terms, like Les Dawson – who's still, I think, an amazing comedian... uh, although we weren't allowed to... you weren't allowed to like him...

Steve's use of the phrase 'Year Zero' is revealing, but it is also a reference to the Killing Fields of Cambodia when the Pol Pot regime carried out a purge of intellectuals, artists, and dissidents. It moreover reminds us of how cultural artefacts are classified by 'cool' youths, who use their internalized counter*cultural* and subcultural frameworks to separate objects into cool/hip and uncool/square categories. The phrase 'Year Zero' also makes an appearance in Stewart Lee's autobiography (Lee, 2010: 1). The alt-space, though non-racist and non-sexist, refused performers from the official world on the grounds of their mainstream credentials, regardless of whether they met the entry requirements of non-racism and non-sexism or not. They were associated with the parental culture and this marked them out as part of an old order, punk's so-called 'boring old farts'.

Resisting the parental culture is common to almost every youth culture, and yet punk differed from the other subcultures because it was constructed on the margins and wore its alienation on its sleeve (Hebdige, 1993). If one was a punk, then admitting to liking Neil Young or the Carpenters was considered to be the ultimate *faux pas* among one's peers – it was an indicator of 'uncoolness'. When I began performing comedy in 1987, it wasn't considered 'cool' to admit one's admiration of traditional comedians like Frankie Howerd and Tommy Cooper. However, by the early 1990s, one could express such admirations without fear of ridicule or rebuke (often by fellow performers), partly because of the collapse of the boundary between alternative and mainstream – and partly because fewer comedians were coming from fields and spaces that lay outside the official world, unrelated fields, or because they were too young to remember the generational tensions between historical youth cultures and their parental counterparts.

Compère, comedian, and promoter Ivor Dembina (2012 interview) was sceptical of direct comparisons of altcom with punk:

> I mean, I'm not an expert on punk rock, although I was aware… you know… I don't know much about music, but [pause] I don't think anyone ever sat down and said "Oh, that's happening in music, let's take that and try it in comedy". I don't think it worked in that kind of linear fashion. But it was part of a general [pause]… I was gonna say zeitgeist but that kind of thing. I think it… one was a reflection of the other. I mean, punk undoubtedly came first, but the spirit, it was like… yeah, it was more of a reflection…

Ivor opens this extract by declaring that he is not an "expert on punk rock" but is prepared to offer an observation by accepting that punk had an effect more generally on the cultural production. He recognizes that punk as a subcultural form wasn't appropriated for use as a comedic medium but understands its subtle influence on what followed. This is evidenced by his use of the words "zeitgeist" and "spirit [of punk]" and is instructive because it relates back to Mark Kelly's idea of a cultural rupture that took place in punk's wake.

Nick Revell (2013 questionnaire) was happy to connect punk to altcom in one aspect:

> I think there was a feeling that we were to comedy what punk was to rock and roll. So in attitude, definitely.

This attitude, informed by punk's influence, was another marker of differentiation between the alternative comedian and the traditional comedian. The snarling, the swearing, anger, and anti-authoritarianism could be considered as embodied forms of counter*cultural* (or subcultural) capital that came from exposure to punk in the media or as subcultural agents. For Otiz Cannelloni (Korn, 2012 questionnaire), punk appears to have had a deeper influence; one that is tied to his understanding of the counterculture:

> There was a small group of us then and we were very much into the music and attitude. I don't give a fuck was a great help getting on stage at the early Comedy Store – although I didn't come over that way, it was just in the mindset.

Again, the keyword here is 'attitude' and it was this that helped to differentiate the alt performers from their mainstream counterparts. Attitude was a theme that was present in my interviews with Tony Allen and Bob Boyton, the latter of whom says, "what matters is not what the subject is about but what the attitude is" (2010 interview), while Allen (2011 interview) insists, "It isn't about material, it's about attitude". These quotes recall the words of the Eddie Waters character in Trevor Griffiths' television play *Comedians* (BBC, 1979), who tells his students: "It's not the jokes; it's what lies behind them. It's the attitude". Indeed, Mark Hurst (2012 questionnaire) suggested that *Comedians* may have also been responsible for providing alternative performers with ideas:

> I think some of those first alt stand ups like Tony Allen, Alexei Sayle, and Rik Mayall were influenced by the Jonathon Pryce character. But I can't recall ever discussing it with any of them, so I dunno. But it was a before its time piece of theatre and should be part of the story.

Comedians predated punk and altcom, so it is difficult to say for certain if it inspired the early alt performers, but it is worth remembering that in order to create something new, it was necessary as avant-garde artists to make use of what was available. WMC comedians were not role models, therefore the first alt comedians had to make do and draw from a number of sources. *Comedians* arguably acted as a harbinger of the future of British stand-up comedy because it questioned the staleness of traditional stand-up and its use of Others as the butt of jokes.

Ivor Dembina (2012 interview) first became involved in comedy after visiting the Comedy Store on the advice of Jim Barclay, who had performed in one of his plays. He says of this experience,

> [Jim Barclay] kept telling me stories about this new place called the Comedy Store, where people got up and just did five or ten minutes of their own original stand-up comedy material. It sounded very exciting and I went down to see it and I was just blown away... by the newness of it, the, uh, the freshness of it and the kind of post-punk spirit of amateurism, which I really enjoyed... I like... I enjoyed the roughness of the whole, um the whole shebang... if you like...

Ivor uses words like 'newness' and 'freshness' and these resonate with the avant-gardists' perceptions of their art in relation to the staleness of established forms. It is instructive that Ivor should use the term 'post-punk spirit' to describe a comedy experience; he thus seems aware of the rupture that took place in the aftermath of punk and reinforces this by referring to the new comedy's endearing "spirit of amateurism". This 'spirit' cut across the fields of music and cabaret and was one of the guiding principles of the space. It is linked with the tactic of bricolage and is reminiscent of the grassroots communities that gathered around DIY spaces in D. Andrews' (2010) reimagining of Wollen's (1975) seminal work. Therefore, the alt-space is a DIY space, but it is not often associated with art or the avant-garde in the mind of the commentator, critic, or historian, and I would argue this is because, first, suggestions of art tend to be vigorously denied or resisted by many entertainers. Second, there is a general perception that art appreciation is a middle-class pastime (Bourdieu, 1993, 1996). The alternative performers' use of critical theory and deconstruction, two associated aspects of the avant-garde, differentiates them from mainstream comedy. This makes altcom a form of post-punk avant-garde because comedians refused that which was 'naturally' or 'obviously' comedic. Gags, for example, were seen as very obviously comedic and therefore regarded by many alt comedians, me included, as being old-fashioned and belonging to the official world, with all of its tedious predictability.

At this point I would like to turn to the post-punk music space and draw out its structural affinities with altcab. The term 'post-punk' appears to suggest that anything that has been assigned this label simply post-dates punk and was its "repudiating offspring" (Gracyk, 2011: 74). Post-punk was characterized by its attitude to mass cultural production and was defined by its restricted mode of production and its autonomous hierarchical principles. The structural characteristics of post-punk were its amateurism, its willingness to confront social and political issues, and its tendency to play with content and form. According to Reynolds (2005: i–ix), post-punk existed from 1978 to 1984, meaning that it occurred in parallel to the first wave of altcom/altcab; therefore I would argue that the appearance of post-punk music and altcab/altcom is part of a zeitgeist moment, a space that had been opened up by the catalyzing effect of punk, in which anything was possible. Punk's example led to the creation of spaces for the production, distribution, and consumption of counter-*cultural* forms that were excluded from the dominant field of cultural production by the very nature of their restricted mode of production. The most obvious example of these structural similarities existed between post-punk music and altcom. Alt comedians matched their post-punk musical counterparts in terms of their use of form and content. Reynolds (2005: xviii) notes two post-punk bands:

> Gang of Four and Scritti Politti abandoned tell-it-like-it-is denunciation for songs that exposed and dramatized the mechanisms of power in everyday life: consumerism, sexual relationships, common-sense notions of what's natural or obvious, the ways in which seemingly innermost feelings are actually scripted by larger forces.

Alt comedians, like their post-punk musical counterparts, mocked traditional power relations, talked humorously about sexual relationships and consumerism, and challenged dominant comedy aesthetics. However, post-punk should not be confused with the ambiguously labelled 'new wave' – the two are distinct for the following reasons: the former was created mainly by former punks, some of whom had a university or art-school education and utilized Marxist, Situationist, or art theory in the production of their music and lyrics; this is particularly evident in the music of Gang of Four and Wire (Marcus, 1989). Altcab and post-punk refused commercialism, and both constructed their respective products from bricolage by drawing from a diverse array of source material. Some post-punk bands, like the Pop Group, used a form of sonic bricolage by incorporating funk (which was reclaimed from the ruins of disco), free jazz, and dub rhythms and combining them with punk rock to create new sounds. Similarly, alt comedians, in particular, used bricolage to construct their performances, combining words, physicality, music, props, dance, and sometimes poetry. The table below provides an at-a-glance comparison of post-punk music and altcab/altcom.

Table 1

Characteristics	Post-punk music	Altcab
A refusal of predictability	X	x
Avant-garde/Counter*cultural*	X	x
Amateurism DIY/bricolage	X	x
Engagement with ideas/everyday life/politics	X	x
Democratization/egalitarianism	X	x
Use of critical theory and deconstruction	X	x
Fringe left/left libertarian/Marxist/ Situationist-inspired	X	x
Non-racist/non-sexist	X	x
Mocked predecessors		x

Like punk, post-punk can therefore be more broadly described as a counter*cultural* movement rather than being limited solely to a musical genre or a specific subcultural style. In the early years, there were crossovers between alt comedians and post-punk music. For example, Tony Allen went on tour with post-punk bands, the Clash, the Poison Girls, and Crass (Allen, 2011 interview). Allen and Sayle also performed for punks and post-punks at Camberwell School of Art in 1980 (Wilmut, 1989; Double, 1997). Yet playing rock audiences, as I have discovered, is not an easy task when the punters are expecting to see a band, and someone appears onstage to 'talk to them'.

The link between music and comedy can be seen in the example of Lenny Bruce, whose use of improvised riffs, argot, and phrasings was directly inspired by jazz (Magnuson, 1965 video; Baker, 1971 video). In the post-punk era, we can see how the language of rock and its rhythms filtered through to alt comedians. While it is uncertain how many other comedians opened for rock bands, there was much overlap between the punk poetry cohort and the world of post-punk music. Poets like Mark Hurst (2012 questionnaire) opened for post-punk bands like the Human League and played the altcab clubs, thus straddling the worlds of alternative (post-punk) music and alternative entertainment. Britain's traditional stand-up comics, by contrast, were separated from the lived experiences of youth and this is evident in the absence of rock music as an influence and inspiration. This was illustrated when Sayle told Wilmut that

> there was no tradition of rock stand-up comedy in Britain, no one like Richard Pryor or Lenny Bruce, so people didn't understand what you were doing and things could get out of hand fairly easily.
>
> Sayle, quoted in Wilmut, 1989: 22

Here Sayle is describing an experience during his time with Threepenny Theatre[3] and this experience provided him with the substrate for his comedy. If the performers were new to this kind of comedy, then the audiences who witnessed these shows were uncertain of what to expect. British comedy audiences had grown accustomed to the predictability of joke-forms and their butts, and therefore needed to be educated. Post-punk music provided the backbeat for the new British comedy in the same way that rock had done for George Carlin in the 1970s. This is evident in Sayle's choice of stage wear, which was alternately the skinhead and ska rude-boy styles (Campbell, 2018).

Reynolds (2005: xxv) recalls that post-punk overlapped "two distinct phases in British and American politics": the centre-left governments of Jim Callaghan (himself on the right of the party and a Gaitskellite) and Jimmy Carter were displaced by the right-wing governments of Margaret Thatcher and Ronald Reagan. The elections of Thatcher and Reagan marked the end of the post-war consensus and any talk of full employment. Although ostensibly left-wing, post-punk and altcab equally rejected the orthodoxies of the established political right and left parties and attacked both sides. Sex, sexuality, race, class, and Northern Ireland were common motifs that were openly being articulated by post-punk bands and cabaret performers alike. 'Armagh' by the Au Pairs and Gang of Four's 'Ether', for example, comment on the status of prisoners in the Six Counties. The Au Pairs deal

---

[3] Named after Brecht's *Threepenny Opera*.

with the incarceration and alleged torture of women prisoners in Armagh and sing, "We Don't Torture, we're a civilized nation" (Au Pairs, 1981), while Gang of Four examined special category status prisoners in the H Blocks of Long Kesh (now called the Maze) and invite us to look at the "Dirt behind the daydream" (Gang of Four, 1979b). 'Armagh' uses stark imagery and direct language with a funky backbeat to convey the horrors of the British occupation, and such were the establishment's anxieties over its lyrical content that the song was banned in Ireland and received little, if any, airplay on the British 'mainland' – a stark reminder of the state's symbolic violence and how it works to silence oppositional discourses.

Like their post-punk musical counterparts, many alt comedians were sympathetic to the Irish republican struggle. Andy de la Tour (quoted in Wilmut, 1989: 40) frequently commented on Northern Ireland, and was one of the first English comedians to play republican clubs:

> I did quite a lot of stuff about Northern Ireland – it was good satire and the audience used to appreciate it – but sometimes people would respond badly, simply on the grounds of its politics, no matter how funny other people in the audience found it. One of the most exciting experiences I've ever had was a series of gigs in some Republican clubs in Belfast in 1981 – it was very unusual for them to see an English comic making jokes about Northern Ireland that were basically pro-Republican and anti the army presence.

De la Tour's comedy would never have been permitted in the official world because he questioned established notions of nationhood and the dominant discourses surrounding the 'Irish question'. In the simplistic binaries offered by the media, this was a struggle between Catholic irredentists and Protestant loyalists. Questions about the nature of Britain's relationship with Ireland and its continued occupation of the Six Counties were not up for discussion within the official world. Even traditional Irish comedians like Frank Carson found it easier to play up to their English audience's expectations of their Irishness rather than challenge age-old prejudices. Bernard Manning was known for his racist jokes and the Irish were included in his set:

> The Irish have just invented a new parachute...
>
> It opens on impact.
>
>> Anon., told by Bernard Manning in *The Comedians*, 1972

This two-line joke is thematically typical of an Irish joke. Such jokes are very real in the sense that they are, at the same time, *unreal*. That is to say, they are not based on the reality of Ireland, its people, or the history of the British occupation of the country, but rely instead on the notional stupidity and technological ignorance of the Irish. They are thus based on an ideological reading of the country's largely agrarian economy. These kinds of jokes were told, seemingly, to serve as a means of distancing oneself from the very real terror of an Irish republican bombing campaign through the insistence that the Irish were thick in spite of the IRA and INLA's technical competence with explosive materials.

Bob Boyton (2010 interview) echoes de la Tour but adds,

> of course the [Irish] republican struggle was still armed and there was an assumption that you were on the side of that struggle…

Bob does not say who exactly assumed one's commitment to the cause of Irish republicanism. It may be the audience or the state. The Irish republican cause was a deeply unfashionable one in the United Kingdom and, moreover, offensive to the right-wing sensibilities of Conservative MPs and their allies in the media. Therefore, expressing sympathy with Irish republicanism in public carried the potential risk of censorship from the audience, the promoter, or the authorities – even if there was no such intention in the first place. The mere suspicion of IRA sympathies was sufficient grounds for censorship, as Skint Video found out. Brian Mulligan (2013 questionnaire) says:

> we once got pulled from Ealing festival for being pro IRA – as I said at the time even if you played our songs backwards you wouldn't find such a message.

It is hard to ascertain how the promoter of this festival could have read pro-IRA sympathies into Skint Video's set, but this incident reminds us that even the mildest sympathy with Irish republicanism could be seen as politically subversive – more so perhaps after the 1984 Brighton bombing. Here, the symbolic violence of the state was applied through a promoter who believed they were acting in the state's interests by cancelling Skint Video on spurious grounds. Yet it is easy to see how these new upstart performers were seen as 'dangerous' by the authorities in the official world, because of their willingness to address issues that were considered taboo. Traditional performers assiduously avoided such discourses because they saw themselves as being free from politics.

Countercultural Practices and Cultural Conflict

A principal aim of this study was to situate altcab, altcom, and NV within the post-punk counter*cultural* milieu of the late 1970s and 1980s. Given the confusion over the term 'counterculture', I wanted to determine how my participants perceived this word and whether or not they consciously associated it with the alt-space. I was aware that 'counterculture' would be equally as complicated as the word 'culture' (Williams, 1976: 87), and yet I expected to see replies that repeated the generally held assumptions of the word and its connotations of psychedelia and hedonism. To my surprise, post-punk was mentioned three times but only Anvil Springstien (real name Paul Ward) linked his explanation of the counterculture directly to the post-punk movement of the late 1970s:

> Yes. I thought that this, us, we, I, were part of that. We *were* the 'new wave' – that was us, 'post punk', exciting, dangerous, revolutionary, cool…
>
> Ward, 2013 questionnaire

Not only is the counterculture represented in this case by post-punk (and by extension, punk), it is depicted as "exciting", "dangerous", and "revolutionary". Traditional light entertainment, by contrast, was predictable, stale, and devoid of anything revolutionary in terms of its aesthetics and politics; it remained aesthetically conservative. Anvil also uses the term 'new wave' interchangeably with 'post-punk' and this illuminates the confusion over the genres, which have been assigned as classifications by music journalists. Anvil's descriptions of the counterculture allow us to see how it is perceived on both sides of the argument. For the dominant culture, it is represented by the hackneyed image of the dropout who chooses subversion over the 'democratic' process by joining a revolutionary party. It also summons up mental images of hippies, squats, communes, drug-taking, mysticism, and indolence. For those attracted to a counterculture, it is something far more honourable, and this can be seen in the way that Anvil uses the word 'cool', which like 'hipness' is a conscious effort to differentiate oneself from the fustiness of the official space and is similar to Thornton's (1997: 3) formulation of subcultural capital. Yet Anvil also seems to be aware that altcom/altcab was countercultural because it was a "new wave" and broke with the prevailing forms of entertainment.

When replying to the second question, Anvil (Ward, 2013 questionnaire), a Liverpudlian working-class ex-Catholic, explains its effect on him:

> You have to understand that I'd come off a very large post industrial [sic] estate dominated both by unemployment and catholicism [sic] in equal measure. This was my *Renaissance*, my *Enlightenment*, my *world turned upside down*. There were battles to be fought – Thatcher was in power. Did I look cool? I'm sure I looked cool?

Anvil uses words like 'Renaissance' and 'Enlightenment' to describe his countercultural experience as a transformative process that allowed him to transcend a post-industrial inner-city housing estate and the socially repressive practices that tend to be associated with the Catechism. Liverpool was a once-prosperous city that was built on the slave trade and shipbuilding. However, by the late 1970s containerization had closed down the docks, and the shipbuilding that once took place on both sides of Mersey had ground to a halt by the early 1980s (Sykes et al., 2012: 299–318). Consequently, the city witnessed depopulation as well as unemployment, and years of government neglect had exacerbated the situation (Sykes et al., 2012: 299–318). The mention of the struggle against the Thatcher government is also revealing for it suggests that anti-Thatcherism is a countercultural position and, again, it is 'cool' to be *contra* the 'uncool' Thatcher. Coolness can also be read as a symbolic form of counter*cultural* capital because it indicates a competence with counter*cultural* practices and the political ideas that are produced within countercultural formations. Anvil was a political comedian and thus he saw his art in the service of something greater than just entertainment for its own sake, and this is indicated by the clause "there were battles to be fought – Thatcher was in power". Yet it is not clear if Anvil saw his comedy as part of a wider effort on the part of those battles or whether he saw it as carnivalesque. Anvil's testimony also tells us that counter*cultures* are not class-bound, because the message of resistance is a potent one that appeals to restless youths from council estates and suburbia alike. This is arguably because its simple message proposes magical solutions to social injustice and intolerance, while simultaneously accommodating social deviancy, hedonism, and bohemianism.

Counter*cultural* formations, like subcultures, produce their own language and the term used by those who had adopted a relationally 'cool' position within any of the anti-Thatcher countercultural formations wasn't 'political correctness', because this was a term used by the right-wing press to mock the Left; it was 'ideologically sound' or 'sound'. Stewart Lee (2011 interview), who joined the space in 1989, recalls how this word was used:

> then, the highest praise you could have for someone was to call them a 'sound bloke'. "What's he like? Oh, he's sound". What I... and I talked about this in my book... and I remember when I got to college it was the same, but those kind of words had been knocked around on the comedy circuit by people like Kevin Day and Mark Thomas, you wanted to be sound. There was this, kind of, this was a sort of ideological, kind of, imperative.

Ideological soundness was itself a form of cool and was the default position of eighties counter*cultural* and left-wing youth; it provided a sort of philosophical undergirding of the space, which in turn positioned it against the anti-intellectuals and reactionaries of the dominant culture. Indeed, it could be argued that being a left-winger was itself cool. Nick Revell (2013 questionnaire), a comedian from the first wave, also mentions coolness. Except in Nick's case, it is his perceived lack of coolness that concerned him:

> I suppose I was part of it, although I always think I wasn't cool or hardcore enough to be so.

This time the word 'cool' is used in conjunction with the word 'hardcore'. This second word suggests a kind of commitment or dedication to a particular cause, be it setting up communes or engaging in full-time political activism. Irrespective of his perceived lack of coolness, Nick understands the stakes that were involved in the countercultural struggles of the 1980s and could not be more explicit when he was asked to describe them:

> In the early eighties, there was a definite sense of the government enacting a counter-revolution, with dramatic changes being introduced, and clear specific issues to agree or disagree over: union busting, race riots, nuclear weapons. So you felt an identity through what you were against. Same as today, I guess, but it seemed like the opposition was more vocal and there was less apathy. Perhaps because the unions still had a voice. On the other hand – the Tories stayed in power for 18 years!
>
> Revell, 2013 questionnaire

Nick sees the counterculture in rather broad, oppositional terms. Indeed, Nick appears to suggest that this wasn't a homogeneous counterculture; rather, it is a mosaic of counter*cultural* formations, and this is reinforced by the use of the word 'identity', which was bound up with political struggles for racial and sexual equality; membership of trade unions and opposition to nuclear weapons. Furthermore, the sense of public anger towards policing in the inner cities, the cuts to public services, and the presence of American cruise missiles on British soil was palpable, and was expressed politically through protests, occupations, encampments, marches against the rise of the extreme right, and of course, riots. Such subjects were off-limits in the official entertainment world but were welcomed in the alt-space. Taking a position on such matters can also be considered a form of counter*cultural* capital because this kind of knowledge is produced and reproduced through political activism. The official world offered no room for such oppositional discourses because those people who defended its institutions saw it as being 'free from politics'. The Thatcher government's response to opposition was to crush it through the use of legal mechanisms.[4] Draconian legislation was introduced to limit union activity and to outlaw (what were deemed to be) oppositional lifestyle choices, which included the New Age Traveller movement and, in particular, the so-called Peace Convoy. In this light, what Nick says about a right-wing 'counter-revolution' resonates with the Thatcher government's drive to curb the 'permissive society'. Yet we also see that Nick does not naively think that what he or anyone else was doing as performers might have lead to the imminent collapse of the Conservative government. Altcab's value as a revolutionary weapon was confined mostly to carnivalesque.

Brian Mulligan (2013 questionnaire) of Skint Video supports the view that countercultural formations are broadly oppositional and cites particular examples:

> Mainly defined by what it stands against (woody guthrie's idea) – racism, sexism, homophobia – in comedy terms making the subject of your ire that which can be changed ie political views, vanity – freedom of expression

---

[4] This could be witnessed in its reaction to the increased popularity of CND, which involved harassment by Julian Lewis's Coalition for Peace through Security with the ultimate objective of limiting the space within mainstream political discourse for the British Left (Wittner, 1993).

This idea of freedom of expression appears to have been central to the thoughts of many performers. Yet Brian's list of oppositional political discourses is similar to Nick's. It is also interesting that he mentions Woody Guthrie, a socialist, whose music stood in opposition to the excesses of capitalism and whose battered guitar bore the words "This Machine Kills Fascists". The folk music scene was itself counter*cultural* because it was constructed outside the official structures of the music industry and refused the trappings of modernity – especially electric instruments – but also because it embodied bohemianism and established itself on the margins of official culture (Lund and Denisoff, 1971: 394–405). In the 1960s and 1970s, the folk clubs in Britain provided a space for oppositional politics and some alt performers, like Jenny Lecoat, began in the folk clubs. Folk clubs also played host to early alternative theatre companies like CAST (Muldoon, 2011 interview).

When asked his views on whether or not the space was countercultural, Dave Thompson (2013 questionnaire) seems to suggest another form of symbolic violence:

Yes in its early days. But the establishment's way of dealing with the influential artists wasn't to silence them by putting them in gaol. It silenced them by making them rich.

I would tend to agree with Dave's assessment. Altcab's first and second waves were counter*cultural* but by the third wave in 1987, as John Gordillo (2012 questionnaire) also recalls, it was no longer counter*cultural* because it was now subject to greater media exposure. By 1987, the broadcast media were taking an ever-increasing interest in the altcab circuit and had identified the elements (stand-up comedy) which they intended to recuperate and return to the public as slightly dangerous art forms. Channel 4's *Saturday Live* and its successor, *Friday Night Live*, plucked performers from the circuit and made household names of Ben Elton, Stephen Fry, Hugh Laurie, and Harry Enfield, but these programmes and those that followed them ultimately became responsible for forcing standardization onto what was effectively a scene that was operated mainly by amateurs, for amateurs. It is also interesting how Dave tells us how artists have been "silenced by making them rich", an allusion to the recuperative processes of the dominant cultural industry, which first ignored altcab when it was fresh, exciting, and dangerous, but then found ways to make it safe. What is interesting about this extract is Dave's use of the word 'artists' and this suggests that those who performed on altcab's stages saw themselves not as technicians but as artists who approached their work from the position of art rather than a craft that places greater emphasis on technical competency instead of creativity. Bourdieu (1996: 120–124) says there are two kinds of avant-garde: one is consecrated and the other is not. The comedians who appeared on *Saturday Live* were legitimated by television exposure, while the circuit continued to produce avant-garde performers – albeit in smaller numbers until the early 1990s. Normally, this separation occurs between artists of different generations, and the new generation that emerged during the transitional phase (1987–1991) were not avant-garde but mainstream performers who had accepted non-racism and non-sexism as a requirement of entering the new space.

Some performers saw countercultures as having more or less the same properties as the official culture, but inverted in relation to official culture. Dave Thompson (2013 questionnaire) said:

> The counterculture was a massive umbrella, almost as large as the established culture. In terms of cabaret performing we all felt obliged to express a distaste for Margaret Thatcher and the government.

Dave suggests the counterculture is nomenclatural rather than fixed to a moment in time or related wholly to psychedelia and bohemianism. He draws a comparison with the official culture, which itself is no less nomenclatural. Dave's view is redolent of Williams' (1976: 81) definition of the culture as a large but ill-defined entity, but recognizes that, in spite of his misgivings, anti-Thatcherism was a counter*cultural* formation. However, Dave insists that performers were *obliged* to take an anti-Thatcherite position and although there were no codified rules of conduct in the space, there was an assumption on the part of audiences that the clubs and the performers were anti-Thatcher. This theme was extended by Ivor Dembina (2012 interview):

> there was almost an assumption in the audience that you were anti-Tory… you were… you just assumed, even if, you know and most comedians [pause] when it came to taking a political perspective in their material would invariably reveal themselves or said they were anti-Tory [noise as recorder is being moved], um, but a lot of the people who went into lengthy diatribes… or had a, you know, exclusively political content to their act was incredibly small.

If anything, there was an emphasis on the rejection of the dominant cultural aesthetics of the official world with its conservatism and use of humorously veiled symbolic violence. Thus the Thatcher government, like television light entertainment, represented the dominant culture and was, at times, tacitly opposed by performers in the alt-space. Ivor Dembina (2012 interview) echoes Dave's sentiments:

> We were her children… you know, we were Thatcher's children… […] the thing about being a stand-up comedian is you're self-employed, you've got to make your own way, create your own work, travel to where the work is. I mean, we were… you know… we were Tebbit's bicyclists.

The suggestion here is that all performers who earned money by performing on the circuit had unconsciously bought into Thatcher's petit-bourgeois notions of entrepreneurialism by dint of their self-employed status. However, we must remember that self-employment has been a constant feature of working in the entertainment industry for centuries. Even within the alt-space, it wasn't possible for performers to be salaried. The entertainment profession relies on itinerant and temporary labour and the alt-space was no different in this regard. Furthermore, many of the clubs were also run by enthusiastic amateurs who were not supported by Arts Council subsidies; and unlike NV or CAGG, which were supported by public money they could not afford to pay the acts guaranteed fees. Payments were generally made in cash and often on a 'no questions asked' basis. Formal contracts did not exist, and agreements were made on the basis of a phone call. Due to the precarious nature of working in the space, many performers claimed unemployment benefit, which often meant they occupied a space between legality and illegality, while others had day jobs. Mark Kelly (2012 interview) also suggests that this was one of the reasons why performers chose stage names. However, for all their apparent status as self-employed businesspeople, there is no reason to suggest that they were not committed to the principles of social justice and political action – which was especially the case with the Miners' Strike of 1984–1985. For some like Andy Smart of improvising double act, the Vicious Boys, the Miners' Strike was a defining moment in his life and the counterculture in which he participated politicized him.

> I read a good newspaper every day and got involved with campaigns, marches, demos. Lead to me joining Red Wedge.
>
> Andy Smart. 2013 questionnaire

Andy's idea of a "good newspaper" may well be a liberal broadsheet like the *Guardian* rather than a tabloid like the *Sun* or the *Daily Mirror*. There is also a sense that, like Anvil, he sees countercultures as transformative, and this led him towards political activism. Improvisation was a new comedy form that was based mainly on Keith Johnstone's (1989) Theatresports concept, and was popularized by the success of Channel 4's *Whose Line Is It Anyway?* The popularity of this new form of comedy saw the birth of the Comedy Store Players in October 1985 and led to a flowering of improvisational companies including London's own version of Theatresports. Indeed, there were venues that were entirely devoted to improv – Late at the Gate and the Hurricane Club being two notable examples.

Ian Saville (2013 questionnaire) admitted that he "was at the 'hippy' end of the counterculture" but had "discovered political ways of looking at the world", adding that although he didn't join a political party, he "was close to the Trotskyist view of the world". Hippies were one of the visible subcultural faces within the 1960s countercultural milieu and as McKay (1996: 6) reminds us, "subcultures feed the counterculture". In this instance, it is also easy to see how subcultures and countercultures become entangled with one another and thus conflated as one and the same thing. The fashionability of long hair for men in the late 1960s and the 1970s could lead to an assumption that any long-haired male was a hippy. Yet conversely, those men who wore their hair short could be seen as skinheads, 'straights', or worse, undercover policemen or the 'narcs' of the drug squad. This fashionability or coolness also extended to politics and the "Trotskyist view of the world", that Ian mentions here, was opposed to the rigid orthodoxy of the relatively 'straight' CPGB because it proposed permanent revolution as a means to continue the initial goals of the revolution. On the one hand, Trotskyism refused Stalin's 'socialism in one country' and was internationalist in its outlook; and on the other, it rejected the Western capitalist model, and was illuminated by the Socialist Workers Party's (SWP) slogan, 'Neither Washington nor Moscow' (McGregor, 2002: 1). The SWP, as I pointed out earlier, was closely involved in RAR and had created the Anti-Nazi League. Yet Ian also recognizes that being at the hippy end of the counterculture did not necessarily entail being a drop-out and he recognizes the value of education in political theory over the hedonism and mysticism of the mass media's depiction of sixties countercultures. He is clear about the production of his counter*cultural* practices.

My practice in theatre related to oppositional forms, which were affected by my reading of socialist theory, and of cultural theorists and practitioners, particularly Bertolt Brecht

Ian Saville, 2013 questionnaire

Ian's familiarity with Brecht was commonplace within the political theatre space (Itzin, 1986: 6). Ian had worked with Broadside Mobile Workers Theatre but was sacked, "apparently" because he was "not a good enough performer". He continued to work with individual members of Broadside after the company had lost its Arts Council grant, and it was during that time (1981–1982) that he developed his socialist magician act (Saville, 2013 questionnaire). Ian took the counter*cultural* capital that he had acquired with Broadside and carried it with him in the transverse migration from the socialist theatre space to the alt-space when he began performing at NV shows, which welcomed ideologically sound entertainment that wasn't overly didactic.

Yet for all the apparent freedoms within this new entertainment space, there was a sense from some performers that they were being censored. The freedom of expression that Brian Mulligan mentions is challenged by Dave Thompson (2013 questionnaire), who identifies the possible culprit:

> There was less freedom of speech in the alternative cabarets of the '80s than there is on the comedy circuit today. The limitations to freedom of speech came from the right-on socialists in the audience, not from the government.

Whatever issue one had with the capitalist system or the Conservative government, it was impossible to operate within the official space because of the way in which the old guard worked to exclude innovatory forms of entertainment and discourses that challenged conventional socio-political thinking. Although there was space provided for oppositional political views, this cannot necessarily be seen as 'free speech' in and of itself. On the contrary, there was a general feeling among the space's agents that some forms of language and political opinions were unacceptable. However, the notion that we can say what we like is false: free speech is not enshrined in statute, and English and Welsh defamation laws make it easy for powerful and wealthy people to shut down discourses they find unacceptable. Dave believes the "limitations to freedom of speech" came solely from "right-on socialists in the audience", though this is not wholly supported by the evidence: performers censored themselves and other performers, and club proprietors also engaged in censorship. Jongleurs, for example, had a reputation for censoring performers (Darrell, 2010, Allen, 2011, and Kelly, 2012 interviews). Indeed, in 1998, the club sent a memo to its regular performers advising them to avoid material relating to Princess Diana's death and stating that anyone caught contravening this diktat would not be booked in future.

Sometimes, what appeared to be censorship could also be seen as a misreading of the performer in question. This can occur because of a misinterpretation of the performer's textuality: this can be either their persona or their words. Character comics can often be read literally rather than as a grotesque caricature of a performer's observations. In this case, the habituses of performer and audience are mismatched. WMC and commercial cabaret audiences and promoters were unlikely to tolerate overtly political comedians because the official space was regarded by its inhabitants as apolitical and had been conditioned to expect the safety of a predictable and notionally politically disinterested format. Therefore, the idea of censorship wasn't limited to the alt-space, it happened everywhere.

Alt-spaces were constructed partly in response to the symbolic violence of the official world. In the official world, racism and sexism – considered 'just a bit of fun' or the ubiquitous 'banter' – were part of a natural law that governed entertainment, which itself was paradoxically deemed to be free from ideology by the legitimating authorities within the official world. The *doxa* of the alt-space was therefore inverted in relation to the official world and was constructed as non-commercial, even anti-show business, rejecting the social conventions of its dominant cultural counterpart, and appearing as a carnivalesque mirror image. Its inhabitants established their own parallel institutions of production, distribution, and legitimation. The alt-space was also characterized by its use of language as a means of making a semantic distinction between itself and the old world of official entertainment.

Making Distinctions

Traditional comedy and light entertainment of the 1970s were mentioned by many of the participants, and the words they used to describe the official world indicate an unconscious understanding of the avant-garde. The word 'alternative', particularly, acted as a means of signification and differentiation, reminding audiences, promoters, performers, and journalists that they inhabited a second world of entertainment that opposed the predictability and staleness of the official world. When asked what they thought the terms 'alternative comedy' and 'alternative cabaret' meant to them, the participants' responses were broadly similar. Randolph the Remarkable (real name Phil Herbert; 2013 questionnaire) told me:

> 'alternative' came about as we were an alternative to mainstream white stand ups. larry grayson, kenneth williams, frankie howerd, hattie jaques [*sic*] – all things 'carry on'.

Phil presents us with a binary choice between the 'alternative' or the 'cool', and the mainstream or the 'straights'. Yet while 'alternative' was used as a marker of differentiation, there appears to have been few, if any, alternatives to the word 'alternative'. There was 'underground' and in many respects, this suited the embryonic space but for whatever reason it wasn't used. Notably, the word 'alternative', while it is an important marker of distinction for the performers themselves, wasn't universally adopted by them (Craig, 2000: 1–20). CAST, for example, preferred the term 'NV', not just because it suited their format, but for other reasons that are explained in the next chapter. The word 'alternative' had originally been employed in the name of the Alternative Cabaret collective and was later adopted by the journalists to refer to a kind of comedy or cabaret that broke with tradition. Dave Thompson, who opened the Alley Club at the Horse and Groom in central London in 1985, preferred to use the term 'new comedy' to describe his club (Thompson, 2013 questionnaire). Nevertheless, 'alternative' established itself as a term of reference and came to represent a distinction between the old and the new, the uncool and the cool, and the fresh and the stale. Randolph's point is reiterated by Andy Smart (2013 questionnaire):

> It marked us out as different. I'm very proud to have been part of it. It didn't get rid of Thatcher, but it did marginalise Jim Davidson, and Bernard Manning and other racist and sexist comics.

Being 'different' was an important marker to the alternative performers and we can see this reflected in members of a particular subculture, who used style and argot to mark themselves out from the rest of the crowd (Hebdige, 1993). Difference hinged on a notion of authenticity that was predicated on the belief that writing one's own material was more 'real' than reproducing the industrially produced jokes told by the 'uncool' traditional comedians.

Although the alt-space's comedians may have marginalized some traditional acts, it is worth remembering that Jim Davidson still managed to get work, first in sitcoms like *Up the Elephant and Round the Castle* (Thames Television, 1983–1985) and then later in gameshows like *The Generation Game* (BBC1, 1995–2001) and *Big Break* (BBC1, 1991–1998), and has maintained a relatively high profile ever since (IMDb website entry, 2016). Manning, Ken Goodwin, and others returned to the WMC circuit. Yet Andy also recognizes comedy's limitations as a potential instrument of social and political change, demonstrated here by the mention of opposition to Thatcher. However, this would deny satire's role as a form of passive resistance, for while satire is unable to raise a weapon in open revolt, it has the potential to raise social and political consciousness in its audiences and can exist as part of an overall strategy of cultural and political resistance (Mascha, 1998: 69–89).

For John Gordillo (2012 questionnaire), the terms 'alternative cabaret' and 'alternative comedy' can be located in a specific moment in time:

> Yes but purely as description of what was happening until – at latest – the early '90s. It describes a shift in the comedic targets/power relationships – a move away from the frilly shirted racists & hacks that came before.

John references the traditional comedians' sartorial style as well as their reinforcement-through-joking of the dominant power relationships. He suggests the 'alternative' label ceased to have any meaning in the late 1980s and this can be attributed to the newer comics' symbolic cultural capital, which they imported into the space during the transitional period, militating against so-called political correctness. As a 'dominant discourse', altcab and the attitudes that were articulated around it were faced with a dominant cultural backlash from around 1984, with the Conservative-supporting press publishing often-apocryphal stories of 'political correctness gone mad'. Women's, gay, and ethnic-minority rights were regarded by these papers and those who read them as evils that would limit individual freedoms.

Mark Hurst[5] (2012 questionnaire) points out some of the drawbacks and perceptions of the 'alternative' label:

> There were very different ideas and expectations, especially as you moved around the country as to what 'alternative' meant. I don't

---

[5] Formerly Mark Miwurdz.

mean literally, but, what it was a byword for. Some people thought it meant they were going to see political comedy, some thought it was just middle-class arty, and to others, it meant 'loads of swearing'.

Of course it was all those things a lot of the time. What it was supposed to be, I suppose, was a signal saying, 'Non racist, non sexist'. I was ok with the label myself.

It is telling that Mark uses words like 'arty' and 'middle-class'. These words reveal the way in which many people perceived the divide between altcab and traditional entertainment, yet they also remind us how art appreciation and production are perceived as middle-class pastimes or occupations (Bourdieu, 2003). S. Friedman (2010: 1–3) observes that the divide between altcom and traditional comedy was a cleft between not just old and young but working class and middle class. He argues that the working classes tend to have lower levels of cultural capital and thus make their comedy judgements based on their class habitus (Friedman, 2010: 1–3). However, one's appreciation for cultural forms is contingent on independent variables, and having come from a mixed American–British working-class background, my exposure to American stand-up in its commercial and counter*cultural* forms transcended the supposedly class-based tastes of British comedy consumers (Friedman and Kuipers, 2013: 180–195). Therefore, given my levels of a more specialized cultural capital in the shape of the Firesign Theatre, I found the references in Oxbridge humour easy to understand.

Bernard Manning represented the official world and was mentioned more than any other traditional comedian. This was particularly the case when performers spoke of their differences with the old-school performers and why they felt altcom was a necessary antidote to what they saw as the staleness of the official world. Mark Kelly (2012 interview) admits

I'd never considered being a comic, because I'd associated comedy, obviously, with Bernard Manning and so on…

The suggestion that altcom, in particular and as distinct from performance art or street performance, was an art form is contestable. I would argue that, in Britain, art is viewed with a certain degree of suspicion by many people. I put this question to Stewart Lee (2011 interview):

R.C. So true… Ummm… I wanted to ask you about how you see your work; do you see it as art?

S.L. Um, it's useful for me to see it as art. Um, because I'm not able to compete... um... well, I probably could now actually in the last year have really changed but, you know, you're basically, you basically construct a set of terms so that you'll feel comfortable with, don't you and I think if your goals are to be on mainstream telly, you have to be selling out stadiums and whatever, then you'll always be frustrated but, so you move your goalposts around and my goalposts were, you know, can I'd done so badly when I was with Avalon and I'd done so badly financially out of having co-written the theatrical hit of the decade, that actually I'm... um moved my goalposts to "can I make art and not lose money and make a living?" You know... but if you say in your brain that it's art first and foremost, then you go "oh I've just done a good piece of art and I didn't lose money. Brilliant". You know, but if your thing... if your thing is you want to be famous and successful, you're always going to be disappointed.

Even here, Stewart attempts to distance himself from the idea that his work could be construed as art. He reluctantly concedes that it is "useful" for him to see it that way but only as a means of making a distinction. However, he also acknowledges a kind of truth that comes with small-scale art production: that if one has a choice either to stick to one's artistic principles or to produce work for mass consumption or for fame, then taking the latter route may lead to riches but will not be as fulfilling. Yet his use of the term 'selling out', although here related to stadium tours, has a double meaning. For within countercultures and subcultures, the act of 'selling out' can be seen not only as an act of betrayal but also as the conversion of one's counter*cultural* capital into symbolic cultural capital.

Producing Talent and Reproducing Counter*cultural* Capital

In 1982, the embryonic circuit lost many of its major acts to television. These performers were members of the Comic Strip, who had migrated to Channel 4 and BBC2 with, respectively, *The Comic Strip Presents...* and *The Young Ones*. Although Ben Elton wasn't a member of the Comic Strip, he joined the migration when he became one of the writers for *The Young Ones* (Hamilton, 1981; Wilmut, 1989). During the latter part of 1982, cabaret courses were established at the Crown and Castle and Jackson's

Lane Community Centre to produce the next generation of performers. These courses self-consciously referred to themselves as 'cabaret' rather than 'comedy' courses and promised to teach novices "cabaret techniques" (McGillivray, 1990: 165). Jackson's Lane's entry in the *British Alternative Theatre Directory* (McGillivray, 1990: 165) says

> Beginners can learn cabaret techniques and established acts can try out new material (Booking essential).

The phrase "cabaret techniques" may sound rather ambiguous these days, but in the 1980s, the word 'cabaret' was used as a means of differentiation between the new entertainment and established forms of entertainment. Jackson's Lane remained a popular choice with novices until 1990, when the professionalization of comedy led to the proliferation of stand-up comedy courses, the biggest of which was Jill Edwards' comedy course based at City Lit in London, which tended to produce what I disparagingly referred to as 'identikit comedians'. It became easy to identify comedians that had attended a Jill Edwards course because of the way they presented themselves onstage and the jokes they told about themselves. This reminds us of the role the art schools play in the reproduction of legitimate artists, who learnt the same techniques that may have been taught for decades or centuries, but who produced no artworks that challenged the status quo. Art schools were often rejected by political-aesthetes as places that perpetuated the dull, stale, and impotent work of the past. Cabaret workshops reproduced counter*cultural* capital through the inculcation of the space's ethical framework. Workshop leaders provided informal guidance and allowed performers to develop their own style. Cabaret workshops covered topics like improvisation, writing, and compèring over the course of 11 hour-long sessions. Yet despite the use of the word 'cabaret', these courses tended to produce comedians of all kinds rather than performance poets, for example. Jugglers and more unusual acts tended to come from Covent Garden, where there's long been a street-performance tradition. Wendy Lee (2013 questionnaire), Julie Balloo (2012 interview), and Dreenagh Darrell (2010 interview) attended the course at Jackson's Lane, while Bob Boyton (2010 interview) attended a course run by Jean Nicholson at the Crown and Castle in Dalston a year earlier. For the performers who chose this route to the circuit, these courses also provided them with their first gigs. Cabaret courses like these were not certificated, and novices were taught by performers who were already working on the circuit (Boyton,

2013 Facebook conversation).[6] Therefore, the only qualifications they possessed were their stage experiences and their seniority, rather than a certificate that demonstrated their pedagogical competence. Instead, workshop tutors were legitimated by their students, who recognized the value of their experience. Some tutors were less enthusiastic about teaching than others, as Julie Balloo (2012 interview) explains:

> they had guest teachers in those days and the first teacher was Julian Clary, who was very nervous about teaching because he doesn't like teaching. He's quite shy really… he just wanted to do his act. So, he talked a little bit and then he said "Does anyone want to get up and do anything they've got?" So, I just jumped up out of my seat and did my Miss Australia and I didn't realize that would appeal to him and he absolutely loved it and, of course, it immediately appealed to him.

As this extract shows us, the emphasis was on support rather than formal instruction. Students were encouraged to perform material they had written and were given guidance and encouragement. Tutors had no formal training, and this is evidenced by the reluctance of Julian Clary to 'perform' the role of cabaret teacher. His role as he saw it was to act as a mentor and provide advice. Cabaret courses like these also reveal the supportive nature of the space – something mentioned by many of my participants, who began working in the space before the transitional period began. Yet the workshop idea breaks with individual informal guidance and places it in a setting that is not dissimilar to the stand-up comedy course in Griffiths' *Comedians* (BBC, 1979). This informal mode of learning reveals how capital is produced and circulated within countercultural spaces: a need arises for the production of particular experts or artists, and pedagogies are organically created to cater for this need.

Other performers, like me, were autodidacts and it is certainly the case that the first wave of performers taught themselves the basics, sometimes with the assistance of others. Steve Gribbin (2011 interview), who started Skint Video with John Ivens in 1983, sought guidance from a non-comedy source before taking to the stage:

---

[6] Workshop tutors at the Crown and Castle included John Hegley, Roy Hutchins, Andrew Bailey, and Ronnie Golden (Boyton, 2013 Facebook conversation).

we had no idea what we were doing... em... we fell in with a guy called Michael Belbin, who was... um... un... kind of a Media Studies, um... friend of John's, who tried to give us some sort of ideological background...

Like many performers, Steve was new to comedy and his tactic was to consult someone who understood the ideological positions of the government and the opposition. Therefore, Steve understood the *doxa* of the space, but he also identified a need for political satire, while recognizing the importance of relevant theories for the production of satire. Mike Belbin was a lecturer at Goldsmith's College, where Steve, John, and Brian were studying. Yet this is also an example of De Certeau's (1988) concept of bricolage, in which one makes do with what one has to hand. Given there were no models on which to base themselves, Skint Video needed to create something fresh from scratch, and so obtaining information in this way was crucial since the *doxa* of the space required an understanding of subversive politics and art forms, but, moreover, art's role in society more generally. Here we are reminded that the production of avant-garde art demands some knowledge of the artistic medium in which one is working.

Martin Soan, Malcolm Hardee, and the Greatest Show on Legs

Martin Soan (2013 interview) was one of three participants who began performing at a young age; the others were Ian Saville (2013 questionnaire) and Mark Kelly (2012 interview). Martin's route to performing was through the creation of a highly mobile Punch and Judy show. This was the first incarnation of the Greatest Show on Legs and was so called because Martin carried his entire set on his back (Soan, 2013 interview). Malcolm Hardee later joined him as his 'pot man'[7] in 1976 and the pair performed at seaside towns in Southern England and on the street and in pubs around South London (Hardee and Fleming, 1996). The early incarnation of the Greatest Show on Legs could be compared favourably to punk rock because of their 'no frills' approach to performing. Martin's interest in this kind of work stemmed from being "a bit artistic" and having a particular interest in

---

[7] The pot man is responsible for collecting money and is so called because the money is put into a pot or hat that is passed around.

puppetry. The story of how he became interested in the subject is worth quoting in full.

> I'd looked at some old engravings, eh, and at Pepys and the first Italian coming over and its history through the continent; Mr Punch... I mean, Punch was a descendant of various, uh, you know... uh, anti-heroes... Karogöz, Le Grand Guignol... they're all French, Turkish... and then I discovered that there was almost a link back and this [is] where theory separates: one was to China and one was basically to India and I found it fascinating the various research books I got out the libraries in those days... they had pictures of how to make his head and I found, like, the diagrams fascinating and, uh, just the idea of getting a plasticine model of your head and then papier mache-ing [*sic*] it on top. In the diagrams it looked fantastic. In reality, it was a load of old misshapen sodden shit, but it got me on the road and within I suppose about two years, um, I'd made three sets of puppets and ended up with a, you know, really efficient knockabout set of puppets that I really, really loved and I've still got one or two upstairs... ehm, basically made out of foam... and that's why Punch and Judy... it was just... it was lucky that I just got fascinated with its history... I wasn't academic in any way whatsoever, so this was my first piece of research. I hadn't read that much to be perfectly honest – fiction or non-fiction...
>
> Soan, 2013 interview

Martin tells us that he "wasn't academic" but here we have evidence of a specialized form of autodidacticism that manifests itself in a particular interest and reminds us of Bourdieu's (2003) description of the kind of specialized but unguided knowledge acquired by jazz and film buffs. Martin's use of bricolage to create his first puppet tells us that in order to create something new from scratch, one must make use of what is to hand. In the variety and music-hall eras, cultural capital in the form of the knowledge of specialized performance crafts was passed from generation to generation. However, with the disappearance of variety theatres and the concert parties, this knowledge had been lost, thus Martin had to go back to the fundamentals and start from scratch. This tactic corresponds to Wollen's (1975) first kind of avant-garde for its use of DIY to create something new (Andrews, 2010).

By the early 1980s, the Legs morphed into the naked balloon dance for which Martin and Malcolm were best known.[8] Malcolm says the balloon dance was inspired by Howard Brenton's 1980 play *The Romans in Britain*, in which men "were prancing around nude on stage" (Hardee and Fleming, 1996: 107–108). Brenton's play, which explored issues of imperialism and class power, was considered by its critics to be grossly indecent because it featured nudity and a male rape scene, and this led the taste and decency campaigner Mary Whitehouse to object to the play (Brenton, 2006). That was reason enough for Hardee and Soan to create the balloon dance.

> About a week later, I read that Mary Whitehouse *did* like cha-cha music. I thought I know what to do. We'll do a sketch and be naked in it but we'll have cha-cha music and then everybody will be happy. So we ended up with The Balloon Dance.
>
> Malcolm Hardee, in Hardee and Fleming, 1996: 107–108

The balloon dance involved three members, with a third member of the group recruited on an *ad hoc* basis. The most consistent third member of this period was clown Chris Lynam, whose solo routine involves shoving a firework up his bum. In the words of Malcolm, the performance consisted of "dancing the cha while holding two balloons each and swapping them round on the fourth beat to cover [their] genitalia" (Hardee and Fleming, 1996: 107–108). The Legs' use of naked male flesh was daring since it was often commonplace for females to perform nude or semi-nude in strip clubs; this absurd spectacle therefore unwittingly challenged sexist assumptions about nudity by using nude males in a comedy routine. The Legs were, in some sense, a male reimagining of the *tableaux vivants* of the post-war Windmill Theatre, which served as an incubator for the demob comedy of the 1950s. The balloon dance proved very popular on the fledgling circuit and they were eventually invited by Chris Tarrant to perform on *OTT* (Hardee and Fleming, 1996: 107–108). The Legs continued to perform at events around the country and when Malcolm opened the Tunnel Palladium in 1984, the team worked together infrequently, performing only at large-scale events. Due to their infrequent performances, Martin

---

[8] The Greatest Show on Legs also appeared on *OTT* (Central Television, 1981) (Hardee and Fleming, 1996).

decided to form another dance act called 'Two Fingers Cabaret' that included someone he only referred to as "Tony", who was a professional dancer (Soan, 2013 interview). The use of dance as a form of comedy entertainment is rather unusual because the form is usually confined to specialized dance venues rather than upstairs pub rooms. However, it is worth remembering that dance also featured in music hall and variety theatre, as well as the commercial cabarets of Paris like the Moulin Rouge. Eventually, Tony left to take up a job as an "entertainments manager" and Martin continued as a solo act, while retaining the name "Two Fingers" (Soan, 2013 interview). When I saw Martin perform his solo routine for the first time, it was at the Meccano Club at the Camden Head in 1986 and, on that occasion, he performed an escapology routine. I asked him about this:

R.C. You were solo, yeah, cos I remember you doing the escape act…

M.S. Oh, escapology…

R.C. Yeah!

M.S. And that was escapology… what, the joint?

R.C. Yeah.

M.S. And then…

R.C. I remember you going out the window and coming back in… [laughs]

[crosstalk]

M.S. Oh, the other one was to announce the escapology and go on a joint and go "I'm really out of it".

Martin wasn't the first to smoke a joint onstage; CAST also lit them up and passed them around the audience (Muldoon, 2011 interview). This, I would argue, is another counter*cultural* aspect to alternative performance and while it may seem rather passé today, we must remember that the possession of cannabis – a controlled substance – was and still is an arrestable offence. The street performers were especially responsible for some of the most interesting innovations, and we can think of Martin and others like him as "organic intellectuals" (Gramsci, 2003: 5–23) that have been produced within the field of street performance. Furthermore, his use of specialized knowledge allowed him to carve out a distinctive niche for himself that made him stand out from the rest. As Martin (2013 interview) himself says, "If you want to get on, get a gimmick. If you want to be noticed, be different".

Chapter 5

CAST, New Variety, and the Hackney Empire

Preamble

My association with CAST and the Hackney Empire began with my undergraduate work placement there in the spring of 1989. My tutor, Richard Stourac, had suggested the Empire to me when I was unable to find a placement with a community theatre company on Tyneside. My job at the Empire was to review local and national newspapers and cut out any articles that were related to the theatre and file them into an ever-expanding archive. I also dealt with telephone enquiries and performed general administrative duties. When I had some spare time, I would explore the building, sometimes finding myself upstairs in the upper circle, which had been closed for safety reasons (no one knew I was there) or below the stage, marvelling at the amazing machinery. I returned to the Empire for a few months in the summer of 1989 to research potential donors for the theatre and carry out administrative tasks. Even though the shows were going well and the Empire was more popular than ever, life for the theatre was precarious, and the threat of financial ruin was ever-present.

For this case study, I have made use of the Hackney Empire Archives at the University of East London and first-hand testimony in the form of interviews with Roland Muldoon, as well as the work of Catherine Itzin (1986) and Sandy Craig (1980), who wrote about Britain's alternative theatre movement and included informative chapters about CAST's work. Craig was also a local government officer with Hackney Council and was instrumental in facilitating the purchase of the Hackney Empire

(Muldoon, 2013). Roland Muldoon's book *Taking on the Empire: How We Saved the Hackney Empire for Popular Theatre* was published in early 2013 and I have found this useful because it offers a first-hand account of the period that helps to fill in the gaps.

Left-wing Rock 'n' Roll Kids versus the Square Lefties

Although there had been left-wing political theatre in Britain; the WTM, the Unity Theatre, and Joan Littlewood's Theatre Workshop, for example, highly mobile political theatre – the kind of theatre that could simply 'pop up' anywhere – only began in the mid-1960s. Formed in 1965 by husband-and-wife team Roland and Claire (née Burnley) Muldoon, CAST was the first of such companies. Roland came from a working-class Irish Conservative-voting family in Surrey, while Claire came from a working-class Yorkshire family that had been involved in the Independent Labour Party (Muldoon, 2010 interview; Hughes, 2011). The Muldoons and the core of what would become CAST met at the Unity Theatre in Camden, North London, where they worked as stage managers. In 1965, The Muldoons were expelled from Unity for allegedly plotting a coup against the management committee (Craig, 1980; Itzin, 1986; Kershaw, 1992; McDonnell, 2010: 98); the catalyst for their expulsion hinged on a dispute over the nature of Unity's music-hall productions, which Muldoon believed should be updated for a younger generation of left-wing audience. For his trouble, he was labelled a "Freudian Marxist" by the committee (Shallice, 2007). According to Roland (Muldoon, 2010 interview) there was "a generational gap and, you know, we were rock 'n' roll or whatever and they weren't". While Unity may have seen music hall as an authentic working-class form of entertainment (which it was), their approach was somewhat nostalgic and curatorial (McDonnell, 2010). Muldoon's mention of "rock 'n' roll" is instructive because it reveals how important this new music was to the youth of the 1950s and 1960s and how it helped to mark the difference between young people and the parental culture. The BBC, for example, saw rock 'n' roll as a passing fad and the only radio stations to play this kind of music were Radio Luxembourg and, later, the pirate radio stations like Radio Caroline and Radio London. It is likely that Unity regarded rock 'n' roll in a similar light to the BBC and furthermore saw it as being tainted by the conditions of its capitalist relations of production.

Unity was aligned with the CPGB and the Left Book Club, which meant that all matters had to be referred to the CPGB's headquarters on King Street (McDonnell, 2010; Muldoon, 2011 interview). The Muldoons represented the positions held by the emergent New Left, which had begun with the Aldermaston CND March, and were thus in opposition to the altogether more aesthetically conservative position of the CPGB. This was a struggle, as Baz Kershaw (1992: 82) observes, "between the old left and the new left" on the field of political-aesthetic discourse and these generational tensions rested on the fulcrum of rock 'n' roll. We can liken the tension between CAST and Unity to a form of repulsion that occurs between two autonomous poles on the counter-*cultural* sub-field. This repulsion inevitably led to the constitution of a new space of counter*cultural* production that tapped directly into the socio-political concerns of Britain's politically conscious youth. These concerns were increasingly being articulated through countercultural formations like CND, the Anti-Apartheid Movement, and the anti-Vietnam War movement (Kershaw, 1992; Hughes, 2011; Muldoon, 2011 interview). CAST wanted to attract this younger audience to Unity and, in so doing, inject new blood into an ageing British Left that was rather nostalgic and culturally insular.

The Birth of Alternative Theatre

Taking Ray Levine and David Hatton with them (Red Saunders followed later), the Muldoons established themselves at the Working Men's College in Camden, where Roland was now working as a drama teacher, and it was here that the idea for CAST was developed. CAST's philosophy was rooted in what Muldoon calls "archetypical theatre", which works by breaking the fourth wall and playing off the audience by addressing them directly (q.v. Brecht, 1964). CAST developed their theatre with the idea of fitting into folk clubs, where performers played 20-to-25-minute sets, which meant the plays needed to be short and sharp. This technique is what Muldoon refers to as 'presentationalism':

> you present yourself to the audience... talk directly... any scene that you can take in 60 seconds, you can do in 50... cut, cut, cut...
>
> Roland Muldoon, 2011 interview

CAST's style of quick cutting between scenes was primarily influenced by television advertisements with their fast edits and use of slogans acting as anchorage to a series of representational images (Kershaw, 1992; Shallice, 2007; McDonnell, 2010). Theatrical innovations like these had been taking place for decades and it is worth mentioning Vsevolod Meyerhold's spectacles, whose montage style was developed from the cinema (he had been closely associated with Eisenstein) and whose episodic style had an influence on the work of Piscator and Brecht (Stourac and McCreery, 1986). The Muldoons also borrowed the idea of music hall from Unity, which had in Roland's words "kept it alive, more than anybody", adding "Unity Theatre had seen the folk value of the music hall and they had a very good team of people doing this… you know, people like Lionel Bart" (Chambers, 1989; Muldoon, 2010 interview). This reminds us of the crucial role played by Unity and other left-wing companies as a training ground for young playwrights (Chambers, 1989). New technology has an evolutionary effect on theatrical forms: it inspires the artist(s) to render human the machines, the devices, and the very mechanics of industrial production and to co-opt them into a new aesthetic practice – in this case, avant-garde theatre.

Brecht's (1964) concept of scientific or 'epic' theatre extends and synthesizes Meyerhold and Piscator's work to create a kind of theatre that is fully engaged with political discourses and dispenses with the naturalism[1] of the so-called legitimate theatre (Brecht [1964] and Suvin [1972] refer to this as 'bourgeois' theatre, while Bourdieu [2016]) would call it 'commercial'), which is fixated with characters, emotions, and performer hierarchy (leads, principals, chorus, and so on), and is therefore diversionary. Darko Suvin (1972: 72) refers to bourgeois theatre as having an "illusionist" and "individualist" aesthetic, while the epic theatre possesses a "critical" and "dialectical" aesthetic. On the one hand, bourgeois/commercial theatre seeks to exploit the audiences' emotions and on the other, epic theatre seeks to inform and inspire its audiences to take action. Brecht's (1964) use of what he called the *Verfremdungseffekt*, or the 'distancing' or 'alienation' effect, deliberately

---

[1] 'Naturalism' refers to the predominant acting styles of the legitimate theatre that emphasizes the character's emotions, behaviour, and so forth. This kind of acting is often associated with the acting techniques of Constantin Stanislavski. So-called 'method acting' was developed from Stanislavski's technique by practitioners like Lee Strasberg, whose Actors' Studio produced Hollywood names like Marlon Brando and Rod Steiger.

breaks the fourth wall to engage directly with the audience, reminding them that they are watching a play and not a representation of real life. CAST's archetypicalism is therefore a bricolage adaptation of Brecht's *Verfremdungseffekt*, which combined elements of rock 'n' roll, satire, and music hall/variety to create a counter*cultural* kind of popular theatre that spoke directly to their generation but was still anchored in Marxism, despite its rock 'n' roll appearance.

However, to describe CAST as 'agit-prop' is incorrect and misleading, and Muldoon rejects this term as a means of describing CAST's practices. 'Popular theatre' is the term favoured by Roland, seemingly because of its close association with popular culture. CAST's rejection of formal terms like 'agit-prop' is what Bourdieu (1993, 1996) would refer to as "position taking" on the field. Officially, all theatre of this kind was singularly described by authorities as 'street theatre' regardless of whether it was performed on the street (Muldoon, 2013). According to Kershaw (1992: 82), CAST's style was a form of "carnivalesque", because it did not adopt the didacticism of continental agit-prop and was, instead, satirical and adopted a countercultural position of opposing the status quo – regardless of whether it was the authority of the state or the authority of the vanguardist left-wing parties like the CPGB (Muldoon, 2011 interview). Kershaw's (1992) use of the term 'carnivalesque' to describe CAST's work seems to trivialize it and ultimately devalue it against the relatively legitimated work of agit-prop companies like Red Ladder, who Craig (1980: 33) correctly describes as the "epitome of agit-prop". Muldoon prefers to use the conveniently coined term 'agit pop' to describe CAST's work because they used popular cultural forms like rock 'n' roll, while being, at the same time, agitational. As if to reinforce this, CAST's first show was called 'Agit Pop' and featured Adrian Mitchell, Ram John Holder (who played the character Porkpie in the Channel 4 sitcom *Desmond's* in the 1980s), and Janet Street-Porter, whose husband, Tim, operated the lights (Muldoon, 2011 interview). CAST's first proper play was *John D. Muggins is Dead*, which had Roland Muldoon playing the eponymous character, a young US soldier in Vietnam. Muggins was a sort of everyman character who was at everyone's beck and call (Itzin, 1986; Kershaw, 1992; Muldoon, 2010 interview). The name comes from the popular expression 'Muggins' for a 'dogsbody' archetype. This character-incarnation of Muggins was inspired in part by Hašek's *The Good Soldier Švejk* and partly by music-hall song (Muldoon, 2011 interview). Muldoon explains the essence of Muggins:

our character said "Don't talk to me about capitalism. I've eaten Walls sausages all my life"... um... uh... it was that... being cheated and mugged by society with our characters.

Roland Muldoon, 2013 interview

The very mention of "Walls sausages" here is in stark contrast to CAST's main rivals, Red Ladder (originally called Agitprop Street Players), who were formed in 1968 (Shank, 1978; Itzin, 1986; Red Ladder website, 2013). Both theatre companies took antagonistic positions to each other on the new alternative theatre field. CAST was satirical and used elements of popular culture, while Red Ladder's style was more didactic and rooted in the continental tradition of agit-prop; this is particularly evident in their use of Meyerholdian and Piscatorian visual imagery and is best illustrated in their early productions like *The Cake Play*, which was about productivity bargaining (Shank, 1978; Craig, 1980; Itzin, 1986; Red Ladder website, 2013). The central visual theme of this play centred on the cutting and distribution of a massive cake (Craig, 1980; Itzin, 1986). Such visual imagery, while no doubt arresting, was effective yet arguably too alien for average working-class British tastes. CAST understood the value of using popular culture to carry the message, which they rooted in the experience and practice and politics of everyday life – hence the reference to Wall's sausages. Their preference for this kind of approach is inscribed on their habituses and expressed through the use of cultural bricolage in their performances. The Muldoons' social and cultural capital was thus at variance with the more orthodox Red Ladder, not only because of their working-class origins, but because of their knowledge and use of British popular cultural forms.

Muldoon (2013 interview) often depicts CAST as a band of outlaws, who were aligned with no party or group. CAST played unusual venues like universities, technical colleges, and pubs. Additionally, they often opened for bands like the Rolling Stones and Pink Floyd and could thus claim to have some connection with left-leaning youth (Muldoon, 2013 interview). By contrast, Red Ladder became the house agit-prop company of the Trades Union Council (TUC) because of their close association with tenants' groups and trade unions. They were also the first political theatre company to receive Arts Council funding and their application was supported by the TUC, thus they were closely bound to the Labour establishment (Shank, 1978; Itzin, 1986). Muldoon (2013 interview) was under no illusions about CAST's role as mischief-makers: "I didn't ever think it was gonna lead to [laughs] a socialist revolution". However, not taking sides with one leftist faction or another led to accusations from sections of the Left that CAST was being "too countercultural" (Muldoon, 2013 interview). Roland recalls one particular example:

> Ewan McColl came along and he said to us, "You know, you shouldn't take the piss out of Mao Tse-Tung and Fidel Castro at the same time as attacking the enemies"... so we were defence as well... we're satire... you know we're living here... we're talking about working class consciousness here and what they say and all the rest of it...
>
> Roland Muldoon, 2013 interview

Like many counter*cultural* producers of the 1960s, Roland rejected the political vanguardism that characterizes many of Britain's revolutionary left parties and took a sceptical position against sections of the Left that refused to critique authoritarian figures that were considered to be on the same side. In this respect, CAST's position is close to that of the Weimar *Kabaretts*, which critiqued the Right but also pointed out the failure of the Left to respond to new threats and challenges posed by reactionary forces. By describing themselves as satirical, CAST could claim to be rightful inheritors of the anti-establishment positions previously held by the proponents of the earlier satire boom (*TW3*, *Private Eye* et al.), only in this instance, the satirists had come from solid working-class backgrounds rather than Oxbridge or public school. We can also see an echo of the struggle between the old and new that Roland talked about when he and Claire were expelled from Unity, with the old being represented by the CPGB and the orthodox Left, and the new Left represented by new libertarian socialist and anarchist political currents. The left-wing political field with its cast of regulars was now being challenged by upstart new actors that they were powerless to stop. The old guard would be forced to adapt or be consigned to the margins as an irrelevance.

The year 1968 marked a turning point for British theatre generally when the **Theatre Licensing Act** was repealed, meaning that scripts no longer had to be submitted to the Lord Chamberlain's Office (Morrison, 2014). This also meant that improvisation was finally legalized. During this time, CAST formed a brief, but often uneasy, partnership with political playwright John Arden and his partner/wife Margaretta D'Arcy in 1968. Arden wrote a play for CAST using the Muggins character entitled *Harold Muggins is a Martyr*, which as Kershaw (1992: 124) says, became "the focus for a series of epic encounters between three generations of political radicals committed to subversive cultural action". The play premiered on 14 June 1968 at the Unity Theatre and included actors from CAST and Unity, as well as Arden and D'Arcy (Kershaw, 1992; McDonnell, 2010). Arden recruited John Fox (who would go on to found Welfare State International) and Albert Hunt "to turn the approach to the theatre into an environment" (Kershaw, 1992: 124). However, the pressures of a tight schedule exposed the ideological differences between the parties. Unity felt that the spectacles created by Fox and Hunt would "offend the neighbourhood" (Kershaw, 1992: 124), while the Muldoons and Unity were opposed (for very different reasons) to Arden's inclusion in the play of a nude woman. According to Kershaw (1992: 127), "D'Arcy and Arden were keen to question the sexual exploitation of the fashion [for nudity]", which had now been unleashed by the repeal of the **Theatre Licensing Act**. The immediate aftermath of the act's repeal saw many gratuitously exploitative musicals like *Hair* and *Oh! Calcutta* in which nudity was a strong selling point (Barnes, 1969). The inclusion of a stripper was apparently done with the intention of analyzing the sexual exploitation of women (Kershaw, 1992: 127). However, this attempt at analysis was regarded by the Muldoons as being somewhat naive, and although it appeared to be well-intentioned, it was, at any rate, rejected by CAST in the bluntest of terms (Craig, 1980; Itzin, 1986; Kershaw, 1992; McDonnell, 2010; Muldoon, 2011 interview).

After a successful visit to Berlin in 1971, CAST split up in 1972, with Red Saunders taking half the group and going off to form Kartoon Klowns, which later became the foundation of RAR (Itzin, 1986; Muldoon, interview). The split occurred in the middle of filming 'Planet of the Mugs' (CAST had turned down a film offer from Andrew Loog-Oldham, the former Rolling Stones manager), which was never released. However, the main reason for the split was because the Muldoons had become parents and this made touring difficult, which invariably highlighted tensions within the group; money was another concern, but they had also fallen out with each other over the need for an Arts Council grant. McDonnell (2010: 103) notes that during this juncture, "The group sat on the sidelines while fractions within the working class began mobilizing against the new Conservative government, led by Edward Heath". However, CAST had no other choice: the Muldoons had a young child and as Roland (Muldoon, interview) notes facetiously, "they [the rest of CAST] didn't

Figure 4: CAST – *Sam the Man*

want to take their share of babysitting". The Muldoons also needed a regular income to provide for their young family and continue their work, and this forced them into a position where they had to apply for a grant or consider other options. During this time, Roland worked for Counter-information Services (CIS), which specialized in producing "anti-reports" into multinational companies and industrial conglomerates (Muldoon, 2013 interview). Even so, CAST managed to produce one play during this period: *Come in Hilda Muggins* was staged in 1972. Muldoon describes the play as "awkward", one that they had to "drag around the country" (McDonnell, 2010: 104). This was followed in 1975, however, by the play that would cement their reputation as Britain's foremost subversive theatre troupe and eventually secure their future.

Sam the Man was billed as "a Cartoon History of the Labour Party since 1945 to date" (McDonnell, 2010: 104) and was a savage critique of the Labour Party's betrayal of the working class. According to Muldoon (interview), *Sam the Man* was based upon Ralph Miliband's 1973 book, *Parliamentary Socialism*, and listed every twist, turn, and lie of the Labour Party, and it helped to provide CAST with their first ACGB grant of £5,000. The Arts Council grant allowed CAST to work full-time, but it put pressure on them to produce two plays a year; it also meant that they had to recruit new performers to replace those who had departed four years earlier. The Arts Council grant also meant that CAST altered their direction and, in McDonnell's (2010: 104) words, "The revolutionary 'gang' became the revolutionary theatre company".

The Road to New Variety

When CAST received their first Arts Council grant it marked a major change in direction from their earlier plays: not only were they compelled to produce two plays a year, but they also introduced more variety elements to their work. This meant more solo work from Roland, who often addressed the audience in the style of a stand-up comedian. What makes this work different from previous plays is the impact of Gramsci's (2003) theory of cultural hegemony. This is particularly evident in CAST's use of satire as a means of raising consciousness in their audiences as well as making them laugh. *The Prison Notebooks* (Gramsci, 2003) were translated into English by Hamish Henderson in the early 1970s and Roland (telephone conversation, 7 August 2013: 17:39) told me that he had encountered Gramsci's theories through a discussion group while he was involved in CIS (during CAST's hiatus) and later attended a course devoted to his work. This period foregrounds CAST's future direction as variety promoters and alternative impresarios, which is most evident in plays like *Sam the Man*, which makes use of stand-up comedy as a vehicle for radical ideas.

Feminism (second-wave feminism) had become an increasingly important focus of 1970s counterculture and had been formally adopted as a cause by the International Socialists (IS), the forerunner of the SWP, which Roland had joined in the middle of the 1970s but had left shortly thereafter. The IS organized Marxist seminars for CAST to provide them with a theoretical foundation from which to work (Hughes, 2011).

Feminism thus began to feature prominently in CAST's work. This is particularly evident in their 1979 play, *Full Confessions of a Socialist*, that was developed from *Confessions of a Socialist*, which was originally devised in the first quarter of 1976 but not performed until 1978 and happened against the backdrop of ACGB cuts (HE/CAST/SHO/2/1-7). In *Confessions* Roland performs a stand-up comedy version of his Muggins character and opens with the line "I hate my wife and my wife hates me". Here he is parodying the hackneyed set-up of the Northern club comedian's sexist 'take my wife' joke but one audience, in particular, questioned the line's construction. Muldoon explains:

> afterwards they stormed on the stage at Edinburgh [...] and demanded that I change the line to "MY wife hates me, I hate her" and it was all right from then onwards...
>
> Roland Muldoon, 2010 interview

On the other hand, Roland tells us that many men made a literal reading of his character and believed that he was expressing the very things that they were thinking (Harry Enfield's Loadsamoney and Warren Mitchell's Alf Garnett characters have also suffered from this). Roland's Muggins character in *Confessions* was a send up of the trad. comedians of the WMCs and the popular Granada Television series *The Comedians*. *Confessions* mainly discusses automation through the Universal Gottlieb Junction Joint Machine but takes in the contradictory nature of working-class package holidays to Francoist Spain and the failures of Harold Wilson (HE/CAST/SHO/1/1-7). The SWP also recorded the play on audio cassette (HE/CAST/SHO/2/8-11).

The final performance of *Full Confessions* occurred a month before their prescient Gala Evening of Variety at the Star and Garter pub in Putney in May 1979 (*TO* 80, 1979: 21) that featured CAST, Limousine (billed as a "funky seven-piece band"), and the Covent Garden Community Theatre Group (HE/CAST/SHO/2/9/1) and was a benefit for single-parent families. This show took place a month before the Comedy Store opened and provides us with a glimpse of CAST's future direction. It also reveals to us the kind of cultural capital the Muldoons possessed: this wasn't a stand-up comedy event; rather, it was an effort to revivify the moribund genre of variety theatre. Unfortunately, when I asked Roland about this show, he had no recollection of it. Yet this date tells us that the idea of a new kind of live entertainment genre was in gestation and ready to be born. It also tells us that the idea of creating a new form of entertainment cannot be solely attributed to the Comedy Store.

Roland took *Full Confessions* to New York as the guest of that city's Labor Theatre and won the *Village Voice*'s Off Broadway Theater Award (or OBIE). He says that he improvised performances every night and delivered the play "on the mike, a la stand-up comedy, direct to the audience" (Muldoon, 2010 interview). This is where the field of political fringe theatre begins to transform the comedy field but only at the counter*cultural* level. Around this time, Roland had "tentatively" joined Tony Allen's Alternative Cabaret collective, but the late nights were not conducive to family life and he left after seven gigs (Muldoon, 2010 interview). Roland also performed at the early Comedy Store, but he admits that he wasn't well-received by the audience and wasn't used to this (Muldoon, interview). The Comedy Store has always had a reputation for being a difficult gig for anyone performing political or thoughtful material. The clash between aesthetic sensibilities – on the one hand, the alt comedians and on the other, audience members who had been acculturated to accept only gag-driven comedy as legitimate – indicates a mismatch of habituses.

CAST's other plays from this period include *What Happens Next?*, "which warned trade unionists of the dangers of complacency over the issue of race" and was written in conjunction with the ANL (Muldoon, 2013: 25; HE/CAST/SHO/2/1-7), and *Goodbye Union Jack*, a piece that examined Britain's industrial decline, which was both a celebration of TUC General Secretary Jack Jones's imminent retirement, and a pun on his name and status. According to Muldoon, *Goodbye Union Jack* prompted a great deal of late-night debate over the play's title (Muldoon, 2013: 26). Alongside autodidacticism, discussion and debate are important elements in countercultural pedagogy and here we see the role of cultural forms in stimulating debate. This indicates that the play had fulfilled its role in challenging the cultural hegemony and the dominant political consensus. However, *What Happens Next?* attracted controversy and the guarantee against loss wasn't covered by some Local Arts Associations. Roland believed that the decision was a direct result of the group's involvement with the ANL (HE/CAST/SHO/2/1-7). The *Cornish and Devon Post* (9 September 1978) reported that CAST were due to play at the St John's Ambulance Hall in Launceston, but this was cancelled at the last moment and the venue was moved to the White Hart Hotel. A letter from the local Conservative Association published in *Western Morning News* (8 November 1978) read:

CAST, New Variety, and the Hackney Empire

Figure 6: CAST – *Hotel Sunshine*

of cannabis's illegality, the act of handing the audience a massive joint can be seen as an act of subversion in itself: the ideal 'topping off' to a politically subversive play.

Responding to Thatcher's Symbolic Violence

CAST's reputation for subversive acts often attracted the attention of the press and, on one occasion, Roland recalls an incident in 1982, when the *News of the World* (*NotW*) had sent a reporter (described by Muldoon [interview] as a "Benny Hill lookalike") and a photographer to obtain incriminating evidence of CAST's onstage drug-taking and ACGB money being wasted on a simulated assassination of Margaret Thatcher. The journalist did not get his story, but this did not stop him from fabricating one and the following Sunday, the *NotW* reported that CAST had "spent

1981, annual 'Smokey Bear's Picnics' were held in Hyde Park where hundreds of people would gather to smoke cannabis in open defiance of the police. The final picnic was quickly shut down by the Metropolitan Police's SPG.

Figure 7: CAST, Left-wing Teds

£34,000 of taxpayers' money on drugs" (Muldoon, 2013: 115). There was no point in suing the *NotW* for printing a malicious falsehood either, and as Roland says, "I asked the late Paul Foot if I could sue them, and he said you can only complain as they're so powerful they can print whatever they like" (Muldoon, 2013: 115). The printing of sensational stories like these reminds us of the press's contribution to a tapestry of myths and slurs that was deployed as a propaganda weapon to discredit the Left in the eighties. What this also serves to illustrate is how sections of Britain's notionally 'free' press are motivated by sales to the extent that fabrication is often seemingly preferred to producing truthful copy. Conversely, such 'news' items help to reinforce the notion, on the part of the legitimating authorities, that there are such things as 'worthy' (legitimate) arts and 'unworthy' (illegitimate) arts. These classifications seem to accompany the revived nineteenth-century social, but notional, classifications of 'deserving' and 'undeserving' poor. One, the heritage form, is characterized by opera and so on, and nominally deserves funding on account of its legitimacy that rests entirely on its assumed social value. The other, the low cultural form, here apparently characterized by CAST's politically subversive theatre, is afforded no measure of legitimacy.

CAST, New Variety, and the Hackney Empire

Figure 8: CAST – Protest outside the Arts Council of Great Britain's HQ

Muldoon (2010 interview; 2013: 30) says that, despite their lack of funding, CAST saw *Sedition 81* "as a challenge to the New Comedy" and with the Arts Council subsidies now cancelled, CAST was placed on hiatus and the Muldoons migrated to the embryonic alternative space, creating NV as a form of cultural intervention. "We were setting down a marker", insists Muldoon (2010 interview), "because you can't believe that you can have a left idea without something going on". Thus, NV assumed simultaneous positions against light entertainment, old variety, and the Thatcher regime. At this point in time, political comedy on the embryonic altcab circuit was limited to a small number of performers. It is difficult to say with any degree of certainty whether or not CAST were entirely responsible for this shift in attitudes on the circuit. Indeed, Tony Allen was already performing politically subversive material as early as 1979. One thing is for certain: the economic austerity that was being imposed on the country by the Thatcher government was beginning to have a deleterious effect on people's lives. This and the inner-city riots, coupled with the continued occupation of Northern Ireland, were starting to filter through to the altcab circuit and by 1982, we can see that the process of importing political discourse into the new comedy field was more or less complete.

This is evident in Alexei Sayle's appearance on the late-night show *OTT* (Central Television, 1982), in which he delivers stinging diatribes about austerity economics, the ideological turpitude of the Social Democratic Party, and the government's moralizing rhetoric in the aftermath of the inner-city riots. Other performers of this kind would follow, and the altcab and NV circuits were the only spaces that allowed for views like these to be expressed. Indeed, these performances can be described as didactic because the comics conveyed knowledge to their audiences through the medium of humour. This knowledge wasn't available elsewhere because the discourses produced about the riots within the corporate media tended to frame any discussion in terms of criminality. Furthermore, the range of permitted discourse within the mainstream media was narrow and focussed almost exclusively on efficiencies, consumer choice, and personal responsibility as well as Thatcher's quasi-*Poujadiste*[3] notions of entrepreneurialism and petit bourgeois self-denial (Bourdieu, 2003). These positions opposed the so-called 'permissiveness' of the 1960s and 1970s and were fused with idealized notions of Victorian moral conduct. *Sedition 81* was thus an affront to the Thatcher regime's appeal to moral rectitude as well as a subversive marker to the new performers on the altcab circuit.

CAST's main parliamentary nemesis was the Conservative MP Teddy Taylor, then the MP for Glasgow Cathcart (1964–1979) and a prominent member of the reactionary Monday Club. When the Conservative Party won the 1979 general election, Taylor lost his seat but his cause was shared by others in the party who wanted to abolish the ACGB or, at least, restrict its funding to what they considered to be more legitimate causes. Taylor was returned to the Commons in the 1980 Southend East by-election and immediately resumed his witch-hunt against CAST (Muldoon, interview). According to Mike Parker (unpublished newspaper article draft [1], CAST archives, 1986), Taylor said "It is an outrageous waste of money. I'd like

---

[3] *Poujadism* takes its name from Pierre Poujade, the owner of a book and stationers shop in Lot, France, who formed the Union de Défense des Commerçants et des Artisans (UCDA) to organize tax protesters. The UCDA gradually became associated with Poujade himself. The UCDA's loose doctrine was referred to as *Poujadism* and was characterized by anti-intellectualism, xenophobia, anti-parliamentarianism, and petit-bourgeois asceticism (Trouchard, 1956; Bourdieu, 2003). Therefore, any reactionary conservative movement that espouses such beliefs is often described as *Poujadiste* by political commentators.

all grants withdrawn from this theatre company and intend to make representations to the authorities". This view was shared by others in the Conservative Party, most notably Norman Tebbit, the MP for Chingford, who had urged the abolition of the ACGB during the Heath government. CAST was also targeted by James Goldsmith's magazine *NOW!*, which served as a vehicle for Goldsmith's reactionary political views (Muldoon, 2010 interview). Goldsmith, who was known to take a dislike to anyone who questioned his business methods, had been knighted in Harold Wilson's Lavender List[4] and, in 1976, had issued 60 writs against the satirical magazine *Private Eye* with the intention of bankrupting it and imprisoning its editor, Richard Ingrams (Milne, 1986; Bindman, 2007). Few people were willing to confront him. Yet CAST welcomed the negative publicity that Taylor and others had helped to generate for the press and delighted in winding him up, because any publicity, however negative, is often perceived as good publicity and can often work to one's advantage. Indeed, the negative publicity generated by the media over the antics of bands like the Stones or the Sex Pistols only served to enhance their image and increase their popularity. In this respect, CAST's claims to being rock 'n' roll or proto-punk are not without foundation: they were theatre's equivalent of a rock band and used tricks that played upon and enhanced their subversive reputation (De Certeau, 1988).

It was around this time that CAST moved into the Diorama,[5] near Regent's Park. The Diorama, as its name suggests, was a Georgian cinema that was built in the 1820s and had been squatted by a few diverse groups including CAST, the new circus company Ra Zoo, filmmaker Dennis Jarman, and "other fragments of the hard-pressed counterculture" (Muldoon, 2013: 31). At the same time, CAST's funding for its theatre projects was terminated by the ACGB, because the funding body were displeased that money which had been allocated for their play *Hotel*

---

[4] The so-called 'Lavender List' was Harold Wilson's 1976 resignation honours list. Those who appeared on the list were mainly from the political right and questions were inevitably raised as to Wilson's judgement in the list's drafting. The most curious inclusion of all was a knighthood for James Goldsmith, who had been concerned about Britain's 'slide into communism' and had held meetings with former military officers who shared his views and were planning to stage a coup d'état against the Wilson government and install The Earl of Mountbatten as Prime Minister. The coup never went beyond a show of force at Heathrow Airport under the rubric of 'anti-terrorism manoeuvres' (q.v. Curtis, 1999; Kennedy, 2016).

[5] The Diorama is part of the Crown Estate and so technically belongs to the Queen.

Sunshine had been diverted to their NV project (Double, 2020). This meant that the Muldoons had to seek funding from elsewhere (which I will discuss later in more detail). The Muldoons already had a great deal of variety and comedy expertise under their belts, meaning that CAST were better placed than other fringe theatre companies to make a transverse migration from the field of alternative theatre to alternative talent-agency/variety promoters on the border of the new field of altcab. This is indicative of their counter*cultural* competence: being able to spot underground opportunities and to seize upon them by using their DIY skills to create cultural spaces in a way that other companies would have found difficult to execute (De Certeau, 1988; McKay, 1996; Bourdieu, 2003). Muldoon says,

> I mean from my point of view, I won an OBIE in New York (1979–1981) for what was stand-up theatre basically… which was a comedy rant for 60 minutes… um… and they could see it in *The Village Voice*… but they didn't have a problem with that concept at all… if you see what I mean… and I would… and we all were doing sort of stand-up type plays by the end, you know, New Variety began in 1981… and *Sedition* was '81, which was a tour of Britain as a cabaret-comedy show…
>
> Roland Muldoon, 2010 interview

Here, Muldoon mentions "comedy-cabaret" as a distinct form of entertainment and it is possible to deduce that CAST realized what was about to happen to alternative theatre companies and were unconsciously preparing for the time when they would have to leave theatre altogether. The left-wing theatre field was being squeezed; most companies would be forced to relocate, disappear entirely, or take the counter*cultural* capital they possessed and use it symbolically by migrating to the partly legitimated field of touring theatre, as Red Ladder did in 1985.

The Comedy Store has often been credited with breaking altcom to a wider audience and rightly so, but the groundwork had been done throughout the 1970s with acts like John Dowie (who came out of Birmingham Arts Lab) performing in art centres around the country; 20th Century Coyote's appearances at the Band on the Wall in Manchester (Peters, 2013); and CAST's more stand-up-orientated plays towards the end of the decade. CAST's *raison d'être* was different to that of the Store: they were very much part of the counter*cultural* space, while the Store assiduously constructed itself on the margins of the dominant culture. Out of its two promoters, Don Ward and Peter Rosengard, only Ward had some knowledge of the entertainment industry – albeit its seedier side (Cook, 2001).[6] Rosengard was looking for a British version of American stand-up comedy, while Ward's comedy roots were in an altogether more traditional, if not low-brow, field of the performing arts, as the compère of a strip club (Cook, 2001). Thus, we can see that the Comedy Store was the product of Ward's hard-headed business sense and Rosengard's amateurism. The Muldoons, on the other hand, were from working-class backgrounds and had brought their aesthetic dispositions with them to the field of popular entertainment, their cultural capital having been produced in part by their work in alternative theatre.

It is also worth noting that after its move to new premises in March 1983, the Store left its former life as an avant-garde comedy space behind and became a straight stand-up-comedy club. Ward now forbade anything that resembled variety on his stage – this included comedy impressionists, whom some impresarios and comedians tend to regard as 'cheats', because they use their vocal skills rather than jokes to raise a laugh (Balloo, 2012 interview; Gribbin, 2012 interview; Kelly, 2012 interview). However, in 1983, the Store was the only venue to have actually done this; the rest of the clubs referred to themselves as cabaret clubs and offered variety bills. In the same year, CAST began its NV shows at the Old White Horse in Brixton. The pub had a small hall attached to it that had been used as a billiard hall. The Old White Horse had been 'discovered' by their administrator, Warren Lakin,[7] who had driven around London looking for venues. There were many pubs like the Old White Horse in London, whose halls and function rooms had once hosted pub-rock bands but were either being used to store unused equipment or had been turned into games rooms. Many of these rooms would be given new life when they were turned into altcab or NV venues, and most of the time a pub landlord would be happy to allow the room to be used, because it meant increased bar takings.

---

[6] Don Ward was previously the compère and organizer of a strip club but had also worked as an unsuccessful stand-up comedian.

[7] Lakin, a former local Southend journalist, would later go on to manage Linda Smith (he was also her partner) and run the Sheffield-based talent agency Popular Productions in the late 1980s. He later ran Lakin McCarthy Entertainments, also based in Sheffield, but has since retired. http://www.lakinmccarthy.com/about.asp.

The Birth of New Variety

Variety as an entertainment form had been, rightly or wrongly, identified in the public consciousness with the BBC's variety shows like *Seaside Special* and the other variety-*style* programmes, all of which seemed to hark back to a bygone era but had, in reality, been pieced together from scraps of memories and held together with the glue of mythology. *The Royal Variety Performances* on ITV also cemented in the public memory a mythologized continuum of variety that had seemingly existed for eons, but which appeared to live in a hermetically sealed space outside of history. In addition to this, the BBC screened *The Good Old Days*, a Baudrillardian (1994) simulation of music hall that bore a passing resemblance to the form itself. The general public's perception of variety and music hall was thus a somewhat sanitized one that was helped along by this simulation. Indeed, in the WMCs, to which many variety performers had migrated when the theatres had closed, variety was mainly overshadowed by show bands, bingo, strippers, and comedians. Programmes like *The Wheeltappers and Shunters Social Club* (Granada Television, 1975) used the WMC format and usually offered one variety act per show, but they played second fiddle to the racist and sexist jokes of rising star Bernard Manning and the guest comedians who appeared on the show. Many of the variety artistes who played the halls and theatres had been recruited to the new medium of television in the 1950s, but these performers were mainly stand-up comedians or double acts like Morecambe and Wise. The plate-spinners, jugglers, and paper-tearers were mainly left behind and appeared for the occasional television special but, as an entertainment form, variety had been shunted into the sidings. Occasionally rolled out like a vintage steam locomotive on a heritage railway line, it could only remind visitors of its glorious past. Old-style variety was comatose and on life support, and contrary to Michael Grade's thesis on BBC4's *Story of Variety* (BBC, 2012), the concept of variety had actually been kept alive by CAST/New Variety on their circuit and at the Hackney Empire. Grade, for whatever reason, appears to have overlooked this, and I would suggest this is because his background in legitimated entertainment caused him to misrecognize NV as a form of entertainment, possibly because of CAST's reputation for subversive acts.

For the Muldoons, NV was more than just a simple revival of a dead form; it was a fresh version of variety that situated itself in the present and still contained strong traces of rebellion. Significantly, NV was positioned against Allen and Sayle's Alternative Cabaret collective.

Alternative Cabaret was… um… limited in our opinion, because it only had a few acts… you know, it had a theory that it had a few acts who would go on tour, wasn't for everybody… but New Variety was for everybody.

Roland Muldoon, 2013 interview

Alternative Cabaret's roster of performers was small, and many had left for other fields by 1982. Roland's insistence that NV was "for everybody" therefore reveals that it was for all comers rather than a select group of performers that were linked through social capital. NV was also opposed to Alternative Cabaret in another way: it was supported by public money, something which Tony Allen and Alexei Sayle had vehemently opposed, believing that ACGB funding would compromise their art. Furthermore, the employment of the word 'new' as a prefix to 'variety' serves to mark a distinction between the old politically disinterested variety and the new variety. To this end, CAST made a conscious decision to filter out the racists and the bigots (Muldoon, interview) who had cluttered up the television's variety schedules. In this way, the Muldoons applied their judgements, produced through their habituses, to make distinctions and thus lay the foundations for what they saw as a new socially inclusive popular form of entertainment. Its emphasis on variety and its refusal of what Roland saw as an 'alien' entertainment form in the shape of cabaret defined it aesthetically and relationally.

Roland is insistent about variety's socio-political value:

> we keep it alive; so that it can flower again at a time of social confusion [...] you can't believe that you can have a left idea without something going on.

Roland Muldoon, 2013 interview

It is interesting that Roland uses the words "social confusion". We can see this in the socio-political upheavals that are characterized by the constant cultural and ideological battles on the terrain of the class struggle, which had reached fever pitch by the 1980s and had been stoked in part by the Conservative-owned press. The Thatcher government had encouraged people to think of themselves as individuals or entrepreneurs, with no thought for the society in which they lived. Conversely on the British Left, there is a po-faced, self-referential, and inward-looking attitude among some parties, and certain forms of culture (youth culture, especially) tend to be viewed as peripheral or vulgar. Rock or reggae music are seen as having no function other than as diversions, and for some on the Left, 'culture' means aspiring to bourgeois or high-brow culture. In other words, the kind of mass-produced high cultural forms that are produced by what Adorno and Horkheimer (2001) called "the culture industry". Yet left ideas are meaningless if they cannot relate to people's everyday lives, and culture is a means of connecting with those lives and addressing social concerns. Laughter and dancing are closely bound to the body and thus both activities may be seen as 'base' by the more ideologically ascetic Left parties that are hoping to recruit new members. Yet it is culture that holds us together as a society and within whatever communities we happen to belong to; it occupies a crucial role in everyday life. Few but the faithful are prepared to commit themselves to a life of political asceticism and self-denial. There is little point in proselytizing on street corners if the promise of joy and celebration are seen to be absent. In this sense, carnivalesque cultural events serve a very vital function in terms of allowing members to let off steam.

New Variety and Funding

CAST had been running their NV shows in parallel to their theatre work from 1982, but the Muldoons had found that, by 1985, they could no longer continue touring their plays and so instead devoted their attention to their work in NV. From this point onwards, they are known as 'CAST/New Variety' (though they would often use a confusing variety of names). Although CAST had been forced to abandon their theatre work, they harboured serious thoughts of returning to it at some future stage (Muldoon, interview). Meanwhile, they would put most, if not all, of their efforts into their circuit and, eventually, the Hackney Empire.

As well as the Old White Horse in Brixton, NV had a core of eight spaces throughout London. In the early 1980s, CAST/New Variety secured funding from the GLC for a tour of London's 32 boroughs (Muldoon, interview). How they managed to secure funding can be attributed to a mixture of audacity, charm, and serendipity. Tony Banks, then Labour's GLC councillor for Tooting, had written an open letter defending subsidies for the arts and culture in the *Evening Standard*, so when Labour formed the majority on the Council in 1981, Banks became the chairman of the influential Arts and Recreation Committee. Muldoon (2010 interview) tells the story:

> And I wrote to Tony Banks saying "Well, let me help you" and then he... the weird thing was that I was on the tube with my daughters going to meet him and he was there, sitting opposite us and my daughters were so charming and we were so great and [he] was so charmed by us [...] Then I went into the GLC building... into the office and there was this bloke... that I'd been on the tube with... but, anyway, he said "I'm going into the chamber now to get a million pounds when you come back, tell me what you would do with it"... So I divided it by the minimum Equity wage into a million, when he came back I said, "You should employ 200,000 [slight laugh] artists, of which one third will run off with the money, one third will be absolutely fucking useless and the other third will change the world"... you know... and, uh... he didn't do that... but he made it accessible for us to get money...
>
> Muldoon, 2010 interview

Access to GLC funding was vital to the NV circuit because without this, they would not have been able to pay the acts at a rate that was just above the Equity minimum wage (Muldoon, 2010 interview). CAST/NV was one of a handful of promoters who paid the going rate for performers. Other promoters were less generous, and many would operate a sliding scale on which headline acts were paid substantially more money than the support acts or the compère. This financial hierarchy can be traced back to the days of music hall and it was an issue which led to the 1907 performers' strike for better pay (Honri, 1997). Of course, there were less scrupulous promoters who would, in spite of a full house, pay the acts a pittance and pocket the remainder of the takings. Promoters like these did not last long in the business, with word of their underhandedness being spread around the circuit.

Under Labour, the GLC committed itself to arts and culture and took a strong line on equality; and under the leadership of Ken Livingstone, the GLC allied itself to the Rainbow Coalition, which opposed racism, sexism, and homophobia (Campbell and Jacques, 1986; Garnham, 1987). It also pursued green policies and thus opposed Thatcher's neoliberal economic and social policies. The Rainbow Coalition became a target for the right-wing press, which cited its policies as extravagant and indicative of Labour's profligacy in local government. However, London is a multicultural city, and the celebration of these cultures was seen by Livingstone and the ruling Labour group as vital to creating social harmony as well as celebrating the city's diversity. The generosity of the GLC's grants was never matched by those of the ACGB, which were paltry by comparison (Muldoon, 2013 interview). The ACGB was under a new picked chairman, William Rees Mogg, whose view of the arts and culture was based largely on his aesthetic disposition, and his vision was imposed through the policy document 'The Glory of the Garden', which showed a preference for legitimate art practitioners, and also split the ACGB into regional arts boards, making the touring of plays difficult, because a grant application now had to be submitted to each regional board (Dorney and Merkin, 2010). In 1986, the GLC was abolished and responsibility for funding the arts fell to the individual borough councils and Greater London Arts (GLA) (Hipkin, 1986: 41–42). Consequently, the NV circuit was reduced to a core of six venues (including the Hackney Empire), all of them in Labour-controlled boroughs: Lambeth, Hackney, Haringey, Hillingdon, Brent, and Waltham Forest. These venues continued alongside the Hackney Empire until they were each forced to close because of a funding shortfall.

Disseminating the Message/Educating the Public

Publicity is important to any cultural promoter and the way in which the message is disseminated to the public is crucial for attracting audiences. Posters and flyers typically combine images with text, and during the 1980s, publicity materials like these were produced by small-scale operations using DIY methods to save money, since only commercial operations – financially supported by sponsorship and large volumes of door receipts – could afford professional typesetting and printing. CAST's posters were originally hand-drawn and used photographs of the performers, which were juxtaposed with the name of the acts. The Hackney Empire posters adopted the variety block format, and this was a deliberate attempt not only to recall the posters of the music-hall and variety eras, but to make a statement. Muldoon says that they

> did them in a contemporary form, because we knew we were [...] borrowing from the great variety tradition [...] also, we were using

names; the names aren't just a picture, you know, you're gonna have Seething Wells and Paul Merton and… so you needed these kind of distinct dots… which is a fascinating thing to do… cos nobody but nobody was doing anything like that [...] the people look at them and say "Cor, look Frank Skinner" and you know… you know… Eddie Izzard or you know [...] they're all on at the Old White Horse for £2.50 and it's like a variety bill… but a contemporary variety bill… and then along came desktop publishing and then everything changed…

Muldoon, interview

Like CAGG, CAST found that once desktop publishing was introduced, the nature of the posters changed. With the production of digitized promotional materials, the public now came to expect slick, uniformly produced posters with no spatial inconsistencies (however small) or other flaws that gave the posters their character. What is also interesting about CAST's posters and those of the Hackney Empire is what Muldoon (interview) describes as the "subliminal" use of the proscenium arch at the top of the poster (at CAGG, this was a 'masthead'). According to Muldoon (interview), this was done deliberately to plant the seed in the public's mind that what they were about to see was a variety show. It was therefore a very subtle means of educating a public whose habituses had no conception of variety shows as a live form of entertainment. On the other hand, variety was seen as outmoded, possibly déclassé, with old artists appearing occasionally on television on shows like the BBC's *Seaside Special*. Posters like these refuse the aesthetic of the pure gaze and, instead, engage the viewer by providing them with the necessary information to make choices or pique their curiosity to the extent that they may go and see the show being publicized. Alternatively, the graphic design and the information provided on the poster may appeal directly to a viewer, whose habitus may possess a political-aesthetic disposition. Posters and flyers like these give equal space to form and function. CAGG's posters, for example, deliberately recalled the photomontage style of John Heartfield and asked the viewer to consider the form equally with its function (Campbell, 2022).

Roland (Muldoon, 2010 interview) was quick to point out that there is no link between the old and new forms of variety, and that the relationship between the two variety generations is symbolic in both the use of the word itself and the appropriation of old variety's visual language, which

198 A Cultural History of British Alternative Cabaret (1979–1991)

Figure 9: Hand drawn flyer for Wood Green TU Centre

Figure 10: New Variety Benefit poster. Brighton Bottle Orchestra, Attila the Stockbroker, John Dowie, Kevin McAleer, Hope Augustus, the Dinner Ladies

can be seen in the use of the 'variety block' style that was common to music-hall/variety posters (see Figure 10). CAST's posters reveal their cultural capital, which has been symbolically deployed to communicate an educative as well as a promotional message.

If we compare Figure 10 to the classic variety-block posters from the variety era, we can see some similarities. In the Hackney Empire posters of the 1950s, when the variety theatres were at the beginning of their decline, there were nine acts on the bill, most of whom were speciality acts or comedy characters, but no stand-up comedians. If we compare the number of acts on the bill to the poster in Figure 10, we can see there are fewer acts in the new Hackney Empire poster. This was because each performer, apart from the headline act, performed for 20 minutes. In the music-hall/variety era, a performer's set would last a few minutes and during the music-hall era, there was one long show per night, while during the variety era there were two shows an evening. We also see in Figure 11 that there are two stand-up comedians on the bill (Julian Clary, as the Joan Collins' Fan Club, and Paul Merton), while a mixture of character comedians and speciality acts complete the bill. By comparing both posters we see that NV is paying homage to a past form that has been embodied in their habituses, while simultaneously updating the poster design by including an image of the headline act. During the variety era, images of the acts were included by the larger theatres, like the Hippodrome. In this way, the design of Figure 11 emphasizes the generational gap between the old and new forms of variety theatre. This homage to the past is evident in the title "Summer Show", which recalls the summer seasons and end-of-the-pier shows at Britain's seaside resorts.

In addition to the Hackney Empire, CAST operated a circuit of six venues around London that were modelled on variety theatres, meaning the stage was 'end-on' and the seating arranged in rows rather than cabaret style. CAST already possessed a full lighting and sound system, while many of the altcab clubs had rudimentary lighting and sound systems, and although they offered variety, many of these clubs could not employ jugglers, for example, due to ceiling height restrictions. NV shows often consisted of a poet, a comic, a speciality act,[8] and a band to close the evening. Figure 9 is a hand-drawn flyer for a NV show at Wood Green Trade Union Centre. This particular flyer was created using Letraset and pen, and typifies the DIY approach to publicity that can also be found

---

[8] These were often jugglers or street performers.

200 *A Cultural History of British Alternative Cabaret (1979–1991)*

Figure 11: Early CAST presents New Variety flyer for Wood Green Trade Union Centre (1986?)

in CAGG's posters and flyers. NV's hand-drawn posters are indicative of restricted production, and although they were reproduced thousands of times over, they retain the imprint of restricted production. Poster art tends to lack the legitimacy of the consecrated wall art (paintings) displayed in galleries; unless they are part of an exhibition at the Victoria and Albert Museum, for example, posters are assigned a lower social value. Nevertheless, these publicity materials are created by artists, who have had training in graphics at art school or university, and although they lack the glamour and social value associated with legitimated art, they qualify as art of a particular kind, and are consecrated within the tight circles of counterculturalists and avant-gardists.

The bills shown on this flyer (Figure 11) show us the mix of performance styles that could be seen at any NV show. The acts on these bills demand a closer look. There are only three acts that can be described as stand-up comedians. Janice Perry, for example, is a performance artist, while Gary Howard, who appears with veteran comedian John Dowie, is a former member of the a capella group, the Flying Pickets, and the 7:84 Theatre Company. Skint Video, who are

CAST, New Variety, and the Hackney Empire

Figure 12: CAST presents New Variety at the Cricklewood Hotel (1988?)

listed for 2 November, are a musical comedy double act and are given an entire evening. Thus, we can see music being strongly represented and each show features some kind of musical act. One name that stands out is Hank Wangford (real name Dr. Samuel Hutt, who was also a general practitioner), a spoof country and western star, who played alongside Billy Bragg and the Frank Chickens at miners' benefits (Raines, 1988). Wangford, a regular on John Peel's Radio One show, came from a Communist family and his father had been a journalist (Raines, 1988). His band was also popular at the GLC free festivals that were held in open spaces around London in the early to mid-1980s. Here, then, we can see some overlap between performers on these bills and the GLC, which further emphasizes the close relationship between CAST/NV and the former. The door prices here are set at an affordable level and most altcab shows in London never cost more than a couple of pounds. At his time, the Comedy Store and Jongleurs were charging an admission price of around £5.

In contrast to the previous image, the flyer for the Cricklewood Hotel (Figure 12) uses a mix of desktop publishing and handwritten lettering in the individual panels. The dayglo colouring also attracts the eye, making the flyer stand out.

The 23 and 30 October are specifically billed as comedy nights. We can see that 30 October, especially, is not dominated by stand-up comedians and the night mixes poetry, spoof magic, and character comedy, whereas on 23 October there are three stand-up comics and a speciality act. The 16 October is more typical with poet Claire Dowie, comedian–accordionist John Maloney, Red Stripe (formerly of a capella band, the Flying Pickets, and 7:84 Theatre Company) performing a capella and dance, and juggler Steve Rawlings completing the bill. Roland (Muldoon, interview) says that the use of the performers' photographs was a further innovation, and this was later adopted by CAGG in 1989.

Flyposting, although frowned upon by the authorities, was still legal at this point and was CAST's principal method of publicizing their shows. Pete Moreland and Tim Horrocks were charged with the task of covering London in A0-sized posters. Without quite realizing it, however, CAST found themselves involved in what were dubbed "the poster wars" with what Roland (Muldoon, 2013: 62) calls the poster 'mafia', who were working for the recorded music industry and music promoter, Vince Power, of the Mean Fiddler group. These companies banded together and took down the Hackney Empire's posters and pasted up their own, but CAST fought back as Roland explains:

> We adopted the guerrilla strategy of drawing the enemy fire more and more into the Hackney area, where we could react more easily, by printing and posting more than the normal amount [...] Each time we put ours up, they put theirs on top, and then we would put up another one on top of that, to which they would respond by bringing in another poster from Hammersmith or Kilburn (where two Mean Fiddler venues were located), or any one of the other centres from outer London, in order to try and obliterate our posters.
>
> Muldoon, 2013: 62

Eventually, the Empire entered into a truce with the poster companies, which led to the creation of Diabolical Liberties (DL), now a major player in outdoor advertising, to do the flyposting. DL also took on contracts from other promoters and the profits were ploughed into the Empire. However, Hackney Council wasn't pleased with the borough's walls and hoardings being plastered with posters and decided to act, paying for a team to remove them. The Council even tried to pursue the matter in the courts but to no avail (Muldoon, 2013). In an ironic twist, DL accepted a contract from the Council's in-house group, Heart of Hackney, who were attempting to ride the coattails of the International Anniversary Celebration of Pablo Picasso by promoting an "evening of wine, women and song" at the Central Methodist Hall opposite the Empire (Muldoon, 2013: 64). In a stunt to highlight the Council's double standards, Roland, his dog Bengy Cockalorum, and Pete arranged a photo shoot with the *Hackney Gazette*, which showed them putting up a poster for the event (Muldoon, 2013: 64). In the end, the Council's Picasso event attracted few, if any, punters and the show moved to another venue across the road from the Empire. The Council's anti-flyposting team was disbanded shortly thereafter. Pete Moreland returned to the Empire to work as the electrician (gaffer) and Tim Horrocks started running DL as a full-time business.

The Hackney Empire

The Hackney Empire, built in 1901 and designed by the renowned theatre architect Frank Matcham, was owned and managed by the huge Stoll–Moss chain of halls. In contrast, the nearby Hoxton Hall, which was located in a similarly economically deprived area, had been very much a people's music hall, but its legitimacy had been questioned by the authorities and it was closed down under pressure from the police in 1871 (Hoxton Hall website). The Empire had a much larger capacity and a palatial interior; its architectural style was a statement of classiness and upward mobility. Hackney, in London's East End, had always been rather down-at-heel, with a large working-class community and historically high levels of poverty, but this was an increasingly popular form of mass entertainment, for which an analogy with television in the 1950s and 1960s can be easily drawn. Its location was specifically designed to draw in the working classes and the emerging middle classes – especially the petit bourgeoisie – to whom the music halls had increasingly appealed in an effort to clean up in the 1890s. Indeed, as history shows us, no effort on the part of the halls to self-regulate was satisfactory enough for the watch committees and the authorities.

After World War One, the Empire continued as a successful variety theatre until 1956, when Stoll–Moss sold it to ATV for use as a television studio. In 1963, the bingo-hall chain Mecca purchased the Empire and converted it into a bingo hall. However, by the beginning of the 1980s, Mecca had ceased to use it as a bingo hall, mainly because the raked seating was unsuitable for bingo and English Heritage had refused them permission to alter the seating or remove it altogether to fit tables. The condition of the Empire had been deteriorating since it fell into disuse as a major venue and many of the architectural features, like the terracotta domes on the top front elevation of building, were dangerously decrepit and had been removed by Mecca. The interior walls had been thoughtlessly covered with flock wallpaper and paint, which concealed the ornate decorative features. The upper circle was in a serious state of disrepair and unusable, and there was buddleia growing from the masonry at the top front elevation. Anyone taking over the Empire would have to be prepared to spend hundreds of thousands of pounds making good the defects. Hackney Borough Council pursued a different line: they wanted to demolish the building and replace it with a multi-storey car park (Muldoon, 2013 interview).

CAST had originally considered purchasing a 200-seat former cinema in Kilburn but were tipped off about the Hackney Empire by word of mouth. To their surprise, Mecca offered them the building for £1,000 in 1985 but the offer came with certain conditions – namely, that they restored the terracotta domes at the top of the theatre, which Mecca had removed (Muldoon, 2013 interview). Indeed, Mecca had been more than keen to dispose of the Empire because they had been instructed by English Heritage to replace the domes, the cost of which was put at £250,000 each, and because the Empire was a Grade II* listed building, any replacements had to be produced by an approved architectural mason. CAST immediately organized 'dome benefits' to raise the necessary capital but there were many who believed that they would not find the money. Eventually, Andrew Puddephat, the leader of Hackney Council, made the money available to purchase new domes through "planning gain", which came through an increase in land value that is derived from planning permission being granted on the land (Muldoon, 2013: 54).

The reincarnated Hackney Empire was officially reopened on 9 December 1986 on the occasion of its 85th birthday (CAST had formally occupied the building in the previous month). Local people were employed to assist in the running of the Empire. For example, Harry Goodwin, one of the Empire's former doormen, was hired to perform the same role (Muldoon, 2013: 45). Pete Moreland, who joined in 1982, was already running lights and sound for CAST and performed the same jobs at the Empire. Brian Wren, who had joined for *Mrs T and the Red Teds* in 1985, became the theatre manager and Ann Cartwright, who had written her master's dissertation on CAST, was given the role of administrator (Muldoon, 2013: 45–46). The front-of-house team and bar staff were hired on a casual basis (Muldoon, 2013: 45–46).

From the very moment CAST took over the Empire, it was a financial struggle and the theatre was threatened with demolition as early as 1986. The biggest drain on resources was the Empire's much-needed restoration. Roland (Muldoon, interview) admits this is something for which they were not prepared. To oversee the restoration project, CAST established two charities: the Hackney Empire Preservation Trust (HEPT) had a board made up of local residents and others, and was chaired by the poet Benjamin Zephaniah.

Separate to HEPT was the Hackney Empire board of governors, which included performers Mark Hurst, Otiz Cannelloni, and Ian Saville, and promoter Jean Nicholson (all Hackney residents), the latter of whom ran cabaret nights at the Crown and Castle in Dalston, along with what Roland describes as "key workers" from the NV circuit venues (Muldoon, 2013: 56). Muldoon (2013: 56) admits that in HEPT they had "created a trust and a board that was sympathetic to their views". This was vital: for if the Muldoons had created a board and a trust that were antagonistic to their aims, it is unlikely that they would have survived for very long; but having local people on the board of HEPT was crucial in demonstrating their commitment to the community. CAST also based their operations at the Empire, which included NV Management Company (NVM),[9] run by Claire. However, the ever-present threats of demolition and financial ruin meant that HEPT had to widen its network of supporters and find celebrity names who could lend their support to the restoration project. To their credit, CAST had some early success in attracting many high-profile names to their cause, including Michael Caine and Lenny Henry, among others.

---

[9] NVM was the first agency to manage the careers of fledgling altcab artistes who were now beginning to appear on television in ever increasing numbers.

Despite this new support, CAST still had to make a final payment of £50,000 to Mecca and faced a further penalty of £50,000 if they failed to meet the April 1988 deadline. CAST were holding out for a lifeline from Hackney Council that was worth £150,000 and everyone was on tenterhooks. It was during this month that I was on my undergraduate work placement at the Empire, and I was present when the new domes were finally lifted into place. I later chatted to Roland in his office, and on that occasion, he indicated that he saw CAST as a band of South Sea pirates boarding a ship. I wanted to know more:

> You know… and, uh… we had no money and no nothing… you know… we were like… you know… South Sea pirates taking over and having to turn… to look respectable of course… there's people going "The Hackney Empire? My God, who are these people? They're not that terrifying left-wing group that we've heard about or the group we haven't even heard about. Who are these people who've captured this building that we all ignored?" An iconic, historical building that the industry… the commercial industry had said, "We don't want it anymore. We don't want the Hackney Empire. Fuck the Hackney Empire"… the Empire is in Hackney, there's no tube, low-waged area, poverty, East End.
>
> Muldoon, 2010 interview

Muldoon regards CAST as a band of outlaws, which indeed they appeared to be in the eyes of legitimate cultural practitioners. They were not regarded, in the conventional sense, as responsible people; they were seen, mainly because of Teddy Taylor's moral vendetta and the scare stories in the right-wing press, as dangerous subversives. If the Right attacked CAST for being 'dangerous Lefties', then the Left rarely praised them at all. Roland admits "The Left was never turned on by our claim that we were providing a counter-hegemonic challenge to the status quo" (Muldoon, 2013: 65). This position has as much to do with CAST's refusal to be part of one Left group or another. In their early days, they played for any audience on the Left. The many left-wing benefits that the Hackney Empire hosted were also criticized by some on the Left, who questioned the fees they were being charged, forgetting that theatres cannot afford to run on goodwill. Furthermore, the staff still had to be paid and could not be expected to work unpaid.

When word of their acquisition of the Hackney Empire became public, it was inevitable that old-style variety agents, or the "nostalgia clan" as

Muldoon (2013: 96) refers to them, would contact the theatre and ask to put on shows. Muldoon was adamant:

> We, for our part, did not want to encourage their retro ideas. We thought that we should emphasise the gap between old and new variety by not having too much of the old variety on. On the rare occasions when we did let the 'old school' promoters in, they weren't successful, thus proving our case.
>
> Muldoon, 2013: 96

Muldoon recalls one occasion when Jack Seaton brought the British Music Hall Society to the Empire and how he found it difficult to tell these 'old-timers' to refrain from using their 'cheeky chappie' asides (Muldoon, 2013: 96). Roland does speak of one particular old-style show with some fondness. Frankie Vaughan's show had been a great success, though it had only broken even, and Muldoon speaks highly of his professionalism and magnetic stage presence as well as the absence of racism. Frankie Howerd, on the other hand, made a racist joke directed at a group of Asian punters seated in the front row of the Empire when he appeared there in 1989 (Muldoon, 2013: 97). When Roland confronted Howerd's management, they brushed it off by claiming "he was forced [*sic*] to do that when he was working in the clubs" (Muldoon, 2013: 97.) Other old-timers who appeared on the Hackney Empire's stage included paper-tearer Terri Carol, the ventriloquist and magician Terri Rogers and her foul-mouthed dummy, Shorty Harris, and Black American jazz 'hoofer', Will Gaines. Rogers, a transsexual woman, had also appeared in cabaret and made an appearance on Granada's *Wheeltappers and Shunters' Social Club* in 1974. Newer speciality acts, many of whom had come from street performing, were now rubbing shoulders with some of the old-timers who had spent years treading the boards of the old variety theatres. However, it's worth pointing out that this cannot be read as evidence of a direct link between the old and the new forms of variety, and likewise the old and new forms of stand-up. The old and new came from very different aesthetic and stylistic origins and were shaped by very different discourses. The old variety had existed during a time of colonialism, while the new variety had grown up with its consequences, especially the nationalism and the racist discourses that stemmed from postcolonial anxiety, which were embedded in the light entertainment of the period and treated disinterestedly by performers and impresarios alike.

Though Muldoon would reject the label 'avant-garde', the positioning of CAST/NV and the altcab circuit was in direct opposition to nostalgia *inter alia* and appears to indicate a kind of aesthetic disposition that was redolent of the historic avant-garde, in the sense that all such movements demanded a break with the past. The refusal of nostalgia can be traced back to the Muldoons' time at Unity and their opposition to the moribund nature of the latter's music-hall evenings, but it is also present in the countercultures that emerged in the latter half of the seventies with punk and post-punk, and is indicative of a sense of the postmodern avant-garde: the opposition to a romanticized and idealized retelling or reconstruction of the past, rather than opposition to a conservative aesthetic *per se*. The conservative aesthetic is solely concerned with the preservation of the past, and art schools, conservatoires, and similar institutions reproduce the techniques of 'classical' artists through the systematized instruction of their students. On the one hand, the autodidacticism of the Muldoons and others broke with this formal approach to artistic production, and on the other, the variety performers of the past were either too entrenched in their positions to be of any use, or they had died and taken their techniques with them to the grave. Thus, it was only possible to create performances from scratch using bricolage, autodidacticism, or both. The new performers had created their own styles through the use of these techniques, and they were produced and reproduced by groups like CAST/NV either through auditions or talent shows.

In 1987 the Hackney Empire began its annual talent show, the New Act of the Year Show (NATYS), which launched the careers of Linda Smith (the first winner), Stewart Lee, Simon Day (as Tommy Cockles), Paul Tonkinson, Ronni Ancona, and Ardal O'Hanlon (Muldoon, 2013). The creation of this award had two functions: to serve as a rival to the Edinburgh Fringe Festival's prestigious Perrier Awards and to provide a steady supply of new acts for the NV circuit and the Hackney Empire (Muldoon, 2013). Moreover, Roland is adamant that this is not a competition: this is a quest to find acts that are capable of headlining a bill, even though some industry figures are involved in the selection process. The Empire also hosted full shows from up-and-coming performers, like Julian Clary (as the Joan Collins' Fan Club), and productions like *At Home with the Hardys*, which was adapted from Jeremy Hardy's Radio Four programme *Unnatural Acts* (BBC, 1987–1988). In addition to comedy, the Empire also hosted concerts, opera, and an annual Christmas pantomime. The latter production had been part of the Empire's programme since CAST assumed control of the theatre and continues to this day.

In 1989, a fledgling Black comedy scene was beginning to emerge in London under the aegis of David Bryan and Jenny Landreth's Black Comedy, which took place first at the Albany Empire in Deptford and then transferred to the Electric Cinema in Notting Hill, and eventually spread out to other English towns and cities with established African-Caribbean communities (Landreth, 2012 interview). NV, seeing the underground potential of all-Black shows, also capitalized on them and started running the 291 Club,[10] which opened in 1990 and emulated the famous nights at the Apollo Theatre in Harlem. These shows were billed primarily as talent quests; Roland says that they did not want to use the word 'competition', but does not explain why. However, I would suggest that the word 'competition' came with its own social and cultural baggage, and was often associated with battles of the bands and similar gladiatorial contests that offer few rewards for the contestants and which actively reinforce hierarchies.

The 291 Club grew in popularity and was eventually recorded for London Weekend Television (LWT). The show was compèred by Miles Crawford, who also ran a similar show, Cabarave, at the Comedy Cafe in Shoreditch. Some performers found these shows difficult, with the audience being encouraged to let off steam, often on cue for the cameras. Muldoon (2013 interview) says that the quest became a search for new talent, rather than a showcase, and the word was appropriated, particularly, by self-styled 'urban' radio stations like Choice FM, whose target audience was young and Black. Again, we see how the use of alternative language reveals the Muldoons' determination to create a linguistic distance between themselves and the establishment and, by so doing, to carve out new territory for themselves. Furthermore, it also reminds us how neologisms like these percolated into everyday speech, thus illuminating the effect of language on thought and cognition. Indeed, part of the success of RAR was the way it used language to inform and to educate, and this took the shape of graphics and words.

---

[10] The club's name comes from the Hackney Empire's address: 291 Mare Street.

The Decline of the New Variety Circuit

By 1992, CAST/New Variety's reduced circuit of weekly clubs had closed. The Labour-controlled councils that had once supported them cancelled their subsidies. The last venue to close was the Old White Horse in Brixton. The reasons for the councils' funding cuts could easily be blamed on the high cost of implementing and collecting the Poll Tax, which was phased out and replaced by the Council Tax in 1993 – the year after the Conservatives' fourth successive victory. The demise of their circuit did not spell the end for the Hackney Empire, which kept running despite the difficulties of keeping the theatre financially afloat (Muldoon, 2013: 43–45). Roland gradually ceded most of the running of the Empire to others but, crucially, he retained the role of chief executive, meaning that he still had some say in how things were run (Muldoon, 2013 interview). However, the Empire continued to struggle financially even though the shows were more popular than ever.

Financially, the Empire was initially supported by modest grants from the ACGB and Hackney Borough Council, the latter of whom later withdrew their funding in the middle of the 1990s. A typical ACGB grant was around £150,000 per annum and accounted for 12 per cent of the Empire's annual turnover; the rest was made up of door receipts and higher-than-average bar takings. NVM, which was wholly commercial and operated without subsidies, had an annual turnover of £50,000 (Muldoon, 2013: 130). Roland says that the Empire was underfunded – and when we look at the theatre's capacity of 1,200, it is easy to see why: if we look at the neighbouring Theatre Royal, Stratford, which has a capacity of 400, this received an annual grant of approximately £400,000 (Muldoon, 2013: 130). Here again, we see how arts funding was allocated so that those deemed less legitimate were awarded less money than those theatres offering legitimate cultural fare. However, there is another explanation for this: the ACE operates a funding tariff that separates producing venues from non-producing venues (Arts Council England, n.d.). The former applies to theatres that produce new works in house, while the latter refers to venues that stage shows produced by outside companies or individuals.

CAST was self-consciously counter*cultural*; an underground theatre company that took control of the Hackney Empire against all the odds and transformed it from a shabby neglected former bingo hall in a run-down corner of the East End of London into a successful Off West End Theatre.

It would be easy to suggest that they were not entrepreneurial; but while they were certainly naive in the early days of running the Empire, they managed to achieve a great deal with limited resources. If 'entrepreneurial spirit' means keeping running costs down by paying staff a pittance, then this was not CAST. Their entrepreneurialism came from their counter-*cultural* practice of running a successful but cash-starved theatre company. Indeed, they were used to operating on a shoestring budget, but the high costs associated with refurbishing the Empire could not be met solely by the cash donated to the Empire by its patrons, who generously put money into one of the many buckets at the end of the evening; nor could they have managed to achieve this through bar takings alone, which were used to pay staff. The Empire's pay structures were more egalitarian than most, but this did not mean that everyone working for the organization was paid the same; CAST paid themselves a little more than their casual staff because they were taking greater risks (at one point, the Muldoons had to re-mortgage their home to help finance the Empire). Yet, even though pay for front-of-house and casual members of staff was above the Equity minimum wage, tensions developed between CAST's technical staff and the Empire's administrators, with the latter demanding pay parity with the former. Roland admits that he wasn't always comfortable with the role of chief executive because this meant that he was in the unenviable position of having to sack people if necessary, which created an obvious conflict between his socialist impulses and the hard reality of running a business with people they regarded as comrades (Muldoon, 2013: 139–204). The pay issue was eventually resolved but this incident set the stage for future conflicts, for as early as 1990, factions developed within the organization: on the one hand, there were the "Respectables", as Roland (Muldoon, 2013: 139–204) calls them, and on the other, the loyalists who supported CAST and the Empire. The Respectables wanted to seize control of the theatre and turn it into an orthodox provincial theatre staging less riskier shows that, in their eyes, would attract more funding from the Lottery Fund. The loyalists, predictably, wanted to maintain the status quo.

Over the years, these battles would involve Hackney Council, now committed to neoliberalism, which wanted to win some European Union funding for its gentrification projects, and would try and undermine CAST's management of the Empire in the process. One example of how the Council tried to scupper the Empire happened when CAST produced its own box-office system, HEBOS (Hackney Empire Bums on Seats) rather than spend large sums on the approved PASS system.

The Council lobbied the Empire to accept this system, but CAST were adamant. However, some of the Empire's front-of-house team had been secretly colluding with the Council. Although CAST won this battle, more internal struggles would develop when they started applying for Lottery Fund grants, but the fund imposed new people on the Empire – management consultants – one of whom was the last chief executive of the disgraced Barings Bank (Muldoon, 2013: 316–328). Following a fundraising campaign led by Griff Rhys-Jones that raised £15 million, with a further £4 million coming from the Lottery Fund and £1.3 million from businessman Sir Alan Sugar, a large-scale refurbishment of the Empire began in 2001 and was timetabled to be completed in December 2002 (Muldoon, 2013: 233–249). All performances were relocated to the much smaller Bullion Room on 117 Wilton Way, but in 2003, the building contractors working on the refurbishment of the theatre and its adjoining buildings (like the Samuel Pepys pub) went into administration, throwing the project into doubt (Muldoon, 2013: 249). The Arts Council convened an emergency meeting to decide the future of the Empire and it looked for a while as though they would call time on the theatre (Leitch, 2003). The Empire eventually reopened in the following year, on 28 January 2004, but within months the management consultants would stage a coup.

In 2005, Roland was ostensibly forced into retirement (Claire had left during the previous year) and their places were taken by more management-oriented people who were sympathetic to the Respectables. Simon Thomsett, who replaced Roland as artistic director in 1992, left in 2009 by "mutual consent" and was replaced by arts consultant, Claire Middleton. The same year, the Hackney Empire announced that it was going to close for nine months to consider its future. I attended an angry public meeting in November 2010 at which Roland spoke passionately about CAST/New Variety's achievements on a fraction of the money the Empire was now receiving. In spite of its financial problems, the Empire never went dark under the Muldoons. He also noted how the buddleia, which had been removed from the Empire's front elevation in 1986, had now returned to re-colonize the building.

After the Hackney Empire, the Muldoons assumed control of the Cock Tavern in Kilburn (Shallice, 2007). Here, they revived NV and introduced a regular Gramsci Night on Tuesdays in the upstairs room. Unfortunately, this venture did not last long because of the high costs associated with running a pub (Muldoon, 2010 interview). The Muldoons are currently focussing their efforts on New Variety Lives, which continues the New Act of the Year Shows (NATYS) and carries on their original work in variety. They also run regular shows in Ludgershall in Buckinghamshire, where they have made their home (Muldoon, 2010 interview; Muldoon, 2013).

Chapter 6

Conclusion

The history of British popular culture is punctuated by moments that can be thought of as openings or rips in the cultural fabric. Such moments are fleeting and being in the right place at the right time is crucial. These are the moments when new forces make their way onto the field of cultural production and, once they are on that field, it is only a matter of time before they too become the dominant cultural producers. Nevertheless, while they are on the field of cultural production, they change the *doxa* of that field. These are also the moments when new tastes are formed, and this is a two-way process between the producer and consumer. The public becomes aware of new cultural products because they are either marketed, or they are otherwise objectified, even stumbled upon. When rock 'n' roll emerged as one of the new forms of popular music in the 1950s, it was mediated to British audiences through other cultural products like cinema and through records brought back by merchant seamen. Films like *Blackboard Jungle* introduced British youth to rock 'n' roll, while at the same time prompting a moral panic in the press. Similarly, when punk rock became known to a wider audience in 1976, it happened at a point in time when rock music seemed to be out of touch with the realities of the street, the council estate, and the workplace, and was seen by punk rockers as self-indulgent and inauthentic. Punk rock's emergence not only stunned Britain's cultural gatekeepers, but it also prompted a crisis among music producers and the broadcast media, who on the one hand, responded with moral indignation and outrage, and on the other, a sort of cold dismissiveness. Gradually, punk was recuperated and its initial shock effect was neutralized. However, punk's apparent demise created a vacuum that was filled by a new generation of DIY cultural producers, who at the start were the new bands like Swell Maps, Wire, and Gang of Four, who were signed by small DIY record labels like Chiswick, Rough Trade, and Step Forward. They were followed by the first wave of altcab's performers. Punk and dub poetry also emerged during this time, with John Cooper Clarke and Linton Kwesi Johnson leading the pack. Cooper Clarke's poetry was humorous and his work was an inspiration for many aspiring poets and comedians.

Altcab was a different kind of moment, and what made it different was the fact that it was neither a music genre nor a subcultural movement that grew alongside an emergent genre of music. This was a moment in which British light entertainment, which was the last bastion of the parental culture, with its postcolonial attitudes to difference, had been challenged. The old norms of show-business orthodoxy, with its centuries-old codes of aesthetic conduct, laden as they were with postcolonial discourses on identity, citizenship, nationality, and difference, were not only questioned, they were openly mocked; this was in stark contrast to the previous art movements, which deferred or even paid homage to their predecessors. In this sense, altcab was very much like punk. Like rock 'n' roll, altcab wasn't mediated: it was, like music hall before it, a confluence of several cultural strands that included the punk or ranting poets, political fringe theatre, street performers, and performance art. Its cultural parentage, therefore, like that of post-punk music, which existed in parallel, was heterodox and complicated. However, it would be fair to say that altcom, rather than altcab as a movement, was mediated to a wider audience through television shows like *The Young Ones*, *The Comic Strip Presents...*, and *Saturday Live*, the latter of which probably had a greater impact than the former shows.

It is generally assumed by many writers that altcab/altcom began at the Comedy Store in May 1979, but this is disputed; there were moves afoot to create a new kind of comedy as early as 1976. First, there was the Band on the Wall in Manchester, at which Rik Mayall and Adrian Edmondson began performing as 20th Century Coyote. Second, there was Martin Soan and Malcolm Hardee's Greatest Show on Legs, which they performed in pubs and other venues on the south coast of England. Third, John Dowie, late of Birmingham Arts Lab, was playing arts centres around the country. His comedy made use of observations and music rather than standard jokes, with their familiar targets of minorities, women, and the post office. John Dowie was also signed by Tony Wilson's Factory Records as one of its first acts, which links him to the post-punk movement. Finally, CAST's work in popular political theatre made use of stand-up comedy and variety theatre to inform and entertain audiences, and this set them apart from agit-prop companies as well as legitimate theatre.

In the beginning, the alt-space was underground and mostly hidden from view. Those who knew about this new field, the subcultural and counter*cultural* cognoscenti, were of a similar aesthetic disposition to those people who had specialized knowledge of not only fringe theatre, but also minor and obscure rock bands, continental philosophy, anarchism, and socialism. Thus, the audience's habituses and those of the performers were matched. From 1979 to 1982, the circuit was at its rawest, but was also small and, towards the end of this period, on the brink of collapse. Then, from 1983 to 1986 there was a flowering of acts, most of which were ranting poets, street performers, and musicians. From 1986 to 1990, there was an explosion of stand-up comedians, who would go on to dominate the altcab circuit until its transformation into the comedy circuit, but this was a circuit that was, for the most part, centred on London and the southeast, with outposts in Manchester, Bradford, Leeds, Bristol, and Newcastle.

As the cabaret circuit evolved into the comedy circuit, professionalization became standardization, and the routes of progression were limited. At first, the novice performer could buy a copy of *Time Out* each week, look for work in the Cabaret or Comedy section, and contact the club promoters who would give them an open spot. This was the case until 1990 or 1991. If the performer didn't die, they would be invited back to perform a half-spot of ten minutes until they eventually were named on the bill. By the early 1990s, the number of clubs that offered open spots had shrunk, and the ones that continued to offer them were usually the bigger clubs, which by the latter part of the decade had become chains: these were the Comedy Store, Jongleurs, and a few others. Towards the end of the century, a separate open-spot circuit emerged to fulfil the need for new comedians. The poets, jugglers, magicians, and oddball acts who had populated the circuit were squeezed out, and there are two reasons for this: many of the newer clubs didn't have enough ceiling clearance for jugglers and it was cheaper to put on stand-up comedians. Speciality acts found it hard to break onto a circuit full of stand-up comedians. In addition, there was a growing number of professional stand-up comedy courses, which supplanted the cabaret courses like those at the Crown and Castle and Jackson's Lane Arts Centre, the latter of which was the only such course to survive into the 1990s. These professional comedy courses acted like a conveyor belt, producing hundreds of new comedians per year; many of them possessed roughly the same performance methodology and this often meant that these comedians visited the same topics as other new entrants.

I realize that the word 'counterculture', like the word 'culture' itself, is difficult to pin down, but it is useful to think of counterculture as a space or a realm that is either a mirror image of the official cultural space or an inversion thereof. For example, the avant-garde is countercultural because it operates outside the consecrated means of cultural production and seeks through revolutionary means to challenge the pre-eminence, authority, and seniority of the old guard. Avant-gardists make use of DIY and experimentation to innovate and create, while others strip down forms to their elements and assemble them from below. The countercultures and avant-gardists that emerged in the wake of World War Two – the Beats, the hippies, the Situationists, the punks, post-punks, and so on – all made use of bricolage as a means of expression. It's no secret that the work of the Situationist International had an impact on punk and this was mediated to the general public by Malcolm McLaren, the manager of the Sex Pistols, who had spent the summer of 1968 in Paris; but he wasn't the only one to have adopted Situationist techniques. Tony Wilson of Factory Records actively made use of them too and so did the post-punk bands like Wire and Gang of Four. It is reasonable, therefore, to conclude that not only did youth culture and rock 'n' roll have an influence on altcom and altcab, so too did the avant-garde. It is worth remembering that stand-ups like Sayle, for example, had been exposed to Situationist ideas through art school and the upheavals of the mid- to late 1970s. In so doing, the alt performers like him introduced a new language to the entertainment field through their deployment of cultural and counter*cultural* capital, expressed as political comment or surreal takes on current affairs or continental philosophy.

While in the 1980s parliamentary politics became more right-wing and effectively froze out any oppositional discourses, the alt-space provided room for dissenting views to be expressed, often in the crudest of terms. However, this doesn't mean that the alt-space was full of performers shouting, "Down with Thatcher", as Steve Gribbin rightly pointed out, because the amount of expression of overtly political views through comedy was small. Nonetheless, non-racism and non-sexism were political positions that were taken in relation to the racism and sexism in the official space. That the alt-space existed was enough in itself; it was a space in which performers were freed from the constraints of the kind of audience expectations found in the WMCs; thus, if they wanted to express anti-Thatcher points of view, they were allowed to do so. Nonetheless, the election of the Thatcher government and its effect on the discourses within the alt-space cannot be understated, and it was generally assumed that cabaret performers were anti-Thatcher. Of course, this doesn't mean that performers were generally supportive of the Labour opposition either. I personally attacked Kinnock's Labour Party from the pulpit of the stage, and I had my reasons for doing so: instead of renewing itself, the Labour Party, which had been defeated in three successive general elections, took the decision to race the Tories to the bottom. Officially, Labour refused to support the year-long Miners' Strike and offered no resistance to the Poll Tax, and this proved to be disastrous; the effects of its political cowardice have lingered well into the twenty-first century. Nevertheless, the Miners' Strike and the Poll Tax were rallying points and, in many cases, the first taste of political activity for the performers – especially those performers who were regulars on the NV circuit.

The numbers of overtly political comedians remained small despite the massive expansion of the circuit and the increased numbers of stand-up comedians. I always detected a reluctance to admit to being political from my participants, and the word itself, like the word 'ideology', has been laden with a good deal of baggage, much of it created by the official media. Yet we all 'do' politics at some level, even if we aren't necessarily conscious of it. For my own part, I was opposed to Thatcher but I always insisted that I was political in the broadest possible sense, and when I began my comedy career, I was determined to use my art to comment on society and politics. For example, being Black meant that I could have either taken the Bill Cosby line and not mentioned race at all or I could have taken the Dick Gregory route and talked about it. I chose to do the latter. In any case, both positions are political: one is passive and the other active. Even the trad. comedians, who would have denied being political, took a political position by at least pretending to be apolitical.

In this book, I've offered a distinction between the confusing and often-interchangeable terms 'altcom', 'altcab', and 'cabaret'. I take the view that 'altcab' and 'cabaret' referred to the movement and the space provided by the clubs that opened to cater to a new demand for new and experimental forms of entertainment. 'Altcom', on the other hand, was coined by the media to describe a new kind of comedy performance that didn't fit into the previous category of stand-up comedy. Stand-up comedians in the alt-space never called themselves 'alternative comedians'; that name was given to them by the press. Indeed, many comedians, including myself, rejected the label. We should recall this wasn't the first time that the media coined a name for an emergent cultural phenomenon that defied not only expectations but prior experience of such things. The same thing happened with punk, post-punk, and the new romantics youth cultures, and it's worth pointing out that the word 'alternative' had been used since the 1960s as an adjective to preface nouns to describe cultural activities like print, theatre, and music that diverged from commercial cultural production – alternative press, alternative theatre, alternative music, and so on. In each case, there was a suggestion of newness or opposition to orthodoxy. Altcab as a movement, therefore, marked a distinction between itself and the decaying remnants of variety, which could still be seen on television light-entertainment shows like the BBC's *Seaside Special* and *The Black and White Minstrel Show*. Yet the most visible manifestation of the altcab movement wasn't the ranting poets, jugglers, or the a capella bands, for all their popularity with cabaret audiences; it was the comedians – and it was because of their visibility as writers and performers on television shows like *The Young Ones* and *Saturday Live* that the entire movement has been labelled 'alternative comedy'.

It is also worth remembering that altcab was mainly a youth-led movement, because of the relatively young ages of most of the performers. Nevertheless, as in the case of punk and post-punk, there were older participants: for altcab, these included Arnold Brown (43), Roland Muldoon (35), and Tony Allen (32); and for punk, U.K. Subs' frontman Charlie Harper (32), Crass's Penny Rimbaud (34), as well as the Stranglers, whose ages ranged from 26 (Hugh Cornwell, the youngest) to 37 (Jet Black, the oldest). During the 1950s, Bill Haley was 29 when his band's song 'Rock Around the Clock' was in the pop charts. For my part, I was 29 when I first performed stand-up and 32 when I made my first appearance on the London circuit, and thus older than many of my contemporaries, who were in their early twenties or, as in the cases of Victoria Coren Mitchell and Alex Langdon, their late teens.

In 1979, the performers of altcab's first wave were amateurs, who had no prior experience of performing stand-up comedy. This had to be learnt by using bricolage: making use of one's cultural and counter*cultural* capital and combining it with one's own performance skills, acquired from working in alt theatre. It was the same for me: I used my cultural and counter*cultural* capital, taken from my knowledge of American comedians, which I combined with my talent for mimicry, my physicality, and my acting skills. By the time of the third wave, the game had changed and performers who had no experience of the struggles of the 1960s and 1970s joined the circuit, thus shifting the *doxa* on the field towards its commercial pole. This meant that there was less space for experimentation and innovation and, as one comedian put it to me, there was less margin for error. Indeed, it is possible to argue that it was television that had the greatest impact on the altcab movement. Thus, many former ranting poets had converted themselves into stand-up comedians and more leftfield acts were finding themselves faced with either converting to stand-up or leaving the circuit. Performers like Steve Murray the Teddy Bear Trainer simply faded away, while some like Woody Bop Muddy had already set up their own clubs and continued to perform into the mid-1990s and beyond.

The contribution of CAST to this live entertainment scene has been largely overlooked and often reduced to footnotes or a brief mention. Yet if it had not been for them, the comedy industry as we know it today may not have existed. In 1981, with the closure of Alternative Cabaret and the exodus of the space's star performers to television, the circuit was on the brink of collapse. CAST stepped into the vacuum and created New Variety using its cultural and counter*cultural* capital, and in so doing set down the marker for others to follow. Indeed, CAST had some experience of variety: Roland Muldoon had been using stand-up comedy as a theatrical device in the years before the opening of the Comedy Store. It was CAST who provided a space for variety performers, some of them drafted from Covent Garden's cohort of street performers, and others, like Will Gaines and Terri Rogers, who came from the defunct variety theatres. Variety was thus seen, by some, as a remnant of Britain's past and had been ostensibly forgotten. Britain's youth had not grown up with the kinds of performers who appeared on television in the 1950s and 1960s. On some level, light entertainment was as fusty, insular, and reactionary as the mainstream politics of the time. In this sense, it mirrored the progressive rock of the 1970s, which was out of touch and self-indulgent. The Muldoons, therefore, introduced the younger generations to variety, but this wasn't the variety of the variety theatres, it was a new kind of variety that was informed by contemporary discourses rather than the aesthetic discourses of the 1950s.

Therefore, CAST's NV circuit may have borne a closer resemblance to variety theatre than much of the altcab circuit or the Store. This is because it was shaped by the Muldoons' political-aesthetic dispositions as theatre practitioners and variety/music-hall enthusiasts, as is apparent in their choice of name for the project and the way in which they reconstructed variety as an entertainment format. Although it was consciously set apart from the rest of the alt-space, NV was part of the same movement. The Muldoons rejected the word 'cabaret', describing it as a foreign and rather different format. Yet it is easy to lazily label all of it as 'cabaret' without appreciating the essential difference in formats, which is most evident in the choice of room layouts for both NV and cabaret. CAST's cultural capital influenced the choice to consciously adopt variety theatre's seating style for their clubs rather than the more intimate cabaret style; while the stage was 'end on' to imitate the proscenium arch of the variety theatre. Altcab clubs varied in their seating arrangements, and in my experience, the cabaret seating style was dominant. Although Jongleurs' original venue in Battersea used a thrust stage, the seating itself was cabaret style. The Comedy Store, on the other hand, utilized a mix of theatre-style and cabaret seating.

Yet for all its similarities to altcab in terms of the performers that appeared on their stages, NV differed in other ways. First, the use of the name 'CAST' to preface 'NV' can be seen as a brand, which had symbolic counter*cultural* value in the eyes of their audiences. CAST's work as political theatre practitioners and their subversive reputation contributed to their value as producers of a particularly counter*cultural* entertainment form. Second, NV was subsidized[1] and, unlike the rest of the space, performers were paid the Equity minimum wage (Muldoon, 2013). The same could not be said for many other clubs, most of which operated a door split, which was a share of the box-office takings: this could range from £200 to as little as £5, depending on the size of the club and the honesty of the promoter. The Store and Jongleurs offered guaranteed fees which amount to £100 or more per appearance. In this sense, NV also opposed the large-scale commercial producers like the Comedy Store and Jongleurs in terms of business practices and their class habituses. Yet the Hackney Empire, despite being run by CAST, was a commercial enterprise, as could be seen when its profile was raised considerably by *The 291 Club* (LWT 1991–1993). Indeed, the Muldoons never avoided media exposure

---

[1] NV received its funding from the Greater London Council and the councils of the boroughs in which its regular shows were located. The Hackney Empire was subsidized by Greater London Arts and the London Borough of Hackney.

and courted it either through their infamy as artists or their possession of the new form of entertainment that had a marketable value. Therefore, by the time they had taken possession of the Hackney Empire, it is arguable that the Muldoons had made a transverse migration once again from the alternative space to the official world. The subsidized productions notwithstanding, the Muldoons remained true to their subversive origins and acted as the custodians for oppositional entertainment forms. Thus, when positioned against the rest of the mainstream entertainment field, they continued to at least appear counter*cultural* or underground.

This leads me to the structural similarities between altcab and post-punk. First, it is necessary to mention how the cultural interventionism begun by RAR continued in the alternative space and post-punk music as non-racism and non-sexism. This cultural interventionism is particularly evident with NV, where a form of ideological vetting took place to weed out anyone whom they regarded as a potential reactionary. In this sense, the Muldoons are very much like the post-punk band the Pop Group, who performed a similar screening process for prospective band members. Therefore, we should not view post-punk as a vaguely defined set of genres that post-dated punk but as a countercultural movement that was characterized by its opposition to cultural orthodoxy and commercial hierarchies. This brings us to the structural affinities between post-punk music and the alternative space. Fragmentation, avant-garde tendencies, the creation of new genres, bricolage, and political engagement are present in each form. This is evident in the performers' willingness to experiment and tackle social and personal–political issues that were not permitted expression in the official world, and its democratization of live entertainment. Formal contracts were dispensed with, and the middlemen (accountants, marketing executives, and so forth) were eliminated. However, it was inevitable that this democratization would be resisted by the commercial players that proliferated towards the end of the decade, because by the middle of the 1990s, the space was fully commercialized and its countercultural elements recuperated as slightly risqué forms of comedy.

Counter*cultural* capital was used in its symbolic form within performances to make statements of authenticity, but by the late 1980s this was absent from those who had no experience of political and social activism or bohemianism. Although Sayle wasn't overtly political, he came from a Communist background, while Tony Allen had experience of opening squats and was, and still is, a regular speaker at Speaker's

Corner in London's Hyde Park. Andy de la Tour also had a background in political activism (his elder sister, Frances, was a member of the Workers Revolutionary Party). Other performers who had experience of political theatre also utilized their counter*cultural* capital to write material and inform their performance styles. The same could also be said for recreational drug use, for one could not talk about any drug without having taken it oneself. This differed vastly from traditional comedians, who only mentioned drugs as a means of questioning a person's mental abilities or judgements. This, I would argue, was an aspect of the alt comedian's work that was inspired by the examples of both rock stars and countercultural figures. Thus, the linguistic and stylistic associations with the world of rock music weren't accidental, and many performers, whether they were comedians, poets, or jugglers, had been influenced by rock music (and possibly reggae and later hip-hop), even if only at an unconscious level. In contrast, rock 'n' roll and youth culture, more generally, had a marginal effect on the light entertainment of the official world, by which they were either mocked or lampooned. One exception was Freddie Starr, the former lead singer of the Merseybeat group, the Midniters, who performed impressions of Elvis Presley and Mick Jagger on television after being 'discovered' on *Opportunity Knocks* (Thames Television) in 1970 (IMDb entry, 2016). CAST, for example, used their love of rock 'n' roll not only as part of their performances, but as a means of identification and differentiation. They opened for rock bands like the Rolling Stones, and this helped to secure their place in the history of the countercultures of the 1960s (Doggett, 2008). Many of the punk poets also continued to open for post-punk bands. For my own part, I acknowledge the impact of post-punk music on my work as a stand-up comedian, which was manifested much later in my rejection of commercial practices and my insistence on discussing broadly political issues, but particularly race, war, and consumerism.

This leads me to the subject of race and difference on the circuit. I realize that what I have written may be hard for some people to accept, but it was equally hard and painful for me to write about it – and it needs to be stated: for all its claims to being non-racist and non-sexist, I experienced racism from some audiences and promoters. This was usually expressed as astonishment at my refusal to perform 'black' – and as I indicated in 'The Wrong Kind of Black Man?', there are many different ways to be Black, so I chose not to conform. This was mainly because I had always instinctively resisted being labelled or straitjacketed, but also because I had been influenced by African-American figures like Paul Robeson, Dick Gregory, and Richard Pryor. However, despite this, there were no Black people of mixed heritage in the public eye to whom I could relate; it was as though they were invisible. I therefore had to forge my own path and create my own identity, which is Black in every sense but defies a prescriptive form of Blackness delineated by racial purists, both Black and White, against whom Ellison's narrator in *Invisible Man* had militated.

The 1980s was a decade in which anything seemed possible: seizing control of a performance space, producing charming, handmade publicity materials with wobbly typesetting; the DIY venues and attitudes, the amateurs, the fun, the excitement, and the danger. All of this happened against the backdrop of social, cultural, and political tensions as well as the ever-present possibility of nuclear annihilation. If you wanted to get up on stage and repeatedly hit yourself over the head with a drinks tray while singing 'O Sole Mio' and doing fart noises with your other hand tucked under your armpit, then the only person stopping you from doing that was you. This was, I insist, redolent of 1880s Parisian cabaret-artistique, because of its amateurs, its opposition to convention, its early refusal of commercialism, and its innovations. For without the innovations in the alt-space, it is possible to imagine trad. comedy and old-fashioned light entertainment persisting much longer.

The performers who participated in the altcab movement may not have been conscious or aware of the fact that they were a part of a great social and cultural change. Altcab, along with RAR and other socio-cultural movements, helped to transform cultural discourse for a generation. No longer was it acceptable to use minorities as a butt of jokes nor was it viable to accept obviousness or that which appeared to be 'natural'. That said, we are now witnessing a backlash from reactionary cultural voices who are determined to reverse all the gains made by progressive forces in the 1980s and 1990s. Under the rubric of the 'war on woke', these voices are given succour and encouragement from Conservative politicians and right-wing media outlets. This must be resisted at all costs. Perhaps the time is right for a new cabaret revival?

Bibliography

Adorno, T. and Horkheimer, M. (2001). 'The Culture Industry: Enlightenment As Mass Deception'. In M.G. Durham and D.M. Kellner (eds.), *Media and Cultural Studies Keyworks*. Oxford: Blackwell.

Anderson, B. (1989). *Imagined Communities: Reflections on the Origin and Spread of Nationalism*. London: Verso.

Anderson, L. (2006). 'Analytic Autoethnography'. *Journal of Contemporary Ethnography* 35(4): 373–395.

Andrews, D. (2010). 'Revisiting the Two Avant-Gardes'. *Jump Cut: A Review of Contemporary Media* 52 (Summer). Available at: http://www.ejumpcut.org/currentissue/andrews2A_Gs/text.html [accessed 24 September 2010].

Andrews, M., Squire, C., and Tamboukou, M. (eds.) (2013). *Doing Narrative Research*. London: Sage. Available at: http://www.sagepub.in/upm-data/56417_Andrews__Doing_Narrative_research.pdf [accessed 26 January 2016].

Appignanesi, L. (1984). *The Cabaret*. London: Studio Vista.

Arts Council England (n.d.). 'Information Sheet: Touring and Grants for the Arts'. Available at: http://www.artscouncil.org.uk/sites/default/files/download-file/Touring_and_Grants_for_the_Arts_Feb2016.pdf [accessed 25 July 2016].

Attardo, S. and Pickering, L. (2011). 'Timing in the Performance of Jokes'. *Humor* 24(2): 233–250.

Baddiel, D. (1989). 'Demystification Corner'. *Comedy Pages*, March, Issue 1.

Bainbridge, L. (2007). 'Ten Right-Wing Rockers'. *Guardian*, 14 October. Available at: http://www.guardian.co.uk/music/2007/oct/14/popandrock2 [accessed 12 May 2012].

Bakhtin, M., and Iswolsky, H. (trans.) (1984). *Rabelais and His World*. Bloomington, IN: Indiana University Press.

Bal, A. S., Pitt, L., Berthon, P., and DesAutels, P. (2009). 'Caricatures, Cartoons, Spoofs and Satires: Political Brands as Butts'. *Journal of Public Affairs* 9(4): 229–237.

Barnes, C. (1969). 'Theater: "Oh, Calcutta!" A Most Innocent Dirty Show'. *New York Times*, 18 June. Available at: https://www.nytimes.com/books/98/05/10/specials/tynan-calcutta.html [accessed 22 January 2016].

Baudrillard, J. (1994). *Simulacra and Simulation*. University of Michigan Press.

Bebber, B. (2014). 'The Short Life of Curry and Chips: Racial Comedy on British Television in the 1960s'. *Journal of British Cinema and Television* 11(2–3): 213–235.

Bennett, T. (2007). '*Habitus Clivé*: Aesthetics and Politics in the Work of Pierre Bourdieu'. Institute for Culture and Society Pre-print Journals. Available at: http://www.uws.edu.au/__data/assets/pdf_file/0003/365394/Bennett_HabitusClive_ICS_Pre-Print_Final.pdf [accessed 30 May 2014].

Bindman, G. (2007). 'Goldenballs'. *New Law Journal*. Available at: http://www.newlawjournal.co.uk/nlj/content/goldenballs [accessed 3 August 2013].

Bourdieu, P. (1986). *The Forms of Capital*. Available at: http://www.marxists.org/reference/subject/philosophy/works/fr/bourdieu-forms-capital.htm [accessed 29 July 2013].

Bourdieu, P. (1996). *The Rules of Art: Genesis and Structure of the Literary Field*. Stanford University Press.

Bourdieu, P. (2003). *Distinction: A Social Critique of the Judgement of Taste*. London: Routledge.

Bourdieu, P. (2016). *The Field of Cultural Production: Essays on Art and Literature*. London: Polity.

Bourdieu, P., and Wacquant, L.J.D. (1992). *An Invitation to Reflexive Sociology*. Chicago: University of Chicago Press.

Bourdieu, P., and Wacquant, L. (2003). *Symbolic Violence*. Available at: http://cges.umn.edu/docs/Bourdieu_and_Wacquant.Symbolic_Violence.pdf [accessed 29 February 2016].

Bowler, A. (1991). 'Politics as Art: Italian Futurism and Fascism'. *Theory and Society* 20(6) (Springer): 763–794.

Boyle, B. and Charles, M. (2010). '"Tightening the Shackles": The Continued Invisibility of Liverpool's British African Caribbean Teachers'. *Journal of Black Studies* 42(3): 427–435.

Brecht, B., and Willett, J. (trans.) (1964). *Brecht on Theatre*. London: Methuen.

Brenton, H. (2006). 'Look Back in Anger'. *Guardian*, 28 January.

Breton, A. (2010). 'First Surrealist Manifesto (1924) and Second Surrealist Manifesto (1929)'. In M.B. Gale and J.F. Deeney (eds.), *The Routledge Drama Anthology and Sourcebook: From Modernism to Contemporary Performance*. London: Routledge.

CAIN at the University of Ulster (nd). *Chronology of the Conflict*. Available at: http://cain.ulst.ac.uk/othelem/chron/ch81.htm [accessed 22 April 2011].

Campbell, B., and Jacques, M. (1986). 'Goodbye to the GLC'. *Marxism Today*.

Campbell, D. (2013). 'Back to the Future'. *British Journalism Review* 24(2): 47–51. Available at: http://bjr.org.uk/data/2013/no2_campbell [accessed 13 July 2015].

Campbell, R. (2016). *Comic Cultures: Commerce, Aesthetics and the Politics of Stand-Up Performance in the UK 1979 to 1992*. PhD, University of East London.

Campbell, R. (2017). 'Post-punk and Alternative Cabaret: Avant-garde, Counterculture and Revolution'. *Punk & Post-Punk* 6(3): 359–376.

Campbell, R. (2022). 'The Story of Cabaret A Go Go'. In *Alternative Comedy, Now and Then*. London: Springer.
Camus, A. (1982). *The Outsider*. London: Penguin.
Carrington, B. (2008). '"What's the Footballer Doing Here?" Racialized Performativity, Reflexivity and Identity'. *Cultural Studies – Critical Methodologies* 8(4) (November). Sage Publications [accessed via csc.sagepub.com].
Carter, P. (1985). 'Striking the Right Note'. *Marxism Today*, March: 28–31.
Chambers, C. (1989). *The Story of Unity Theatre*. London: Lawrence and Wishart.
Chang, H. (n.d.). *Autoethnography as Method: Raising Cultural Consciousness of Self and Others* [Word document].
Cherrington, R.L. (2009). 'The Development of Working Men's Clubs: A Case Study of Implicit Cultural Policy'. *International Journal of Cultural Policy* 15(2): 187–199.
Chester, L. (1986). *Tooth and Claw: The Inside Story of Spitting Image*. London: Faber & Faber.
Chin, T.S. (1997). '"Bullers" and "Battymen": Contesting Homophobia in Black Popular Culture and Contemporary Caribbean Literature'. *Callaloo* 20(1): 127–141.
Christie, I. (2008). 'Histories of the Future: Mapping the Avant-garde'. *Film History* 20: 6–13.
Clarke, P. (1999). 'Rise and Fall of Thatcherism'. *Historical Research* 72(179): 302–322.
Cohen, D. (2008). 'The best comedy club, ever…'. Available at: http://www.chortle.co.uk/correspondents/2008/10/03/7525/the_best_comedy_club,_ever [accessed 26 June 2014].
Cohen, P., and Gardner, C. (eds.) (1982). *It Ain't Half Racist, Mum: Fighting Racism in the Media*. London: Comedia.
Cook, W. (2001). *The Comedy Store: The Club that Changed British Comedy*. London: Little Brown.
Craig, C. (2000). *Alternative Comedy and the Politics of Live Performance*. PhD, Royal Holloway College, University of London.
Craig, S. (ed.) (1980). *Dreams and Deconstructions: Alternative Theatre in Britain*. Ambergate: Ambergate Press Limited.
Crang, M., and Cook, I. (2007). *Doing Ethnographies*. Sage.
Critchley, S. (2002). *On Humour*. London: Routledge.
Dawson, A. (2005). '"Love Music, Hate Racism": The Cultural Politics of the Rock Against Racism Campaigns, 1976–1981'. *Postmodern Culture* 16(1) (September). Available at: http://pmc.iath.virginia.edu/issue.905/16.1dawson.html [accessed 14 February 2014].
De Certeau, M. (1988). *The Practice of Everyday Life*. London: University of California Press.
De Saussure, F. (2019). *Course in General Linguistics*. London: Bloomsbury.
Debord, G. (2005). *Society of the Spectacle*. Detroit: Black and Red.
Desmond, J., McDonagh, P., and O'Donoghue, S. (2000). 'Counter-Culture and Consumer-Society'. *Consumption, Markets and Culture* 4(3). Available at: http://www.crito.uci.edu/noah/NOAH/CMC%20Website/CMC%20PDFs/CMC4_3.pdf#page=40 [accessed 13 July 2013].

Doggett, P. (2008). *There's a Riot Going On: Revolutionaries, Rock Stars and the Rise and Fall of '60s Counter-Culture*. Edinburgh: Canongate Books.
Dorney, K., and Merkin, R. (2010). *The Glory of the Garden: English Regional Theatre and the Arts Council 1984–2009*. Cambridge Scholars.
Double, O. (1991). *An Approach to Traditions of British Stand Up Comedy*. PhD, University of Sheffield.
Double, O. (1994). 'Laughing All the Way to the Bank? Alternative Comedy in the Provinces'. *New Theatre Quarterly* 10: 255–262. Available at: http://journals.cambridge.org/action/displayAbstract?fromPage=online&aid=2340432&fileId=S0266464X00000555.
Double, O. (1997). *Stand Up! On Being a Comedian*. London: Methuen.
Double, O. (2005). *Getting the Joke – The Art of Stand-Up Comedy*. London: Methuen.
Double, O. (2007). 'Punk Rock as Popular Theatre'. *New Theatre Quarterly* XXIII(1) (February): 35–48.
Double, O. (2013). *Britain Had Talent: A History of Variety Theatre*. London: Palgrave Macmillan.
Double, O. (2014). *Stand Up: On Being a Comedian*. A&C Black.
Double, O. (2015). 'What do you do?' *ephemera: theory & politics in organization* 15(3): 651–669.
Double, O. (2020). *Alternative Comedy: 1979 and the Reinvention of British Stand-Up*. London: Methuen Drama.
Duncan, M. (2004). 'Autoethnography: Critical Appreciation of an Emerging Art'. *International Journal of Qualitative Methods* 3(4): 28–39.
Ellis, C., Adams, T., and Bochner, A. (2011). 'Autoethnography: An Overview'. *Historical Social Research / Historische Sozialforschung* 36(4(138)): 273–290 [accessed via JSTOR].
Ellison, R. (1965). *Invisible Man*. London: Penguin.
Elms, R. (2005). *The Way We Wore*. London: Picador
Epstein, R. (1998). 'Imprisonment for Debt: The Courts and the Poll Tax'. *Journal of Social Welfare & Family Law* 20(2): 165–175.
Evans, E.J. (1997). *Thatcher and Thatcherism*. London: Routledge.
Fanon, F. (1986). *Black Skin, White Masks*. London: Pluto Press.
Fanon, F. (2001). *The Wretched of the Earth*. London: Penguin.
Fiske, J. (2000). *Understanding Popular Culture*. London: Routledge.
Fosse, B. (1972). *Cabaret* [film]. 20th Century Fox.
Foucault, M. (1977). *Discipline and Punish*. London: Penguin.
Fowler, B. (1999). 'Pierre Bourdieu's Sociological Theory of Culture'. *Variant* 2(8): 1–4.
Freud, S. (1966). *Jokes and Their Relation to the Unconscious*. London: Routledge and Kegan Paul.
Friedman, M. (2004). *Capitalism and Freedom*. London: University of Chicago Press.
Friedman, S. (2009). 'Legitimating a Discredited Art Form: The Changing Field of British Comedy'. *Edinburgh Working Papers in Sociology* 39 [accessed via JSTOR].

Friedman, S. (2010). 'The Cultural Currency of a "Good" Sense of Humour: British Comedy and New Forms of Distinction'. *British Journal of Sociology* 62(2): 347–370. Available at: http://openaccess.city.ac.uk/2035/ [accessed 7 October 2013].

Friedman, S., and Kuipers, G. (2013). 'The Divisive Power of Humour: Comedy, Taste and Symbolic Boundaries'. *Cultural Sociology* 7(2): 179–195.

Gamble, A. (1980). 'Thatcher – Make or Break'. *Marxism Today*, November.

Garber, M. (1997). *Vested Interests: Cross-Dressing and Cultural Anxiety*. London: Routledge.

Garbutt, R. (2014). 'Aquarius and Beyond: Thinking through the Counterculture'. *M/C Journal* 17(6). Available at: https://doi.org/10.5204/mcj.911.

Garnham, N. (1987). 'Concepts of Culture: Public Policy and the Cultural Industries'. *Cultural Studies* 1(1): 23–37.

Geertz, C. (1973). 'Thick Description: Toward an Interpretive Theory of Culture'. In *The Interpretation of Cultures: Selected Essays* (pp. 3–30). New York: Basic Books.

Giappone, K.B.R. (2012). *The Masks of Anarchy: A Theoretical Study of the Intersections between Punk and Alternative Comedy*. PhD, University of Kent.

Giappone, K.B.R. (2018). *The Punk Turn in Comedy: Masks of Anarchy*. London: Springer.

Gilbert, D. (2005). 'Interrogating Mixed-Race: A Crisis of Ambiguity?' *Social Identities* 11(1): 55–74.

Gilmore, M. (2012). 'Cover Story Excerpt: David Bowie'. Available at: http://www.rollingstone.com/music/news/cover-story-excerpt-david-bowie-20120118 [accessed 5 June 2013].

Gilroy, P. (1987). *There Ain't No Black in the Union Jack*. London: Hutchinson.

Gilroy, P. (2007). *There Ain't No Black in the Union Jack*. London: Routledge.

Goodyer, I. (2003). 'Rock against Racism: Multiculturalism and Political Mobilization, 1976–81'. *Immigrants & Minorities* 22(1): 44–62.

Goodyer, I. (2009). *Crisis Music: The Cultural Politics of Rock against Racism*. Manchester University Press.

Gracyk, T. (2011). 'Kids're Forming Bands: Making Meaning in Post-Punk'. In *Punk and Post-Punk*. Bristol: Intellect. Available at: http://www.ingentaconnect.com/content/intellect/punk/2011/00000001/00000001/art00005 [accessed 30 May 2014].

Gramsci, A. (ed.) (2003). *Selections from the Prison Notebooks*. London: Lawrence & Wishart.

Greenslade, W. (2005). *The Goon Show*. BBC Worldwide.

Hall, S. (1979). 'The Great Moving Right Show'. *Marxism Today*, January: 16–23.

Hall, S. (1980). 'Thatcherism – A New Stage?' *Marxism Today*, February: 26–28.

Hall, S. (1982). 'The Long Haul'. *Marxism Today*, November: 18–24.

Hall, S. (ed.) (1997). *Representation: Cultural Representations and Signifying Practices*. London: Sage.

Hamilton, I. (1981). 'The Comic Strip'. *London Review of Books* 3(16) (3 September): 20.

Hardee, M., with Fleming, J. (1996). *I Stole Freddie Mercury's Birthday Cake* [ebook].

Haritaworn, J. (2009). 'Hybrid Border-crossers? Towards a Radical Socialisation of Mixed-Race'. *Journal of Ethnic and Migration Studies* 35(1) (January): 115–132 [accessed via JSTOR].

Hattenstone, S. (2021). 'Interview: Gina Yashere on Riches, Racism and US Success: "I Don't Like to Boast, but I'm Doing Very Well!"' *Guardian*, 12 July 2021 [accessed 18 July 2021].

Hayek, F.A. (1983). *The Road to Serfdom*. London: Routledge and Kegan Paul.

Hebdige, D. (1993). *Subculture: The Meaning of Style*. London: Methuen.

Hennessey, T. (2013). *Hunger Strike: Margaret Thatcher's Battle with the IRA, 1980–1981*. Irish Academic Press.

Hesmondhalgh, D. (2007). *The Cultural Industries* (2nd ed.). Los Angeles, CA; London: SAGE.

Hewison, R. (1984). *Footlights! A Hundred Years of Cambridge Comedy*. London: Methuen.

Hillier, B. (1970). *Cartoons and Caricatures*. London: Studio Vista.

Hipkin, B. (1986). 'Putting the Popular Back into Culture'. *Marxism Today*, April: 41–42.

Honri, P. (1997). *Music Hall Warriors: A History of the Variety Artistes Federation*. London: Greenwich Exchange.

Horn, G.R. (2007). *The Spirit of '68: Rebellion in Western Europe and North America, 1956–1976*. Oxford University Press.

Houchin, J. (1984). 'The Origins of Cabaret-Artistique'. *Drama Review* 28(1) (French Theatre, Spring): 5–14 [accessed via JSTOR].

Hughes, C.P. (2011). *The Socio-Cultural Milieux of the Left in Post-War Britain*. PhD, University of Warwick.

Hurst, L. (2013). 'The Local Comedy Club'. Available at: https://www.leehurst.com/the-local-comedy-club/) [accessed 13 May 2023].

Ilott, S. (2019). 'Encounters with the Neighbour in 1970s' British Multicultural Comedy'. *Postcolonial Interventions: An Interdisciplinary Journal of Postcolonial Studies* 4(1).

Itzin, C. (1986). *Stages in the Revolution: Political Theatre in Britain Since 1968*. London: Methuen.

Jameson, F. (1991). *Postmodernism, or, the Cultural Logic of Late Capitalism*. Duke University Press.

Johnstone, K. (1989). *Impro: Improvisation and the Theatre*. London: Methuen.

Keay, D. (1987). 'Interview with Margaret Thatcher'. *Woman's Own*, 31 October: 8–10.

Kelly, M. (1989). 'No Politics Please – We're British'. *Comedy Pages*, March, Issue 1.

Kent, N. (1978). 'This Year's Esperanto. John Cooper-Clarke, the Poet Who Came in from the Cold'. *New Musical Express*, 11 November.

Kershaw, B. (1992). *The Politics of Performance: Radical Theatre as Cultural Intervention*. London: Routledge.

Kift, D. (1996). *The Victorian Music Hall: Culture, Class and Conflict*. Cambridge University Press.

Kravitz, S. (1977). 'London Jokes and Ethnic Stereotypes'. *Western Folklore* 36(4) (Western States Folklore Society): 275–301 [accessed via JSTOR].

Lachmann, R., Eshelman, R., and Davis, M. (1988). 'Bakhtin and Carnival: Culture as Counter-culture'. *Cultural Critique* (pp. 115–152) [accessed via JSTOR].

Lahiri, D. (2001). 'I don't think I can die before I find out what happened to my son'. *Guardian*, 15 May.

Lancaster, G., and Brierley, G. (2001). 'A Comparative Study of the Emergence of Marketing Culture within Three Formerly Nationalised Companies'. *International Journal of Public Sector Management* 14(4): 341–371.

Lane, J.F. (2000). *Pierre Bourdieu*. London: Pluto.

Lee, S. (2010). *How I Escaped My Certain Fate – The Life and Deaths of a Stand-Up Comedian*. London: Faber and Faber.

Leitch, L. (2003). 'Future of Hackney Empire in the Balance'. *Evening Standard*, 11 July: 20.

Lewis, J. (2013). Personal blog. https://www.julianlewis.net/cheshire-vc-and-the-cnd/3772:introduction-the-reason-for-this-website-section-2013-08-27 [accessed 27 August 2014].

Lidington, T. (1987). 'New Terms for Old Turns: The Rise of Alternative Cabaret'. *New Theatre Quarterly* 3: 107–119. Available at: http://journals.cambridge.org/abstract_S0266464X00008605 [accessed 15 November 2013].

Lippitt, J. (1994). 'Humour and Incongruity'. *Cogito* 8(2): 147–153. Available at: http://uhra.herts.ac.uk/bitstream/handle/2299/3989/900211.pdf?sequence=1 [accessed 13 April 2016].

Lippitt, J. (1995a). 'Humour and Release'. *Cogito* 9(2): 169–176. Available at: https://uhra.herts.ac.uk/bitstream/handle/2299/3990/900209.pdf?sequence=1 [accessed 13 April 2016].

Lippitt, J. (1995b). 'Humour and Superiority'. *Cogito* 9(1): 54–61. Available at: http://uhra.herts.ac.uk/bitstream/handle/2299/3991/900210.pdf?sequence=1 [accessed 11 April 2016].

Lund, J., and Denisoff, R.S. (1971). 'The Folk Music Revival and the Counter Culture: Contributions and Contradictions'. *Journal of American Folklore* 84(334): 394–405 [accessed 25 February 2022].

McDonnell, B. (2010). 'Jesters to the Revolution: A History of Cartoon Archetypical Slogan Theatre (Cast), 1965–85'. *Theatre Notebook*, 1 June: 96–113 [accessed via Google Scholar, 12 November 2013].

McGillivray, D. (ed.) (1989). *British Alternative Theatre Directory – The Complete Guide to Fringe Companies and Venues*. London: Conway McGillivray.

McGillivray, D. (ed.) (1990). *British Alternative Theatre Directory 1990/91 – The Complete Guide*. London: Conway McGillivray.

McGregor, S. (2002). 'Neither Washington nor Moscow'. *International Socialism Journal* 97 (Winter).

McKay, G. (1996). *Senseless Acts of Beauty: Cultures of Resistance since the Sixties*. London: Verso.

McNeil, D. (2011). 'Black Devils, White Saints and Mixed-Race Femme Fatales: Philippa Schuyler and the Winds of Change'. *Critical Arts* 25(3): 360–376.

Mally, L. (2003). 'Exporting Soviet Culture: The Case of Agitprop Theatre'. *Slavic Review* 62(2) (Summer): 324–342 [accessed via JSTOR].
Marcus, G. (1989). *Lipstick Traces: A Secret History of the Twentieth Century*. London: Faber and Faber.
Marinetti, F. T. (2010). *The Futurist Manifesto* (1909). Available at: https://www.societyforasianart.org/sites/default/files/manifesto_futurista.pdf [accessed 1 May 2020].
Marx, K. (1977). *The Eighteenth Brumaire of Louis Bonaparte*. Moscow: Progress Publishers.
Marx, K. (2002). *Theses on Feuerbach*. Marx/Engels Internet Archive. Available at: https://www.marxists.org/archive/marx/works/1845/theses/theses.htm [accessed 12 September 2011].
Mascha, E. (1998). 'Political Satire and Hegemony: A Case for Passive Revolution During Mussolini's Ascendance to Power, 1919 to 1925'. *Humor: The Journal of The International Society for Humor Studies*.
Merriam, S., and Tisdell, E.J. (2015). *Qualitative Research: A Guide to Design and Implementation* (4th ed.). London: Wiley.
Mintz, L.E. (1985). 'Standup Comedy as Social and Cultural Mediation'. *American Quarterly* 37(1): 71–80.
Moore, X. (1982). 'Guerrilla Voices England's Grey Unpleasant Land'. *New Musical Express*, 6 February: 15–16.
Morrison, M. (2014). *A Critical History of the Soho Theatre: 1968–1975*. PhD, University of Westminster, London.
Muldoon, R. (2013). *Taking on the Empire: How We Saved the Hackney Empire for Popular Theatre*. Manchester: Just Press.
Mullen, J. (2012). 'Anti-Black Racism in British Popular Music (1880–1920)'. *Revue Française de Civilisation Britannique (French Journal of British Studies)* 17(2): 61–80.
Murray, L. (2007). *Teach Yourself Stand-Up Comedy*. London: Hodder Education.
Myers, L., and Lockyer, S. (2011). '"It's about Expecting the Unexpected": Live Stand-up Comedy from the Audiences' Perspective'. *Participations* 8(2) (November).
Newcastle Fringe (1987). 'Free Programme of Events', 7–24 October.
Parkin, C. (2007). 'Counterculture in Ladbroke Grove'. *Time Out*, 13 August. Available at: http://www.timeout.com/london/music/counterculture-in-ladbroke-grove [accessed 9 September 2015].
Peters, L. (2013). 'The Roots of Alternative Comedy? The Alternative Story of 20th Century Coyote and Eighties Comedy'. *Comedy Studies* 4(1): 5–21. doi:10.1386/cost.4.1.5_1.
Purdie, S. (1993). *Comedy: The Mastery of Discourse*. Hemel Hempstead: Harvester Wheatsheaf.
Quirk, S. (2015a). 'Preaching to the Converted? How Political Comedy Matters'. *Humor* 29(2): 243–260. ISSN 0933-1719.
Quirk, S. (2015b). *Why Stand-Up Matters: How Comedians Manipulate and Influence*. Bloomsbury Publishing.

Raines, H. (1988). 'LONDON; A Singing Doctor Works the Land Between Ridicule and Reverence for Nashville'. *New York Times*, 6 March.
Ray, G. (2007). 'Notes on Bourdieu', on *Transform.eipcp.net* [web page]. Available at: http://transform.eipcp.net/correspondence/1169972617#redir#redir [accessed 22 December 2015].
Reed-Danahay, D. (2005). *Locating Bourdieu*. Bloomington, IN: Indiana University Press.
Regester, C. (1994). 'Stepin Fetchit: The Man, the Image, and the African American Press'. *Film History* 6(4): 502–521.
Renton, D. (2002). 'The Life and Politics of David Widgery'. *Left History* 8(1).
Renton, D. (2006). *When We Touched the Sky: The Anti-Nazi League, 1977–1981*. London: New Clarion Press.
Reynolds, S. (2005). *Rip It Up and Start Again: Post-Punk 1978–1984*. London: Faber and Faber.
Ritchie, C. (1997). *Stand-Up Comedy and Everyday Life*. PhD, University of London, Goldsmiths College.
Robbins, D. (2000). *Bourdieu and Culture*. London: Sage.
Rudin, R. (2007). 'Revisiting the Pirates'. *Media History* 13(2–3): 235–255.
Russell, D. (2013). 'Glimpsing La Dolce Vita: Cultural Change and Modernity in the 1960s English Cabaret Club'. *Journal of Social History* 47(2): 297–318.
Rye, J. (1972). *Futurism*. London: Studio Vista.
Saville, I. (1990). *Ideas, Forms and Developments in the British Workers' Theatre, 1925–1935*. PhD, City University, London.
Sayle, A. (2010). *Stalin Ate My Homework*. London: Sceptre.
Segel, H. (1977). 'Fin de Siècle Cabaret'. *Performing Arts Journal* 2(1) (Spring): 41–57 [accessed via JSTOR].
Senelick, L. (1974). 'Politics as Entertainment: Victorian Music Hall Song'. *Victorian Studies* 19(2) (December): 149–180 [accessed via JSTOR].
Shallice, J. (2007). 'Keep Throwing Stones'. In *Red Pepper*. Available at: http://www.redpepper.org.uk/Keep-throwing-stones/ [accessed 14 October 2014].
Shank, T. (1978). 'Political Theatre in England'. *Performing Arts Journal* 2(3) (Winter): 48–62. MIT Press [accessed via JSTOR].
Shiach, M. (1989). *Discourse on Popular Culture*. London: Polity Press.
Skint Video (1989). 'The Swell of the Crowd'. *Comedy Pages*, May, Issue 1.
Small, S., and Solomos, J. (2006). 'Race, Immigration and Politics in Britain: Changing Policy Agendas and Conceptual Paradigms 1940s–2000s'. *International Journal of Comparative Sociology* 47(3–4): 235–257.
Smith, A. (2013). 'Arts Council Announces £11.6m of In-Year Cuts'. *Stage*. Available at: https://www.thestage.co.uk/news/2013/arts-council-announces-11-6m-of-in-year-cuts/?sector=funding-matters [accessed 22 March 2015].
Smith, C.P. (2000). 'Content Analysis and Narrative Analysis'. In T. Reis (ed.), *Handbook of Research Methods in Social and Personality Psychology*. Cambridge University Press.
Smith, E. (2011). 'Are the Kids United? The Communist Party of Great Britain, Rock Against Racism, and the Politics of Youth Culture'. *Journal for the Study of Radicalism* 5(2). doi:10.1353/jsr.2011.0017.

Spencer, N. (2015). 'Craig Charles: My Family Values'. *Guardian*, 29 May [accessed 3 July 2021].

Spry, T. (2001). 'Performing Autoethnography: An Embodied Methodological Praxis'. *Qualitative Inquiry: QI* 7(6): 706–732.

Stewart, G. (2013). *Bang! A History of Britain in the 1980s* [e-book]. Available at: http://uel.eblib.com/patron/FullRecord.aspx?p=1352337 [accessed 3 March 2014].

Stewart, T. (1976). 'Heil and Farewell'. *New Musical Express*, 8 May: 9.

Stourac, R., and McCreery, K. (1986). *Theatre as a Weapon*. London: Routledge and Kegan Paul.

Street, J. (2007). *Politics and Popular Culture*. London: Wiley.

Street, J., Hague, S., and Savigny, H. (2008). 'Playing to the Crowd: The Role of Music and Musicians in Political Participation'. *Political Studies Association Journal* 10(2): 269–285.

Strinati, D., and Wagg, S. (1992). *Come on Down? Popular Media Culture in Post-War Britain*. London: Routledge.

Strinati, D., and Wagg, S. (eds.) (2004). *Come on Down? Popular Media Culture in Post-War Britain*. London: Routledge.

Sturges, P. (2015). 'The Production of Comedy'. *SAGE Open* 5(4). 2158244015612521.

Suvin, D. (1972). 'The Mirror and the Dynamo'. In L. Baxandall (ed.), *Radical Perspectives in the Arts*. London: Pelican.

Thatcher, M. (1999). 'Pinochet Was this Country's Staunch, True Friend'. Text of speech to Conservative Party Conference fringe meeting reproduced in *Guardian*, 6 October. Available at: http://www.theguardian.com/world/1999/oct/06/pinochet.chile [accessed 21 September 2015].

Thoday, J. (2014). Interview on 'Such Small Portions' website. Available at: http://www.suchsmallportions.com/person/jon-thoday [accessed 6 March 2014].

Thornton, S. (1997). *Club Cultures: Music, Media and Subcultural Capital*. Cambridge: Polity Press.

Touchard, J. (1956). 'Bibliographie et chronologie du poujadisme'. *Revue Française de Science Politique* 6(1): 18–43.

Tracy, S. (2012). *Qualitative Research Methods: Collecting Evidence, Crafting Analysis, Communicating Impact*. Hoboken: Wiley.

Turner, A.W. (2010). *Rejoice! Rejoice! Britain in the 1980s*, e-book. Available at: http://uel.eblib.com/patron/FullRecord.aspx?p=898827 [accessed 3 March 2014].

Urry, J. (1995). *Consuming Places*. Psychology Press.

Vaneigem, R. (1967). *The Revolution of Everyday Life*. Available at: http://library.nothingness.org/articles/SI/en/pub_contents/5 [accessed 9 March 2010].

Vorspan, R. (2000). 'Rational Recreation and the Law: The Transformation of Popular Urban Leisure in Victorian England'. *McGill Law Journal* 45: 891.

Wagg, S. (ed.) (1998). *Because I Tell a Joke or Two: Comedy, Politics and Social Difference*. London: Routledge.

Wagg, S. (2002). 'Comedy, Politics and Permissiveness: The Satire Boom and its Inheritance'. *Contemporary Politics* 8(4) [accessed via JSTOR].

Wall, S. (2008). 'Easier Said than Done: Writing an Autoethnography'. *International Journal of Qualitative Methods* 7(1): 38–53.
Watt, D. (2007). 'On Becoming a Qualitative Researcher: The Value of Reflexivity'. *Qualitative Report* 12(1): 82–101. Available at: http://files.eric.ed.gov/fulltext/EJ800164.pdf [accessed 12 October 2015].
Webb, J., Schirato, T., and Danaher, G. (2002). *Understanding Bourdieu*. London: Sage.
Widgery, D. (1986). *Beating Time: Riot 'n' Race 'n' Rock 'n' Roll*. London: Chatto and Windus.
Williams, R. (1976). *Keywords: A Vocabulary of Culture and Society*. London: Fontana.
Wilmut, R. (and Rosengrad, P.) (1989). *Didn't You Kill My Mother-in-Law?* London: Methuen
Witkin, S. (2014). *Narrating Social Work through Autoethnography*. New York: Columbia University Press.
Wittner, L. S. (1993). *The Struggle Against the Bomb. Volume 1: One World or None: A History of the World Nuclear Disarmament Movement Through 1953*. Stanford: Stanford University Press.
Wollen, P. (1975). 'The Two Avant-Gardes, first published in *Studio International*, November/December 1975'. Available at: http://www.medienkunstnetz.de/source-text/100/ [accessed 24 September 2010].
Wolmar, C. (1987). 'Taxation Tangles'. *Marxism Today*, October.
Woodroofe, K. (1975). 'The Irascible Reverend Henry Solly and His Contribution to Working Men's Clubs, Charity Organization, and "Industrial Villages" in Victorian England'. *Social Service Review* 15–32 [accessed via JSTOR].
Zack, N. (2010). 'The Fluid Symbol of Mixed-Race'. *Hypatia* 25(4): 875–890.
Zeldin, T. (1973). *France 1848–1945. Volume 1: Ambition, Love and Politics*. Oxford: Clarendon Press.

Interviews

Allen, T. (2011). Interview [in person], Notting Hill, London, 3 November.
Balloo, J. (2012). Interview [in person], Hackney, London, 14 April.
Boyton, B. (2010). Interview [in person], Camden, London, 15 November.
Bryan, D. (2012). *Black Comedy Club* [in person], West Norwood, London, 12 June.
Darrell, D. (2010). Interview [in person], Stockwell, London, 2 April.
Dembina, I. (2012). Interview [in person], Lambeth, London, 12 May.
Golden, R. (2012). Interview [in person], Tottenham, London.
Gribbin, S. (2011). Interview [in person], Lewisham, London, 5 April.
Gribbin, S. (2012). Interview [in person], Lewisham, London.
James, N. (2011). Interview [in person], Hammersmith, London, 12 April.
Kelly, M. (2012). Interview [in person], National Theatre, London, 12 June.
Landreth, J. (2012). *Black Comedy Club* [in person], Clapham, London, 21 May.

Lee, S. (2011). Interview [in person], Leicester Square Theatre, London, 21 January.
Lyttle, C. (2011). *Cabaret A Go Go* interview [in person], Hammersmith, London, 8 August.
Muldoon, R. (2010). *CAST/Hackney Empire* interview [in person], Paddington, London, 5 December.
Muldoon, R. (2011). *CAST/Hackney Empire* interview [in person], Paddington, London, 10 November.
Sneddon, P. (2012). Interview [in person], Institute of Education, London, 4 March.
Soan, M. (2013). Interview [in person], Peckham, London, 12 May.

Questionnaires

Clayton, S. (2013)
Darrell, D. (2013)
Gordillo, J. (2012)
Herbert, P. (2013)
Hurst, M. (2012)
Korn, J. (2012)
Lee, W. (2013)
Marshall, J. (2013)
Mulligan, B. (2013)
Rawlings, S. (2013)
Revell, N. (2013)
Saville, I. (2013)
Smart, A. (2013)
Thompson, D. (2013)
Toczek, N. (2013)
Ward, P. (2013)
Wilding, W. (2013)

Facebook Conversations

Boyton, B. (2013). Personal communication.
Boyton, B. (2014). Personal communication.
Cresswell, C. (2015). Personal communication, 20 January.

DVDs, Videos, Television Programmes

Baker, F. (1971). *Lenny Bruce Without Tears*.
BBC (2005). *25 Years of the Comedy Store – A Personal History by Paul Merton* [DVD]. SMG TV Productions for the BBC, BBC2, 2005.
BBC (2006). *Lenny Bruce is Dead*. BBC Radio 2, 25 July 2006: 2030.
BBC (2010). *Festivals Britannia* [TV programme]. BBC4, 17 December 2010: 2100.
BBC (2012). *Punk Britannia 'Pre-punk 1972–1976'* [TV programme]. BBC4, screened 9 June 2012: 2100.
BBC (2012). *Punk Britannia 'Punk 1976–1978'* [TV programme]. BBC4, screened 8 June 2012: 2100.
BBC (2012). *Punk Britannia 'Post-punk 1978–1981'* [TV programme]. BBC4, screened 15 June 2012: 2100.
Ben Elton: Laughing at the 80s (2011). [TV programme]. Tiger Aspect Productions, Channel 4, 28 December 2011: 2300.
Bill Hicks: Revelations (1993). [Film]. Directed by Chris Bould, BBC4, screened 27 August 2011: 2340.
Black and White Minstrel Show, The (1978). Final show [TV programme]. BBC, BBC1, 30 June 1978. Available at: http://www.youtube.com/watch?v=KoYOraDt1_k [accessed 10 June 2013].
Boom Boom... Out Go the Lights (1980). [Self-recorded DVD]. BBC, BBC2.
Boom Boom... Out Go the Lights (1981). [Self-recorded DVD]. BBC, BBC2.
Dave Allen: God's Own Comedian (2013). [TV documentary]. BBC2, 5 May 2013: 2200.
Eddie Izzard: Believe (2010). Directed by Sarah Townsend [TV programme]. BBC2, screened 18 December 2010: 2300.
Ladies and Gentlemen, Lenny Bruce! The Godfather of Modern Stand-up (2006). [DVD]. Best Medicine Comedy.
Love Thy Neighbour (1972). 'The TUC Conference' (Series 2, Episode 5). Thames Television, 9 October 1972. Available at: http://www.youtube.com/watch?v=syqsRqv3hPQ [accessed 12 May 2013].
Magnuson, J. (1965). 'Lenny Bruce performance, Basin Street West'.
Marti Caine at the Wheeltappers and Shunters Social Club – Granada TV (date unknown). Recorded 1975. Available at: https://www.youtube.com/watch?v=x_Wo_a_2y-o [accessed 21 September 2015].
Mayfair Set, The (1999). Directed by Adam Curtis [online video]. BBC. Available at: http://www.youtube.com/watch?v=5U-sNn28dJk [accessed 12 March 2011].
Monty Python's Flying Circus, 'The Philosophers' Football Match', on YouTube (published 2 March 2015). Available at: https://www.youtube.com/watch?v=B6nI1v7mwwA.
Story of Variety, The (2011). Presented by Michael (Lord) Grade [TV programme]. BBC4, 26 March, 2011: 2100.
Story of Variety, The (2012). Presented by Michael (Lord) Grade [TV programme]. BBC4, screened 31 May 2012: 0215.

Wheeltappers and Shunters' Social Club, The (1974). Featuring Terri Rogers and Shorty [TV programme]. Granada Television. Available at: http://www.youtube.com/watch?v=k-waR3ucboo [accessed 13 April 2013].

Discography

Au Pairs (1981). *Playing with a Different Sex*. Human Records.
Carlin, G. (1973). *Occupation: Foole* [mp3]. Little David/Atlantic.
Carlin, G. (1974). *Toledo Window Box* [mp3]. Little David/Warner Brothers.
Clash, The (1979). *London Calling!* [Music CD]. London: CBS.
Clash, The (1980). *Sandinista!* [Music CD]. London: CBS.
Dexys Midnight Runners (1980). *Searching for the Young Soul Rebels* [mp3]. London: EMI.
Firesign Theatre, The (1969). *How Can You Be in Two Places at Once When You're Not Anywhere at All?* Columbia Records.
Firesign Theatre, The (1974). *Everything You Know Is Wrong*. Columbia Records.
Gang of Four (1979a). *Damaged Goods EP* [vinyl record]. Edinburgh: Fast Records.
Gang of Four (1979b). *Entertainment!* [Music CD]. London: EMI.
ICA Recording (1989). *Didn't You Kill My Mother-in-Law?* [panel discussion]. 15 June 1989.
Public Enemy (1991). *Apocalypse 91... The Empire Strikes Black* [Music CD]. New York: Def Jam.
Ride (1990). *Nowhere* [Music CD]. London: Creation.
Ride (1992). *Going Blank Again* [Music CD]. London: Creation.
Scott-Heron, Gil (1980). *Re-Ron* b/w *B-Movie* [Vinyl 12-inch single]. New York: Arista.
Scott-Heron, Gil (1988). *Pieces of a Man* [mp3]. New York: RCA.
Specials, The (1979). *The Specials* [Music CD]. London: Two Tone.
Spin Doctors (1991). Pocket Full of Kryptonite [mp3]. New York: Epic.
Wire (1977). *Pink Flag* [Music CD]. London: Harvest.
Wire (1978). *Chairs Missing* [Music CD]. London: Harvest.
Wire (1979). *154* [Music CD]. London: Harvest.

Miscellaneous

David Bowie at Victoria Station, June 1976. Available at: https://www.youtube.com/watch?v=X1SxU83bpkU.
Geoffrey Howe's resignation speech. HC Deb (13 November 1990). *Hansard*. Vol 180, cc461–5.

Index

291 Club 66, 115n, 209, 222

absurdism 72, 80, 81
a capella 37, 43, 67, 208, 210, 228
activism 141, 159, 160, 164, 231, 232
activists 138, 142
aesthetics 149, 155
  in comedy 118, 144
African-American 86, 88, 89, 122, 127, 113, 233
African-Caribbean 4, 33, 115, 118–120, 209
agencies 64, 112, 117
agit-prop 27, 39, 44, 91, 183, 184, 225
Agitprop Players 184, 241
Agraman (John Marshall) 54
Ali, Altab 134, 183
Allen, Dave 80, 131
  Dave Allen Show, The 80
  Dave Allen at Large 80
Allen, Tony 1, 21, 38, 52, 132, 133, 142, 145, 187, 193, 220, 223
Allen, Woody 78, 119
alternative cabaret/altcab (genre) 11–13, 15–21, 23, 26, 27, 29, 30, 42, 43, 46, 57, 63, 65, 70, 74, 77, 78, 80, 82, 122, 136, 137, 143, 146, 147, 152–154, 157, 161, 168, 169, 195, 196, 198, 199, 207, 209, 213, 216, 224–231, 233
Alternative Cabaret (collective) 30, 142, 190–191, 201, 229
'Alternative Seaside Special' 59, 101
amateur (and amateurs) 2, 10, 18, 21, 62, 139, 140, 143, 144, 145, 153, 155, 220, 225
amateurism 128, 139, 191
  see also Port Stanley Amateur Dramatic Society
Amazing Mr. Smith 62
anarchism 138, 217
anarchists 9, 132, 134, 177, 183, 184
Anti-Apartheid Movement 95, 132, 134, 179
Anti-Nazi League (ANL) 14, 15, 17, 19, 22, 25, 27, 164, 182, 191
Anti-Poll Tax League, Anti-Poll Tax Union 63, 69, 71, 102
anti-racism 10, 26, 67
art 9, 24, 25, 90, 92, 107, 123, 128, 129, 143, 150, 154, 161–162, 193, 200, 219
  art appreciation 143, 161
  art cabarets 21
    see also cabaret-artistique
  art centres 190

art forms 5, 9, 22, 153, 165
art movements 216
art practitioners 196
art production 162
art schools 14, 137n, 163, 208
art theory 144
performance art 161, 216
Arts Council of Great Britain (ACGB) 180, 181, 185, 188, 189, 193, 196, 210
Attila the Stockbroker 44, 56, 138, 206
Au Pairs, the 146–147
autodidacticism 127, 182, 186, 208
autoethnography 3–6, 7, 9, 73, 74
Avalon (talent agency) 56, 60, 104, 162
avant-garde 2, 9, 18, 84, 129, 140 -143, 145, 154, 158, 165, 166, 174, 191, 208, 218, 223

Baddiel, David 56, 59
Bailey, Andrew 45, 46, 66, 164n
  see also Podomovsky
Balloo, Julie 136, 144, 171, 172
Banana Cabaret 50, 56, 71, 72, 77, 129
Baxter, Stanley 80
Benn, Tony 36, 49
British Broadcasting Corporation (BBC) 9, 26, 30, 38, 64, 91, 101, 103, 104, 139, 172, 180, 200, 216
Black and White Minstrel Show 16, 111, 120
Black Comedy (comedy club circuit) 17, 30n, 61, 64, 97, 101–102, 109, 119n, 120–121, 209
blackface 16, 16n, 111
bohemianism 150, 153, 154, 223
Boom, Boom… Out Go the Lights 38
boom, satire 139, 185
Bourdieu, Pierre 16, 17, 19, 31, 83, 136, 143, 148, 151, 162, 169, 174, 182, 183, 196, 198, 245
bourgeois 182, 196, 202
Bowie, David 21, 22, 137, 239, 248
Boyton, Bob 36, 43, 52, 57, 65, 128, 130, 132, 137, 142, 148, 163

Brand, Jo 5, 52, 57
Brando, Marlon 91, 174n
Brecht, Bertolt 30, 84, 128, 157, 174
Brenton, Howard 167
bricolage 2, 10, 30, 92, 147, 148, 151–153, 173, 174, 175, 183, 184, 216, 226, 223, 228, 231
British Alternative Theatre Directory 11, 50, 56, 163
British Music Hall Society 207
British National Party (BNP) 7, 25, 42, 105–106
Brixton 39–41, 52, 57, 123, 199, 202, 218
broadcast ban (Sinn Féin) 53
Broadside Mobile Workers Theatre 19, 84, 157
Bruce, Lenny 12, 19, 20, 118, 119, 130, 145, 146
Bryan, David 105, 127, 128, 217
Butler, R.A. 53
  Butler Act (1944) 53
butt (of jokes) 33, 39, 89, 133, 151, 154, 233
Buzz Club 62, 63, 133, 134

cabaret 2, 3, 5, 9, 11, 21, 29, 30, 31, 35, 37, 38, 40, 61, 68, 136, 139, 143, 154, 159, 163, 193, 199, 205, 207, 219, 222, 225
  artists, performers 2, 11, 75, 146, 219
  audiences 220
  circuit 18, 24, 35, 46, 51, 62, 108, 217
  clubs 30, 34, 40, 42, 49, 55, 62, 85, 86, 138, 191
  commercial cabaret 158, 168
  courses 74, 84, 128, 162–163, 164, 217
  promoters 36
  section, *Time Out* 27, 36, 45, 48, 49, 61, 64, 68, 69, 114
cabaret-artistique 3, 129, 225
  see also art cabaret

Cabaret A Go Go (CAGG) 86, 88, 103, 155, 197, 200, 202
Cabaret at the Jongleurs (BBC radio show) 9, 51
Cabaret Upstairs, The (BBC radio show) 9, 101
Callaghan, James 16, 16n, 17, 28, 134, 134n, 146
Cambridge Footlights 48, 56
Campaign for Nuclear Disarmament (CND) 27, 40, 41, 44, 95, 132, 134, 152n
cannabis 168, 184, 185n, 176, 192, 193
Cannelloni, Otiz 91, 142, 205
capital
   counter*cultural* 8, 9, 22, 84, 127, 128, 132, 133, 142, 150, 152, 157, 162, 163, 190, 218, 220, 221, 223, 224
   cultural 7, 8, 20, 30, 75, 76, 113, 114, 115, 127, 128, 132, 133, 135, 136, 160, 162, 166, 176, 181, 191, 218, 220, 221, 223, 224
   subcultural 142, 149
   symbolic 2, 22, 134, 150, 160, 162, 223
capitalism 141, 161, 184
caricatures 51, 52, 99, 235, 240
Carlin, George 7, 80, 84, 88, 118, 123, 146
carnivalesque 43, 107, 133, 150, 152, 158, 175, 194
Carrington, Ben 12–14, 127, 129
Carson, Frank 37, 155
cartoons 34, 87, 188, 240
CAST (Cartoon Archetypical Slogan Theatre) 3, 9, 10, 14, 19, 31, 34, 35, 36, 45, 48, 55, 58, 64, 134, 153, 159, 168, 171–213
censorship 148, 158
centre left, the 31, 146
character 14, 22, 24, 31, 32, 74, 90, 99, 101, 102, 108, 113, 115, 118, 123, 126, 127, 132, 150, 166, 183–185, 189, 205, 207, 210
Cheech and Chong 80
Chuckle Club 76, 95
cinema 89–90, 174, 189, 204, 215
circuits, cabaret (also altcab) 10, 11, 13, 18, 19, 21, 27, 34, 35, 36, 37, 42, 46, 47, 51, 52, 57, 58, 59, 61, 62, 64, 67, 68, 69, 75, 101, 102, 108, 109, 114, 123, 125, 132, 136, 153, 154, 155, 162, 163, 167, 187, 188, 195, 208, 217, 219, 221, 224
   Black 10, 61, 121
   Chitlin (African-American) 119
   comedy 5, 51, 73, 74, 108, 114, 120, 122, 123, 151, 157, 217
   London 10, 19, 21, 27, 36, 37, 42, 46, 47, 48, 50, 52, 58, 64, 68, 102, 104, 109, 114, 118, 219, 221
   New Variety (NV) 35, 45, 66, 188, 192, 194, 195, 196, 199, 205, 208, 210, 219, 221
   open spot 68, 126, 217
   working men's club, old-school 2, 13, 69, 160
circus 1, 37, 40, 49, 92, 189
City Limits 2, 36, 64, 70
Clapton, Eric 14
Clary, Julian 164, 199, 208
Clash, the 134, 145
class, social 4, 73, 123
   see also middle class
   see also working class
classification, classifications 54, 80, 117, 157, 194
Clayton, Simon 71, 83, 117, 122, 138, 145, 246
clowns 74, 85, 175
Coconuts (US comedy club chain) 77
colonialism 207
   colonialists 81, 118
   colonies 110
   colonizers 100, 111n

comedians (including stand-up) 2, 5, 6, 7, 12, 15, 18, 20, 22–24, 27, 28, 34, 35, 36, 38, 39, 45–53, 57, 59–61, 62, 65–70, 72, 74, 77, 79, 80, 81, 84, 86, 92, 93, 94, 95, 96, 98, 99, 101, 102, 104, 105, 106, 108, 114, 120, 123, 124, 125, 126, 136, 140–141, 143, 146, 147, 151, 154, 160, 163, 180, 182, 191, 192, 199, 200, 202, 216, 217, 218, 219, 220, 221, 224
    African-American 78, 80
    alternative (alt) 10, 12, 19, 28, 69, 74, 131, 137, 142, 143, 144, 145, 146, 147, 220, 224
    American 20, 69, 84, 88, 127, 130
    Black 10, 61, 78, 81, 119, 120, 121, 122, 119, 121, 122
    Black British 5, 6
    British 80
    character 23, 24, 199
    female 118
    Irish 80, 131, 147
    mainstream 20, 118
    mixed-heritage 120
    old-school 29
    political 118, 150, 158, 219
    traditional (includes working men's clubs) 13, 23, 25–26, 92, 100, 127, 130, 141, 142, 159, 160, 161, 181, 224
    white 81, 102, 116, 117, 120, 122
Comedians (play) 13, 20, 21, 150, 151, 172
Comedians, The (Granada Television programme) 2, 9, 10, 17, 89, 189
comedy 2, 3, 4, 5, 7, 9, 10, 12, 13, 18, 22, 23, 25, 26, 29, 30, 35, 36, 38, 39, 55, 56, 57, 58, 60, 63, 64, 68, 72, 75, 76, 77, 78, 80, 82, 84, 90, 93, 94, 97, 98, 104, 106, 107, 112, 124, 125, 126, 131, 139, 141, 142, 143, 145, 146, 147, 150, 152, 156, 161, 163, 167, 168, 182, 216, 219
    aesthetic 59, 60, 118, 144

alternative (altcom) 2, 13, 60, 61, 114, 159, 160, 220
    Black 9, 30n, 61, 64, 101, 114, 119, 122, 209
    British 161
    as career 62, 74, 86, 122, 126, 219
    comedy club chains 125
    comedy courses 62, 84, 163, 164, 218
    'demob' 131, 167
    Hollywood 105n
    lunchtime 55
    panel shows 18
    political 46, 161, 187, 218
    racist 13, 25, 26
    radio 131
    sexist 13, 26
    stand-up 1, 3, 4, 5, 20, 24, 34, 35, 36, 40, 46, 47, 48, 49, 62, 74, 77, 84, 94, 102, 125, 126, 133, 143, 146, 153, 163, 164, 180, 181, 182, 191, 217, 219, 220, 221
    television 80–81, 102
    traditional, mainstream 23, 24, 99, 131, 143, 158, 161, 225
comedy-cabaret 50, 60, 190
Comedy Store 20, 26–31, 34, 37, 43–45, 48, 50, 54–57, 60, 61, 63, 65, 67, 70, 72, 77, 127–130, 133, 150, 151, 164, 189, 190, 198, 199, 209, 224, 225, 229, 230, 237, 247
Comic Strip (collective) 29, 30, 60, 62, 162
Comic Strip Presents..., The 9, 30, 162, 216
communism 96, 189n
Communist Party of Great Britain (CPGB) 127, 132, 137, 140, 145, 156, 164, 173, 175, 177, 181, 183, 185
compères 20, 22, 32, 34, 42, 55, 57, 61, 62, 63, 64, 88, 141, 191, 195
Condell, Pat 44, 57, 65

Confessions of a Socialist 19, 181
  see also *Full Confessions of a Socialist*
Connolly, Billy 20, 28
Cook, Peter 131
Cook, William 22, 29, 37, 40, 46, 47
consecration 154, 200, 218
conservatism, stylistic 10, 77, 146, 163
Conservative Party 14, 23–25, 27, 36, 48, 49, 59, 61, 73, 103, 115, 143, 156, 160, 165, 186, 190, 196, 197, 218, 233, 244
consumerism 90, 144, 224
contracts 26, 27, 155, 223
Cooper, Tommy 80, 130, 141
Cooper Clarke, John 18, 36, 57n, 82, 130, 216
Cosby, Bill 78, 219
counterculture 2, 15, 80, 142, 149, 152, 154, 155, 156, 180, 183, 189, 218
counterrevolution 27, 151, 152
Courgettes, the (cabaret vocal group) 42, 43
Crawford, Miles 115, 209
Cresswell, Addison 46
crime 35, 39–41
Crown and Castle 42, 45, 72, 170–172, 213, 225
culture 2, 13, 23, 26, 27, 32, 35, 75, 80, 82, 84, 85, 87, 88, 108, 115, 118, 120, 127, 128, 130, 137, 140, 146, 148, 149, 157, 159, 161–163, 180, 183, 184, 199, 202–204, 223, 224, 226, 232, 245
  cultures 2, 13, 14, 28, 87, 100, 148, 149, 204, 228, 236, 239, 241, 244
  dominant 27, 76, 107, 110, 122, 132, 149, 151, 155, 191
Curtis and Ishmael 74, 110

Daltrey, Roger 14
dance 62, 144, 153, 175, 176, 210
Darrell, Dreenagh 38, 43, 52, 136, 137, 163
Davidson, Jim 159, 160
Davy, John 37

Dawson, Les 23, 92, 130, 140
De Certeau, Michel 76, 107, 138, 165
De la Tour, Andy 29, 36, 155, 156, 232
Debord, Guy 140
deconstruction 143, 145
Dembina, Ivor 36, 56, 58, 59, 128, 129, 141, 143, 154, 155
Dexter, Felix 5, 75, 114
Diorama (cinema) 197
DIY (Do It Yourself) 2, 34, 129, 140, 143, 145, 166, 190, 196, 199, 216, 218, 225
  see also bricolage
Dodd, Ken 80
Double, Oliver 3, 5, 24, 74, 97, 98, 102, 107
Dowie, Claire 61, 210, 213, 220
Dowie, John 12, 29, 190, 198, 200, 216
Downstairs at the Kings Head 32, 62, 105
doxa 20, 21, 23, 32, 46, 89, 166, 173, 223, 229
Draylon Underground 67
drugs 123, 129, 186, 224
  drug-taking 149, 185
dub (music genre) 34n, 82, 145, 216

Earth Exchange Cabaret 32, 34, 35, 478, 55, 56, 89, 128
Edmondson, Adrian 34, 38, 224
education 10, 21, 22, 61, 136, 140–145, 152, 164
Ellison, Ralph 9, 79, 81, 127, 233
Elton, Ben 46, 60, 153, 162
end-of-the-pier 100, 207
Enfield, Harry 51, 53, 161, 189
Enterprise Allowance 128
erudition 105, 118, 127
ethnography 11–13, 127, 235
European Union 41, 65, 96, 211
expectation 14, 118
  expectations 9, 14, 37, 81, 83, 89, 110, 111, 113, 114, 117, 124, 126, 127, 130, 133, 155, 168, 227, 228

Factory Records 216, 218
Falklands War 38, 41, 45
Fanon, Frantz 100, 109, 112, 113
far right, the 6, 14, 15, 17, 26, 30, 134
fascists 15, 106, 153
festivals 26, 58, 66, 141, 142, 156, 209
Fetchit, Stepin 105n, 113, 243
fields (social space) 8, 11, 13, 56, 122, 141, 143, 193
films 5, 7, 13, 77, 78, 215
Firesign Theatre 80, 161
Flying Pickets (vocal group) 34, 35, 200, 202
folk clubs 12
Foundation, the *see* Fundation, the
free speech 59, 157
Friday Night Live 51, 53
Fundation, the 27, 34, 56, 57

gags 31, 77, 88, 101–103, 107, 110, 133, 138, 139, 151
Galton, Francis 109
Gang of Four (band) 18, 144, 146, 147, 216, 218
Gang of Four (British political faction) 31
gatekeepers 6, 215
gaze 112, 113
　pure 197
　scopophilic 110, 113
gentrification 37, 211
Ginsburg, Allen 129
GLC Giro Show 48, 49
Golden, Ronnie 23, 46, 47, 53, 59, 130, 136, 164n
Goldsmith, James 189
gong show (format) 20
Gong Show (US television show) 20
Goon Show, The 33, 88
Grade, Michael 200
Grahame, Peter 40, 70
Granada Television 10, 189, 200
grants 61, 197, 204, 218, 220
Greatest Show on Legs, The 20, 50, 173, 175, 224

Gribbin, Steve 25, 42, 140, 164, 218
Griffiths, Trevor 12, 13, 84, 142, 164
Grunwick dispute 18, 32
Gulf War (1991) 67, 106
Guthrie, Woody 160, 161

habitus 8, 9, 76, 113, 127, 161, 197
Hackney Council 171, 202, 204, 206, 211
Hackney Empire 9, 10, 58, 59, 64, 65, 66, 68, 91, 102, 115n, 194, 196, 197, 199, 202, 203–209, 210–212, 222–223
Hackney Empire Preservation Trust (HEPT) 205
half-caste (slur) 111
Hancock's Half Hour 139
Hardee, Malcolm 12, 42, 54, 62, 65, 103, 126, 165, 167, 216
Hardy, Jeremy 46, 66, 130, 208
Haritaworn, Jin 118, 120, 121
Harris, Pete 70, 71, 76
Hay, Malcolm 52, 57, 59, 61, 66, 67, 70, 114, 125
Hayridge, Hattie 60
Healey, Dennis 27, 28
Heartfield, John 197
Heath, Edward 178, 189
Hebdige, Dick 10, 22, 146, 240
hedonism 157, 158, 164
hegemony, cultural 2, 188, 190
Hegley, John 53, 54, 99, 172
Hell, Buddy 94, 95, 105
Henry, Lenny 46, 52, 75, 80, 81, 122, 205
Herbert, Phil 135, 136, 138, 144, 167
　see also Randolph the Remarkable
Heseltine, Michael 65
Hey, Stan 30, 31
Hicks, Bill 73, 131, 135, 138
hierarchies 10, 217, 231
hierarchy 30, 112, 117, 182, 203
Higher Education 10, 61, 144, 145
hippies 80, 157, 164, 226
Hitchin, Hertfordshire 90, 91, 142

Hitler, Adolf 21, 22
Hollywood 79, 85, 90
homelessness 96
homophobia 52, 195
Hope, Bob 12, 130
Howe, Geoffrey 55, 65
Howerd, Frankie 96, 149, 167, 215
Hoxton Hall 19, 203
Huddle, Roger 14
humour 26, 31, 67, 72, 77, 78, 80, 81, 107, 121, 125, 130, 131, 188
    Oxbridge 131, 161
    political 107, 131
    racist 130
    subversive 131
Hurd, Douglas 53, 65
Hurst, Lee 59, 72
Hurst, Mark 12, 56, 57, 58, 59, 66, 105, 130, 136, 137, 142, 146, 205
Hutchins, Roy 45, 164n
Hyde, Sheila 75
hypodescent 100, 110, 120

identity 6, 9, 10, 25, 46, 73, 102, 108, 110, 111, 118, 151, 152, 216, 225
ideology 17, 38, 132, 158, 219
imagination 13, 31n, 109
imperialism 109, 167
impressionists 40, 91, 191
impressions 78, 84, 90–91, 93, 97, 124, 224
improvisation (comedy) 53, 124, 156, 163, 177
incongruity (humour theory) 94, 108
Independent Television (ITV) 43, 51, 55, 115n, 192
industries, cultural 13, 24, 62, 139
industry, comedy 4, 5, 11, 106, 221
industry, music 153, 202
innovation 23, 126, 132, 168, 174, 202, 221, 225
inspiration 46, 65, 92, 93, 154, 224
intellectuals 125, 148, 176
    organic 168
International Socialists (IS) 180

Ireland, Northern Ireland 25, 36, 49, 53, 61, 154–156, 195
Irish 9, 25, 36, 37, 61, 88, 89, 121, 133, 137, 139, 155, 156, 180
Irishness 37, 155
Irish National Liberation Army (INLA) 17, 54, 148
Irish Republican Army (IRA) 49, 63, 156
    Provisional Irish Republican Army (PIRA) 17, 54
Itzin, Catherine 10, 145, 179
Izzard, Eddie 62, 63, 65, 68, 197

Jackson's Lane Arts Centre 37, 163, 217
James, Noel 57
Jay, Paul (Eugene Cheese) 87
Jenkins, Roy 31n, 51
Joan Collins Fan Club 207, 216
    see also Clary, Julian
Johnson, Linton Kwesi 36, 82, 216
Johnstone, Keith 53, 156
jokes 4, 24, 25, 26, 39, 69, 81, 92, 107, 125, 131, 142, 147, 148, 159, 163, 191, 192, 216
    joke-tellers 25, 80, 130
    joke-telling 12, 39, 125
    mother-in-law 23, 125
    racist 92, 147
Jongleurs 37, 38–40, 43, 45, 45, 48, 49, 55, 57, 69, 121–122, 125, 158, 201, 217, 222
journalists 21, 114, 128, 149, 159, 183
    music journalists 149
judgement 6, 113, 161, 193, 224
jugglers 37, 39, 40, 50, 51, 92, 163, 199, 217, 220, 224
Jungr, Barb 43

Kabaretts 21, 177
Karno's Kabaret 34, 35
Kartoon Klowns 14, 178
Kelly, Mark 37, 38, 130, 136, 139, 155, 161, 165
Kempinska, Maria 37, 38, 121

Kerouac, Jack 129
Kershaw, Baz 84, 173, 175, 178
Kinison, Sam 123
Kinnie, Kim 29, 40
Kinnock, Neil 41, 44, 94, 95

Labour Party 7, 15–17, 27–28, 31, 35, 40, 41, 44, 49–50, 51, 63, 64, 65, 94, 134–135, 176, 180, 183, 194, 195–196, 210, 219
lad comedy 59, 125
Ladbroke Grove 21, 134, 183, 184
Lakin, Warren 191
Lamont, Norman 106, 107
Landreth, Jenny 97, 119
language 7, 58, 80, 85, 100, 115, 129, 131, 145, 147, 150, 157, 158, 197, 209, 218
Late Show, The (BBC television show) 9, 97, 101
laughter 76, 96, 98, 104, 124, 194
Lawson, Nigel 60
Lecoat, Jenny 55, 153
Lee, Stewart 5, 39, 56, 151, 161, 208
Lee, Wendy 57, 138, 163
left-libertarianism 135, 138
legitimacy 186, 200, 203
legitimation 21, 158
Lenahan, John 76
libertarian socialists 9, 135, 177
light entertainment 16, 40, 81, 131, 220
Linden, Andy 57
Liverpool 33, 72, 77–79, 90, 133, 150
Luby, Chris 62, 62n
Lynam, Chris 60, 167
Lynch, Kenny 81
Lyttle, Clive 86

magicians 52, 68, 157, 207
Manchester 24, 41, 54, 92, 125, 190, 216, 217
Mandela, Nelson 58
manifestos 26, 41, 50, 125

Manning, Bernard 24–25, 26, 52, 92, 147, 159, 160, 161, 192
marketing 39, 223
Marx, Groucho 78, 130
  see also Marx Brothers
Marx, Karl 128, 133, 135, 138
  Marxism 130, 133, 175
  Marxist 42, 135, 144, 145, 172, 180
Marx Brothers 78, 130
Mary Whitehouse Experience, The 56, 59
mass-production 25, 97, 194
Mayall, Rik 12, 26, 30, 142, 216
McDonnell, Bill 3, 178
McKay, George 140, 156
Mecca (bingo halls) 204, 206
Meccano Club 48, 57, 168
mechanics institutes 117, 137n
media 5, 6, 21, 25, 27, 41, 54, 56, 73, 89, 94, 100, 135, 142, 147, 148, 153, 188, 189, 215, 220, 222, 225
  Media Studies 165
Melville, Pauline 21
Merton, Mrs (Caroline Ahearn) 93
Merton, Paul 197, 199
Meursault (character) 73, 124
middle class 23, 30, 49, 83, 100, 103, 105, 123, 137, 143, 161
Miliband, Ralph 95, 180
Militant Tendency 17, 28, 95, 133
Miners' Strike 44, 95, 155, 219
minorities 7, 216, 225
minstrelsy 111
  see also blackface
Mirza, Jeff 114
Misty in Roots 17, 18
mixed heritage 4, 5, 72, 81, 100, 109, 110, 111, 111n, 112, 113, 118, 120
  mixed parentage 110
  mixed race 33, 76, 110–111, 119, 120
Monty Python's Flying Circus 25, 80, 131
Moreland, Pete 202, 203, 204
Mountbatten, Louis, Earl of 17, 189n

Index

Muggins (character) 175, 177, 178, 179, 181
mulattos, mulattas 111n, 100, 111, 113
   tragic (literary trope) 100, 113
Muldoon, Claire 172, 177, 205, 212
Muldoon, Roland 34, 171, 173, 175, 176, 177, 181, 190, 193, 220, 221
Mulligan, Brian 148, 152, 157
music 1, 9, 10, 23, 55, 56, 58, 72, 76, 83, 90, 97, 98, 99, 140, 143, 145, 172, 201, 216
   alternative 220
   folk 153
   Irish 129
   live
   music papers 14
   popular 215
   post-punk 29, 144, 145, 146, 216, 223
   punk 141, 142
   reggae 194
   rock 2, 138, 146, 194, 215, 224
   soul 14
   and timing 98, 99
   world 54
music hall 3, 16, 19, 35, 39, 111, 166, 168, 172, 174, 175, 192, 195, 196, 199, 203, 208, 216, 222
musicians 11, 15, 25, 35, 49, 50, 92, 127, 128, 136, 217

name-dropping 23, 127
nationalism 33, 77, 207
nationalized industries 19, 32, 94
National Front 7, 14
Nazis 13, 14, 89
   neo-Nazis 13, 14
Neave, Airey 17
négritude 78, 82
neoliberalism 16, 24
New Variety (NV) 3, 9, 10, 19, 32, 34, 35, 45, 58, 64, 66, 101, 149, 155, 157, 159, 171–213
   New Variety Performers Agency (NVPA) 56

Newcastle-upon-Tyne 7, 74, 75, 84, 85, 86, 89, 94, 99, 105, 121, 217
Newman, Robert (Rob) 64, 67
Nichols, Peter 30, 36, 48
Nicholson, Jean 171, 213
non-racism 55, 59, 108, 141, 154, 218, 223
   non-racist 12, 75, 140, 145, 224
non-sexism 55, 59, 108, 141, 154, 218, 223
   non-sexist 75, 140, 145, 224
nostalgia 2, 13, 24, 81, 206, 208
novices 21, 27, 37, 126, 163, 217

objectification 8, 38, 89
obviousness 39, 225
oddballs 62, 66, 67, 72, 217
Off the Kerb (talent agency) 45–46, 56, 60, 104
official world 3, 24, 75, 111, 141, 143, 147, 148, 152, 155, 158–159, 161, 223, 224
old-fashionedness 13, 15, 81, 83, 130, 131, 143, 225
Onemanandabox 99, 100
orthodoxies 146, 156, 216, 220, 223
Other, the 73, 102, 110, 112, 116, 120, 121
Othering (social process) 18, 81, 125
out-of-town gigs 58, 127, 133
Outer Limits, the (comedy pairing) 29
Oxbridge 25, 56, 117, 123, 137, 177
   humour 131, 161

Paisley, Ian 91
Paramount City 51, 101, 102
parody 45, 89
patriotism 6–7
performers 9, 10, 17–20, 28–31, 37, 43–48, 51, 53, 54, 56–58, 60, 62–64, 66–78, 83, 99, 100, 110, 112, 116, 117, 122, 126, 127, 130, 135–138, 140, 143, 145, 149–151, 154, 156, 160–163, 165–167, 169–173, 176, 181, 188, 195, 196,

200, 201, 203, 204, 207, 209, 210, 213, 215–217, 224–233
permissiveness 196, 244
  permissive society 35, 61, 160
personas 22, 94, 110, 111, 116, 166
petit bourgeois 163, 196
Phillips, Emo 112
physicality 30, 92, 96, 153, 229
pidgin 24, 126
Pinochet, Augusto 60, 88
Pit Dragon 45
Pleasance 111, 112
Pledge of Allegiance 76
Podomovsky 53, 74
poetry 9, 18, 38, 44, 65, 82, 90, 153, 154, 210, 224
  punk 74, 146
  ranting 36
poets 18, 23, 43, 44, 56, 57, 65, 90, 100, 138, 154, 171, 224, 225, 228, 229, 232
  punk 82, 224
  ranting 12, 36, 130, 216, 217, 220, 221
political-aesthetic, the 9, 133, 135, 173, 197, 222
political correctness 15, 55, 60, 66, 67, 75, 158, 168
politics 15, 19, 22, 24, 28, 31, 46, 47, 67, 86, 107, 118, 145, 146, 147, 148, 149, 152, 156, 176, 183, 219
  far-right 15
  left-wing 14, 15, 24, 38, 129, 131–136
  mainstream 221
  oppositional 153
  parliamentary 117, 218
  right-wing 24
  subversive 165
Pop Group, the 145, 223
Port Stanley Amateur Dramatic Society 38, 48, 49
positioning 19, 20, 45, 46, 147, 216
  positions 14, 19, 22, 46, 55, 114, 173, 181, 184, 185, 195, 196, 216, 226, 227

postcolonialism 34, 89, 116, 117, 119, 215, 224, 240
postmodern 22, 67, 216
post-punk 10, 17, 23, 36, 37, 68, 80, 90, 137, 143, 146, 151–155, 157, 216, 224–126, 228, 231, 232, 236, 239, 243, 247
Poujade, Pierre 188n
Powell, Enoch 21, 22, 59
practice 15n, 83, 88, 98, 104, 134, 157, 174, 176, 211
  practices 2, 6, 8, 9, 12, 22, 110, 128, 138, 149–150, 156, 175, 222, 224
  practitioners 2, 157, 174n, 196, 206, 222
pre-alternative period, scene 20, 67
prisoners (Maze/Long Kesh) 28, 41, 146, 147
privatization 19, 50, 60n, 63, 94
producers 9, 15, 20, 21, 30, 40, 101, 102, 177, 215, 216, 222
products 20, 46, 47, 70, 92, 98, 118, 121, 147, 199
professionalization 76, 171, 225
proscenium arch 197, 222
psychedelia 82, 149, 154
punchlines 88, 94, 98
punk 2, 10, 13, 18, 21, 26, 27, 72, 82, 86, 87, 95, 107, 129, 138–146, 165, 183, 184, 208, 215, 216, 218, 220, 223
punks 13, 14, 21, 72, 127, 138, 144, 145, 218
  peacock 60
  progressive 60
punters (audience members) 39, 54, 73, 74, 122, 145, 203, 207
puppets 43, 52, 166

qualifications 8, 27, 83, 137, 164

race 4–6, 9, 14, 18, 33, 73, 75–77, 79, 108–111, 119, 120, 151, 182, 219, 224
  Race Relations Acts (1965, 1968, 1976) 134

Index

racism 4, 10, 16, 27, 77, 109, 114, 116, 119, 152, 158, 195, 207, 218, 224
  racists 117, 120, 160, 193
radicalism 32, 180
Radio Caroline 82, 172
Radio Fiona 82
Randolph the Remarkable 42, 70, 74, 135, 167
  see also Herbert, Phil
Rawlings, Steve 39, 67, 130, 136, 138, 202
Reagan, Ronald 146
reactionary 2, 24, 25, 27, 134, 138, 177, 188, 188n, 189, 221, 223, 225
Red Ladder (theatre company) 113, 175–176, 190
Red Wedge 49, 155
Rees Mogg, William 204
religion 131
representation 82, 175
republicans, Irish 28, 33, 53, 147, 148
  republicanism, Irish 17, 148
Revell, Nick 27, 47, 53, 60, 142, 151, 151
revolutions 156, 164, 177, 185
  revolutionary 15, 149, 152, 177, 180, 218
Reynolds, Simon 143, 152, 154
rhythm 97–98, 99, 100, 123
Ridley, Nicholas 52, 71, 72, 102–104
Right to Buy (housing policy) 19, 37, 96
right-wing, the 33, 64, 146, 148, 150, 152, 218
  economists 63
  media outlets 225
  press 33, 117, 195, 206
riots 27, 31, 33, 44n, 51, 66, 151, 152, 187, 188
Rock Against Racism (RAR) 14, 22, 26, 30, 49, 156, 178, 209, 223, 225
rock music 2, 13, 22, 44, 59, 60, 74, 83, 124, 127–129, 136, 138, 142, 145, 146, 172–175, 189, 194, 215–218, 220, 221, 224

Rosengard, Peter 20, 21, 29, 191
ruses 76

Sadowitz, Jerry 43, 52, 58, 60
satire 28, 84, 107, 117, 118, 131, 147, 160, 165, 175, 177, 180
  satirists 44, 95, 118, 177
Saturday Live 46–47, 51, 68, 153, 154, 216, 220
Saunders, Red 22, 181, 186
Sayle, Alexei 20, 21, 22, 29, 30, 31, 60, 78, 97, 123, 142, 145, 146, 193, 218, 223
Scargill, Arthur 44
Schuyler, Philippa 113
Screaming Blue Murder 62, 63, 68
Seaside Special 9, 92, 192, 197
Seisay, Kevin 48, 55, 101, 109
self-employment 39, 155
Sex Pistols 129, 183, 189, 218
sexism 16, 152, 158, 195, 218
Simmit, John 119, 119n
Situationist International 72, 135, 144, 145, 218
skinheads 22, 33, 52, 154
Skint Video 42, 45, 46, 56, 59, 62, 148, 152, 164, 165, 200
slapstick 26, 78
small-scale productions 9, 18, 162, 196
Smart, Andy 130, 139, 155, 159
Smith, Arthur 45, 54, 102
Soan, Martin 12, 129, 136, 165–169, 216
socialism 156, 217
  socialists 9, 41, 95, 133, 134, 135, 153, 157, 177, 211
Socialist Workers Party (SWP) 14, 15, 49, 63, 94, 124, 130, 135, 156, 180, 181
  see also International Socialists (IS)
sociology 3, 137
Soviet Union 40, 96
space 2, 3, 8–10, 11, 23, 32, 39, 40, 68, 75, 103, 106, 108, 124, 127–128, 131, 132, 134, 135, 138, 140, 143, 144, 149, 151, 152, 152n, 153, 154,

155, 157, 158, 159, 160, 164, 165, 173, 187, 190, 191, 192, 217, 218, 219, 220, 221, 222, 223, 225
Special Patrol Group (SPG) 17–18, 185n
spectacle 46, 59, 133, 167
spectacle (Situationist concept) 138, 140
Spitting Image 43–44, 52, 56
spot (performance time) 46
   half 217
   open 43, 66, 68, 87, 126, 217
Springstien, Anvil (Paul Ward) 54, 115, 129, 133
squats 149, 223
   squatting 133, 134
stage death 90, 105
stage names 57, 86, 87
staleness 2, 22, 143, 159, 161
Stanislavski, Konstantin 174n
Steel, Mark 46, 66, 67, 130
stereotypes 14, 80, 113, 118, 119, 124, 191, 240
   stereotypicality 83, 122
Stewart, Rod 14
Stoll–Moss 211
Stourac, Richard 83, 171
street performers 10, 20, 168, 199n, 216, 217, 221
strikes (industrial action) 16, 32
   hunger 28, 54, 132
   Paris (1968) 135
structural affinities 98, 135, 144, 223
structures 153, 211
students 137n, 142, 164, 208
style, performance (including comedy) 12, 65, 78, 80, 95, 97, 107, 123, 125, 131, 139, 163, 174, 175, 176, 180, 192, 207, 222
style, sartorial 115, 159, 160
subcultural 140, 141, 142, 145, 156, 216, 217
subcultures 15, 72, 138, 141, 150, 156, 139, 159, 162

sub-fields 18, 21, 30, 37, 39, 173
subsidies 44, 58, 163, 195, 202, 218
subversion 149, 185
subversiveness 25, 53, 76, 118, 130, 131, 148, 165, 178, 179, 185, 186, 187, 188, 189, 192, 222, 223
superiority theory (humour) 26
Sus laws 27, 33
symbolic 197, 222
   symbolic violence 24, 107, 117, 147, 148, 153, 155, 158, 185

talent 2, 7, 36, 46, 50, 56, 64, 78, 79, 83, 84, 106, 123, 162, 221
   talent agencies 56, 106, 108, 109, 190, 191n
   talent shows 20, 64, 208, 209
Tarbuck, Jimmy 81
Taylor, Teddy 188, 189
Tebbit, Norman 111n, 189
   'cricket test' 111, 111n
Teds (subculture) 194, 213
television 9, 15, 18, 20–22, 26, 27, 30, 36, 40, 43, 46, 49, 53, 53, 55, 56, 62, 63, 64, 66, 67, 68, 69, 75, 77, 78, 80, 81, 84, 91, 96, 97, 102, 109, 111, 117, 121, 123, 126, 131, 142, 154, 155, 162, 174, 192, 197, 203, 205n, 216, 220, 221, 224
Thatcher, Margaret 7, 15, 17, 27, 32, 33, 35, 41, 43, 44, 45, 47, 49, 51, 60, 88, 93, 94, 96, 103, 146, 150, 152, 154, 155, 159, 160, 185, 187, 188, 193, 218, 219
Thatcher government 27, 35, 44, 44n, 49, 60, 63n, 150, 155, 187, 193, 219
Thatcherism (also anti-Thatcherism) 7, 46, 96, 150, 154
theatre 12, 20, 32, 66, 75, 83, 84, 120, 129, 142, 153, 157, 171, 184, 186, 189, 190, 191, 194, 211, 220
   alternative 10, 20, 136, 138, 171, 172, 173–180, 220
   commercial 136, 174, 217
   epic 174

fringe 18, 19, 20, 22, 31, 34, 36, 132, 182, 190, 216
Off West End 210
political 10, 26, 35, 176, 182, 190, 216, 217, 224
popular 175
street 133, 175
underground 20, 23, 210
Theatresports 61, 76, 164
Thomas, Mark 5, 53, 57, 59, 60, 62, 66, 118, 151
Thompson, Dave (Igor) 129, 139, 153, 154, 157
timing 25, 98–99
Toczek, Nick 130
Tories 16, 17, 41, 44, 90, 151, 219
Tory Party 27, 50
see also Conservative Party
Tottenham 73, 74
Toxteth 41, 86
trades 145, 184
trade unions 32, 44, 133, 134, 152, 176
see also unions
Tramshed, Woolwich 12, 19, 26, 48
travellers 50
new age 50
Trotskyism 143, 164
Tunnel Club, Tunnel Palladium 42–43, 47, 48, 54, 62, 103, 104, 167

Uncle Tom (slur) 82, 105n, 125
uncoolness 132, 140, 141, 150, 159
underground (cultural) 15, 16, 28, 30, 31, 80, 167, 198, 217, 218, 225, 231
unemployment 32, 33, 63, 150
unemployment benefit 86, 155
Union de défense des commerçants et artisans (UDCA) 196
unions 40, 48, 49, 52, 69, 73, 104, 145, 159, 160, 184, 190, 196, 207, 208, 219, 239
United States 20, 42, 72, 76, 82, 119, 122, 130
Unity Theatre 180–182, 185, 186, 216
Up the Creek 54, 62, 64, 69

Upfront Comedy Club 119, 119n

Vaneigem, Raoul 140
variety theatre 36, 147, 168, 181, 199, 203, 217, 221, 222
venues 1, 2, 11, 30, 64, 104, 119, 121, 123, 125, 139, 156, 168, 176, 183, 191, 196, 199, 202, 205, 210, 216, 225
Verfremdungseffekt 174, 175
Vietnam War 85, 86, 183

Walker, Curtis 13
Walters, Alan 60
Wangford, Hank 201
Ward, Don 20, 29, 40, 62, 120, 191, 191n
Weimar Germany 29, 185
Weir, Peter 34
Welfare State International 92, 186
Welsh people 89, 115, 133, 165
Wheeltappers and Shunters Social Club, The 17, 200, 215
Widgery, David 14, 18, 30
Williams, Charlie 75, 80, 81, 100
Williams, Shirley 39
Wilmut, Roger 10, 11, 20, 60, 68, 245
Wilson, Harold 189, 197, 224
Wire 144, 216, 218
Wood, Victoria 12, 20
Woody Bop Muddy 221
working class 23, 26, 33, 37, 42, 53, 78, 101, 117, 118, 123, 127, 137, 150, 161, 172, 176, 177, 191, 203

Yashere, Gina 6, 122
Young Communist League 132
Young Ones, The (sitcom) 9, 30, 36, 162, 216, 220
youth 15, 20, 146, 151, 172, 173, 176, 215
youth cultures 5, 92, 141, 194, 218, 220, 221, 224

Zephaniah, Benjamin 48, 205

Printed in the USA
CPSIA information can be obtained
at www.ICGtesting.com
CBHW071336260624
10696CB00003B/35